MODELING 101

MODELING 101

Debbie Madison
*Author of **Rider Down and Halloween
Flight 77***

iUniverse, Inc.
New York Lincoln Shanghai

MODELING 101

iUniverse books may be ordered through booksellers or by contacting:

iUniverse
2021 Pine Lake Road, Suite 100
Lincoln, NE 68512
www.iuniverse.com
1-800-Authors (1-800-288-4677)

Because of the dynamic nature of the Internet, any Web addresses, phone numbers, or links contained in this book may have changed since publication and may no longer be valid.

The views expressed in this work are solely those of the author and do not necessarily reflect the views of the publisher, and the publisher hereby disclaims any responsibility for them.

ISBN: 978-0-595-47660-2 (pbk)
ISBN: 978-0-595-91923-9 (ebk)

Printed in the United States of America

Contents

This chapter explains how and where to get started with a baby or toddler in the modeling industry. It details how much money a baby or toddler gets paid. It gives an overview of what to expect on a photo-shoot and what to expect from your child at a photo-shoot. It explains how to hire an agency and what they expect from you. It lists what you need to buy and/or have for an agency and for a photo-shoot. It lists modeling agencies across the countries that specialize in babies and toddlers. The list is alphabetical, state-by-state and includes each agencies age criteria (example: 3+ or 6+) along with their addresses, e-mail information and phone numbers.

MODELING DOCUMENTS, FORMS, & INCOME TAXES

This chapter explains the ins and outs of working with and/or without an agency. It explains how to independently find modeling work, how to bill clients and how to get paid. In great details and with picture examples it explains how to keep bookkeeping records, what kind of bookkeeping records to keep, and what income taxes are paid on modeling income. This chapter addresses the business end of the modeling profession and has numerous examples to refer to, including modeling contracts and receipts

This chapter gives an overview of how modeling and etiquette schools work and what they teach. It lists in alphabetical order, state-by-state the name, address and phone numbers of modeling and etiquette schools across the country.

This chapter explains and gives an overview of how a modeling agency works and how they make money. It explains what commissions and percentages they charge. It details how a model gets paid and who pays them. It explains what expenses are paid for and/or reimbursed by an agency when traveling out of town. It gives an overview of union representation and addresses how and when to join a union. It itemizes the dues and initiation fees that unions charge, along with their names and contact information.

This chapter explains how to recognize a scam and how to avoid them. Detailed examples of numerous scams and how they work including fraudulent agencies, schools and photographers are listed. An overview of how the glitz and glamour of this profession can cloud judgment and how to stay focused. What parties to attend and which parties not to attend.

1

MODELING TYPES & MODELING TERMINOLOGY

At some point and time in our lives we've all dreamed about becoming a model. The general consensus is that we would need to have a perfect, long-legged body along with a beautiful face to become a model.

This is not true. There are many types of modeling careers available, from High Fashion and Glamour models to Petite and Plus size modeling, for both men and women.

A large and growing area of the modeling industry is Character Modeling, or simply put, real life models.

The television commercial industry is constantly dreaming up new sales ideas, and as our country's population ages, a demand for older models is growing for women and even more so for men.

Another growing section of the modeling industry is the ethnic area. African Americans, Asians, Indians, and especially Hispanic models are needed. Not just tall skinny women, but men, women and children of all sizes and ages are now in demand.

You don't have to be a woman or perfect to become a model. You do need to be realistic about what kind of modeling your physique and looks fit into.

This chapter outlines the fourteen different kinds of modeling available and the look or criteria that is needed for each category.

The modeling industry is a multi-billion-dollar industry, and finding out where you fit in is your first step to becoming a successful model.

HIGH FASHION

These models are the highest paid men and women in the industry and are sometimes referred to as, "supermodels." They model famous designer clothes, makeup and jewelry. They are the men and women you see every day on your televisions, magazine covers and billboards.

FEMALE MODEL: Should be 14 to 19 years old with a minimum height of 5'9" and weigh about 115 lbs. You must have a great body in perfect proportions with an attractive look, a flawless complexion, healthy hair, and have long legs, especially the portion from the knee to the ground.

MALE MODEL: Should be a minimum of 6 feet to 6'2" tall. You should weigh 140–185 lbs. and be between the age of 20–35 years old. You must have a clear complexion, thick hair, and long legs. You need to be in excellent physical condition, have a waist no larger than 34," and be very handsome or have an unusual (sometimes sexy) look.

EDITORIAL MODELING

Editorial modeling is similar to High Fashion modeling, except the models work for a particular publication. In other words you work exclusively or are under a contract to work specifically with one company. The photographers dress the models in a way fashionable to attract the publication's readers. For example, "Easy Rider" would dress the models in leathers and around motorcycles whereas a teen magazine would dress the models in current and hip fashions. The pay is considerably less than High Fashion modeling but the physical requirements aren't as stringent, and the experience opens the door to High Fashion modeling. Height, looks and physique are still very important to succeed in this area.

FEMALE MODEL: Should be 15–20 years old and a weigh 110 to 130 lbs. You should be 5'7" to 5'10" tall, and you must have a great body, well proportioned with an attractive look, along with a flawless complexion and healthy hair.

MALE MODEL: Should be 20–35 years old and weigh 140–185 lbs. You need to be in excellent physical condition and have a well-developed physique that is in good proportions to your height and weight. You need to have a striking or unusual look, along with a clear complexion and thick hair.

FIT OR GLAMOUR MODELING

The main criteria for this kind of modeling are that the models must be stunningly beautiful or sexy in the photograph. There are no weight or height restrictions in Glamour modeling. It includes everything from swimwear and lingerie to elegant evening and formal gowns. The pay varies, but once established, money in this area of modeling is very good. A stunning look is the key to success in this area. If you have a perfect body, or perhaps you have a beautiful, flawless face this is an area of modeling you should pursue.

CATALOG & PRINT MODELING

These models can be paid as much as ten thousand dollars a day or as little as one hundred dollars per hour. It depends upon which catalog or brand name you are working for.

For example, a brand named blue jeans company photo shoot would pay considerably more than a large retail store photo shoot.

One large advantage of Catalog modeling is that you can work in this area for a longer period of time. Women can work from the ages of 15 all the way up to the age of 25. Male models can work even longer, to the age of 30. There are hundreds of photo shoots in this area on a daily basis, and work is a lot more regular here than in High Fashion modeling. Once established in this area, repeat modeling opportunities are very good.

CATALOG & PRINT MODELING

FEMALE MODEL: Should be between 5'8" and 6 feet tall and wear between a size six and a size eight in clothing. A clear complexion is important, along with healthy hair and straight teeth.

MALE MODEL: Should be lean, 5'11" to 6'2" tall and wear a 36–40 regular sport suit. Your weight should be between 140–165 lbs. You should have a well-proportioned body, straight teeth and healthy hair.

RUNWAY MODELING

Runway modeling is well known and a high exposure area of the modeling world. It starts on the runways of your local clothing stores and progresses to the sophisticated world of designer fashions with shows in London, Paris and New York.

If you're tall, naturally very thin and young, this is an area that many modeling agencies specialize in. The pay is based upon the experience of the model and can range from five hundred dollars to five thousand dollars and up per show. Runway modeling in small towns pays a lot less, but the experience and exposure you get are invaluable. Traveling in, around, and out of town is required for this type of modeling.

FEMALE MODEL: Should be 5'9" to 6'1" tall and weigh 100 to 120 lbs. You need to be between the ages of 15 and 25. A lean body is more important than your facial features. You should have long legs and be in great shape.

MALE MODEL: Should be at least 6 feet tall, lean, and have an excellent physique, proportionate to your weight. You should be between the ages of 20 to 35 years old.

PETITE MODELING

The market for Petite modeling is very small. Most petite models have a much better opportunity in commercial modeling. The opportunity for men in this category is even smaller. There are very few companies that specialize in petite clothes and they usually have their own models.

FEMALE MODEL: Should be 5'3" to 5'6" tall and weigh 90 to 100 lbs. You should be in good shape, have a clear complexion, and your body needs to be in proportion to your weight

PLUS SIZE MODELING

Plus Size modeling is an up-and-coming market in the modeling profession. Not everyone is paper thin, and the need for healthy-looking women models is growing daily. The best cities to find work in this area of modeling are New York, Chicago and Atlanta.

The opportunity for men in this area of modeling is almost nonexistent at this time.

FEMALE MODEL: Should be between 18–35 years of age and you should be 5'8" to 5'11" tall. You should wear a full figure size 12 to 16. Size 13 is the standard for the industry.

A clear complexion, straight teeth, along with an evenly proportioned body in respect to your weight, is a must.

INTERNATIONAL MODELING

International models travel to foreign countries for photo shoots. You travel for two to three months at a time, then you return home for one to three weeks, then the process repeats itself. Speaking foreign languages is helpful but not required. The ability to quickly adapt to new environments is a must, along with a willingness to travel and be away from home for an extensive amount of time.

A reputable agent is very important in this area of modeling. Pay ranges from the number of days that you are over seas to short and long-term contracts that your agent has negotiated for you.

FEMALE MODEL: Should be 13–22 years old, between 5'8" to 6 feet tall and weigh between 110 to 130 lbs. You must have a clear complexion and be stunning, like models you see in fashion magazines.

MALE MODEL: Should be 21–25 years old, between 5'10" and 6'2" tall, in excellent physical shape, and weigh between 140–185 lbs. You need to have a striking look, along with straight teeth and thick hair.

SPECIALTY MODELING

Sometimes referred to as, "Parts models." Do you have long thin fingers and well-manicured nails? This category of modeling includes all of the body parts you see in magazines and television ads, from pretty feet to masculine male hands. A growing sector in this category is hair care products. If you have the perfect natural wave or thick beautiful hair, then you should pursue this area of modeling. Most agents won't accept a picture of your hair or feet, so remember (in your photo shoots) to accentuate the body part that you want noticed.

CONVENTION & TRADE SHOW MODELING

There are no age, height or weight restrictions in this category of modeling. Most of the work is for women, and the average age is between 19–30 years. A pretty face, long legs, and being in good shape are a must. Most of the time jobs consist of greeting visitors, handing out brochures, or demonstrating products. Jobs range from a few hours to a few days and pay from ten dollars an hour to three hundred dollars per day. Many models start out in this category for both experience and exposure. If you live in a city that has a convention center or that is a tourist stop there is a lot of work available, and opportunities are plentiful in this area of modeling.

CHARACTER MODELING

Sometimes referred to as, "Real Life Models." This category has no gender, age, weight or height restrictions. Ordinary, everyday-looking people are needed for catalogues and commercials.

Do you look like a typical accountant? How about a typical mechanic or truck driver? Even schoolteachers and grandparents are needed for their "typical look."

Jobs are plentiful and growing in this category, especially in the ethnic area, such as African American, Asian, and Hispanic models.

The rate of pay depends upon the length of the job and whether the job is union. It also depends on whether the job is for a local promotion or for a national promotion. Pay ranges from fifty dollars per hour to thousands of dollars per contract for national use.

COMMERCIAL MODELING

Commonly referred to as, "Television Modeling." Just like character modeling, there are no gender, age, weight, or height restrictions. A growing demand for "real looking people" has opened the doors for the general public who normally wouldn't be considered perfect enough for television modeling.

Like character modeling, if you have that everyday look of a typical person (housewife, plumber, etc.), then there is work available for you in this category. A growing area of this division is the Hispanic, Asian and African American models.

The pay varies just like character modeling but tends to be higher than character modeling.

BABY & CHILDREN MODELING

Agencies specializing in children normally have different divisions. A baby, toddler, girls and boys divisions usually ages 3–7 years old, and a boys and girls division ages 8–12 years of age.

A prerequisite in all of the children's divisions is that your toddler or child must be outgoing, animated, and able to speak to a stranger without becoming shy.

NEWBORN MODEL: There are no size, height or weight restrictions. The ideal age is 6 to 9 months old. A baby's head should be proportionate to its body. A calm manner and a willingness to listen, along with a bubbly personality, are what agencies are looking for.

TODDLER MODEL: Should be between the ages of 1–2 years old. There are no size, height or weight restrictions. A great smile and a long, lean torso are important. Large eyes and an outgoing personality are what agencies are looking for. Your toddler must be able to speak to a stranger without becoming shy.

CHILDREN MODELS: Should be 3 to 12 years of age, both boys and girls. Should be slender, on the petite size, and a maximum height of sixty inches tall. Just like toddler models, a great smile, along with an outgoing personality, and a clear complexion (is a must). Children should speak clearly and accurately and not have shy tendencies.

ILLUSTRATION MODELING

This category of modeling is used almost exclusively in Europe and in college art classes. There are no gender, age, height or weight restrictions. A healthy, well-proportioned physique, male or female is normally required. Patience and the willingness to shed your cloths in front of a few or sometimes a crowd of people is a must. You cannot be shy and you must feel very comfortable with your body. The pay varies but tends to be on the very low side of the modeling industry.

Knowing the terminology in the modeling industry is just as important as knowing what type of modeling career you're going to pursue.

At an interview an open call director will not answer your questions and tends to frown upon gabby, inexperienced models.

Don't put yourself into this position. It could mean losing the job.

Refer to the following terms before you go out for an interview. Some of the words will be familiar to you, but might have different meanings. For example, the word, "copy" to most of us means " to duplicate or reproduce." In the world of modeling it has a different meaning; it is the actual words to be spoken on a television commercial.

Many times at auditions you will be required to read a few lines. A career in modeling usually includes trying out for television commercials.

Study these words and terms carefully. Terms that you can't remember should be copied and kept close at hand to refer to when you need them.

Don't panic if a term you've never heard before is used at a try out or photo shoot. A friendly smile and calm manor soothes most mistakes and emanates your professionalism to the industry.

A good rule of thumb is to quietly ask other models around you. (If you don't understand something) Be discreet and ask questions on personal break time. I have found that most models are friendly and enjoy sharing their knowledge.

The words and terms are categorized as follows:

AUDITIONS AND JOB INTERVIEWS
PHOTOGRAPHY TERMINOLOGY
MODELING AGENCY & UNION TERMINOLOGY
TELEVISION & STAGE TERMINOLOGY
FASHION MODELING TERMINOLOGY
OTHER TERMINOLOGY

The words and terms are conveniently listed alphabetically so you can refer to them quickly as needed.

AUDITION & JOB INTERVIEW

ADVERTISING AGENCY: A company that creates advertising campaigns for clients, and selects the models for each of their campaigns.

BOOKING: A specific job engagement or assignment.

CALL: An appointment.

CALL BACK: A second interview for a job that you already auditioned for. It means that you are one of the finalists and have a good chance at the job.

CALL TIME: This is the actual time that you need to be at an interview or studio.

CATTLE CALL: Numerous agencies send a lot of models of a specific type to a casting session. (Example: Tall, leggy, blond, under the age of 30.)

COMPOSITE CARD OR COMP CARD: A postcard-sized card with your picture or pictures on it, along with your name, height, weight, hair and eye color, clothing and shoe sizes. Your agent's name, address and phone number is also included. Also referred to as a Zed card.

DEMONSTRATOR: A modeling job that includes demonstrating a product at a trade show, convention, or store. (Example: spraying perfume or rubbing specialty lotions on hands.)

GO & SEE: A job interview where a model meets the client and shows them his or her portfolio. (Dress to impress from your fingernails to your toenails on these interviews.)

INDUSTRIAL: A type of film production used for sales and/or education purposes. (Example: A film made for executives of a company specifically training them in public relations, hiring and firing of employees, etc.)

LOCATION: A job site outside the studio location where you originally interviewed. (Example: A photo shoot at a lake, the mall, car lots, etc.)

MARKET OR JOB MARKET: Any city or location where there is a lot of work available for your modeling type or specialty.

MODEL BAG: A large tote where all of your makeup, cloths, shoes, and hair care products are stored that you take with you on a job.

MOOD: The feeling you need to project and convey to the camera for a specific shoot. (Example: For a Christmas scene you would need to be joyful and happy, etc.)

MONOLOGUE: A scene performed by one person in front of a client that demonstrates your acting ability.

OPEN CALL: Any and all models can show up for these job interviews, you do not need to be invited as long as you fit the required type. (Example: male 20–30 years old, dark hair, thick build.)

PORTFOLIO: A résumé of pictures in a vinyl or leather book which show your prior work experience, along with photogenic shots that illustrate your versatility.

SCOUT: A person looking for a specific type of model, i.e., tall, short, etc, normally hired by an agency or ad company for a specific campaign.

SIGN IN SHEET: A form you sign in on at an audition when you arrive. It normally asks what time you arrived for the audition.

PHOTOGRAPHY TERMINOLOGY

BACKDROP: The background (colors and scenes) used in a photographer's studio.

CONTACT SHEET: 1 ½" x 1" pictures from a photo shoot used to determine which are the best pictures to blow up.

BLOW UP: Enlarging a photo from a film negative or slide.

DIGITAL CAMERA: A camera that uses computer technology to produce instant digital pictures on a screen. This camera does not use rolls of film like traditional cameras.

FILM: A light sensitive emulsion that records images for use in photography.

HEADSHOT: A photo of a person's head and shoulders only.

¾ SHOT: A photo which includes the top of your head all the way down to about your thighs. It should cover ¾ of your entire body.

FULL LENGTH SHOT: A photo of your entire body from your head down to your toes.
NEGATIVES: Film that has been processed which contains the actual pictures of a photo shoot, before they are blown up.

PRINT: A photograph that has been blown up and has been printed in a newspaper or magazine.

PRINT WORK: The actual photographs taken for most all commercial business in the photography industry, such as mail order catalogs, magazine, newspapers, and glamour photographs.

PROOF: Small copies (1–1/2"x 1") of pictures shot in a photo shoot, used to choose the best pictures for blowing up, usually displayed on 8"x11" paper.

SHOOT: An actual photo session or photo shoot.

SPEC SHOT: A photographer's collection of the best pictures from a photo shoot that he or she hopes to sell to a client.

STROBE: A light that flashes when pictures are taken.

TEST SHOTS, TEST PHOTOGRAPHY: Photos used to start or build a portfolio. A

photographer will give you some photos from a photo shoot as a trade for the use of your time at their studio.

TRANSPARENCIES: The slide form of a photograph.

MODELING AGENCIES & UNION TERMINOLOGY

AGENT OR AGENCY: A third-party negotiator either an individual or a company that receives a percentage of your earnings for the work they find you.

AFTRA: The American Federation of Television and Radio Artist, union for most television performers.

BOOK: To secure a job, used sometimes in the verb sense, "I've booked you a job."

BOOKER: An employee at an agency that sets you up for modeling appointments. This person is usually not your agent.

BOOK OUT: Days or times of the year when you are unavailable to work for your agency that you've told your agency about. (Example: summer vacation your regular job hours, etc.)

BREAKDOWN SERVICE: A listing of stage projects, movies, film and television, along with what types of actors are needed and currently being scouted. This list is only available to agencies.

BUYOUT: A payment of compensation for the use of a print ad or a commercial for a specific period of time.

CANCELLATION: A clause in a contract that guarantees that money is due the agency and model if the booking is cancelled within 24 hours of the scheduled shoot.

CLIENT: A client is the company that hires the ad agency. They pay for the photo and television shoots and for the modeling fees.

COMMISSION: A percentage of a model's fee required to be paid to the agency for representation.

HEAD SHEET: An agency's book or list of models they represent that is sent to prospective clients.

HOLD: When an agency puts you, "on hold" for a job, it means that a client is seriously considering you and wants you to keep a specific future time available for them at an up and-coming photo shoot.

MODEL AGENCY: A company or individual that represents you and finds you work in the modeling profession. In return, you pay the agency a percentage of each booking.

MODEL RELEASE: A contract in which the model gives permission to use photos for a specific ad campaign and/or length of time.

RATES: The hourly, daily, weekly, and other fees charged by the model.

RESIDUALS: Additional money paid when a job or commercial runs for more than a specified number of times. The unions set these amounts.

ROUNDS: Making the rounds, calling on prospective clients for photography and television.

SAG: The Screen, Actors Guild is a union which represents performers in film, video, television programs, and commercials.

SCALE WAGE: Minimum wage set by the unions.

STATS: Statistical information on a model, including height, weight, clothing sizes, hair and eye coloring, etc.

TRADE PAPERS: Publications slanted to the modeling and acting professions which include current trends and employment opportunities including: "NY Casting", "Ross Reports", "Hollywood Reporter", etc.

USAGE: An important term in a contract that specifies how photographs or in what cities commercials will be aired. Additional fees are negotiable for billboard use or national use.

TELEVISION & STATE TERMINOLOGY

ART DIRECTOR: The artist who creates the layouts for ads and illustrations for the model's photo poses.

BLOCKING: The actual physical movements by actors in any scene.

CASTING: Choosing a particular type of model for a specific job. (For example, glamour shoots, bathing suit shoots, etc.)

CASTING DIRECTOR: Selects the final models from zed cards for a specific job.

COLD READING: Reading a script for the first time in front of a client, without being given any time to memorize it.

COMMERCIAL: A promotional advertisement on the television or radio.

COPY: The actual words (in writing) that are to be spoken on a commercial.

EXTRA: An acting job where you have no speaking lines. You usually stand in the background of a scene to add a mood or atmosphere to it.

HAIR STYLIST: A specialist who styles and/or works with your hair as needed at a photo shoot.

MAKEUP ARTIST: A specialist who applies and changes makeup on models before and during a photo shoot.

PRINCIPAL: The main person or model in a scene or photo shoot.

PRODUCER: The person who creates, organizes, and runs a production.

SET: An area at a photography or television studio arranged with furniture and props.

SLATE: To announce or say your name in front of a camera at a commercial audition.

STAGE PARENT: A parent who causes problems on a production or photo shoot by over instructing or pushing his or her child.

STORYBOARD: An illustration on a large board showing each scene of a commercial.

TELEPROMPTER: A monitor which displays the written script, like a cue card, during filming.

TESTIMONIAL: An endorsement of a product or service by a celebrity where the celebrity has personally used and supports the product.

VOICEOVER: Background voices for radio or video, recorded separately in a recording studio and dubbed into visual.

FASHION MODELING

BUYER: A store owner or employee of a large company who purchases clothing from a manufacturer.

CATWALK: A stage, ramp, or walkway models parade on, at or during a fashion show.

CATWALK: A term referring to runway modeling. (Example: "Do you have any catwalk work for me this week?")

COLLECTION: A designer's line of clothing, generally shown at fashion shows.

COMMENTARY: The script used to describe clothes at a fashion show.

DESIGNER: The person who designs and creates the clothes or collection shown at fashion shows.

DRESSER: The people who dress the models backstage at fashion shows.

FASHION COORDINATOR: The person who runs and organizes the fashion show.

FITTING: Trying on clothes before a fashion show for sizing. Typically the morning of the fashion show but sometimes a day or even an entire week earlier.

FIT MODELING: Using models with exactly the same measurements of a designer's sample clothing. (Example: Petite size 6, etc.)

FORMAL FASHION SHOW: By invitation only, highly coordinated with music, lights, designer fashions, and runway models.

INFORMAL FASHION SHOW: Typically in stores or restaurants without a runway.

LINE UP: The position or where a model is to stand at a fashion show.

MARKET WEEK: When seasonal collections of designer clothes are shown to buyers. Some designers use the seasons, spring, summer etc., generally four shows per year.

RUNWAY: A long, narrow, raised platform on which models parade during a fashion show.

SAMPLE: An original outfit or piece of clothing made by a designer that has not been duplicated (one of a kind.)

SHOWROOM WORK: Manufacturers show their lines of clothing to buyers without a fashion show, but with live models.

SPOKESPERSON: A model or person who explains the features of a particular product.

OTHER

CREATIVE DIRECTOR: An ad agency employee who determines the type of models needed for a project.

FASHION TRENDS: The styles and designs in clothing that designers create.

FLIPPER: Temporary teeth put on young children (at photo shoots and commercials) when they've lost a tooth. (baby teeth fall out when we least expect them to.)

FREELANCE: Working in the modeling profession without an agent.

PROMOTION: Advertisement or publicity used to promote a model or a product.

PUBLIC RELATIONS: Creating an image of a person or product for the general public.

TRADE SHOWS: A gathering of companies displaying and promoting their products, generally at a convention center or large hotel.

TRUNK SHOW: Modeling one specific designer line of clothing, typically in small stores or boutiques.

2

ZED CARDS, PHOTOGRAPHS &
YOUR PORTFOLIO

WHAT IS A ZED CARD?

A zed card, also refereed to as a "comp card or composition card," very simply put, is an over-sized postcard with numerous pictures of yourself on it.

They are printed both in black and white and or in color. They are 5–1/2" tall x 8–1/2" long, and you can put up to five photos on each card.

The front of the card should have your most striking pose on it, and it should be a head-shot, which means a picture of yourself from the top of your head to just below your neck.

On the back of the zed card you can put up to four photos or poses. You should have a full body shot (from head to toe), preferably in a bathing suit or tight-fitting outfit to show what your body really looks like.

The other one or two photos should show your versatility. They can be anything from a simple girlish look that shows off your fantastic smile, to wearing a tight pair of jeans that show off your long, slender legs.

By now you should know what kind of modeling you want to pursue. Your zed card is the key to getting work.

If you're a large, heavy truck driver, don't try and hide your body. Zed cards should reflect "the real you." whether it be tall, thin and gorgeous, or short and balding with buckteeth.

Zed cards are given out to potential clients similarly to business cards being given out by bankers or brokers.

In the busy world of modeling only a few seconds are spent looking at each zed card. Agents, producers and scouts see thousands of zed cards each year.

You need to leave a memorable impression in their minds, whether it is for your looks, height, or smile.

Your zed card also needs to have pertinent information about you on it. Specifically for women: your name, height, bust, waist, hips and shoe size, along with your hair, eye color and dress size. If your under the age of sixteen your date of birth also needs to be on the card.

Zed cards for men need to have: your name, suit size, waist, shirt, sleeve-inseam and shoe size, along with your hair color, eye color and date of birth if you are under the age of sixteen.

You can also have your agency's name, address and phone number printed on each zed card.

Steer away from having agency information printed on your zed card. Most agencies have their own stickers that they add to each zed card anyway, and if you change agents within an agency or if you are working for multiple agencies, inevitably the wrong agency name will be on one of your zed cards.

Zed cards are sold in multiples of one hundreds (100,200,500). Do not go out and buy 500 zed cards, even though they are cheaper purchased in a larger quantity.

Start out with one to two hundred cards. If you or your agent's supply runs low, order more, but again, only in small quantities. Remember, in the real world you are constantly changing. Your zed card should reflect those changes. For example, you change your hair color or cut your hair. Having three or four hundred outdated zed cards will not help your modeling career.

Children's zed cards should be updated yearly from newborn to the age of five, then every two years after that.

When a fashion designer picks your zed card showing you with long blond hair and you show up for the interview as a short-haired brunette, do you think you will get the job?

Also update your zed cards as you diversify your look. The more diverse your look, the better chance you have at getting work.

For example: If your zed card picture shows you as a tall, leggy blond on the front, and on the back all of your pictures show similar poses, then you have limited yourself to, "a tall leggy blond job."

Having different hairstyles and colors along with different makeup and clothing all adds up to a better chance at more work.

WHERE DO I GET A ZED CARD?

Printing companies and photography studios make zed cards. Before you call any of these companies it's a good idea to call your local modeling agencies first. Be direct and ask them whom they recommend or use for their models.

If they can't or won't refer you to a company then go back to the phone book and look in the yellow pages under "photograph studios." Call more than one company and compare prices.

There are a lot of companies to choose from and their prices vary. Some companies charge over a dollar for each black and white zed card they print. That is very high. Compare your quotes to the industry average below:

Black and white zed cards are sold in groups of 200 and 500. Rarely will anyone print 100.

They should cost around $110.00 for 200 zed cards and about $ 150.00 for 500 zed cards.

Color zed cards are sold in groups of 100/150/300/500. They should cost about $100.00 for 100 two-sided color cards. For 150 zed cards you should pay around $150.00. For 300 color zed cards you should pay around $250.00, and for 500 color zed cards you should pay about $375.00.

A good rule of thumb to remember is that black and white zed cards should cost about fifty cents each, and color zed cards should cost about one dollar each.

When you are ready to have your zed card printed remember that you need to have reproduction quality photographs to copy onto your zed cards. The mom and pop pictures from your camera at home won't produce the quality of pictures you need.

The pictures should be in a 5x7 format, although smaller sizes are acceptable.

Study the zed card styles on the next page and arrange your four or five pictures in the different formats.

Walk away from the arranged pictures then glance back at them. This will help you figure out which pictures look better and which format look best for you.

Don't forget that you need to have all of your stats ready before you have your zed cards printed.

STATS

WOMEN/GIRLS   **MEN/BOYS**

HEIGHT: _____   HEIGHT: _____

BUST: _____   SUIT: _____

WAIST: _____   WAIST: _____

HIPS: _____   SHIRT: _____

SHOE: _____   SLEEVE: _____

HAIR: _____   INSEAM:_____

EYES: _____   SHOE: _____

DRESS: _____   HAIR: _____

D.O.B. _____   D.O.B. _____
(children only)   (children only)

Zed Card Formats

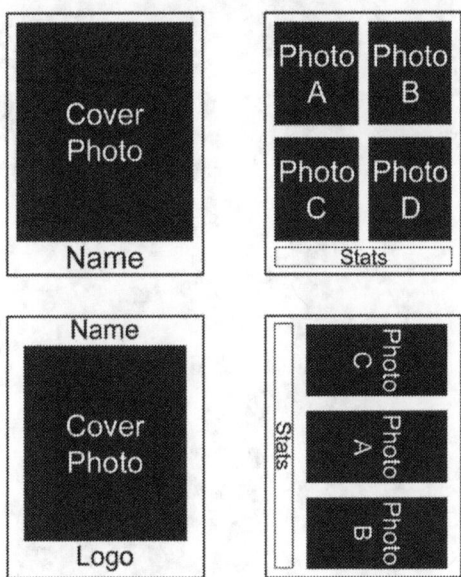

There are other zed card formats available. These are the most common formats used. Ask the company printing your cards what formats they have available.

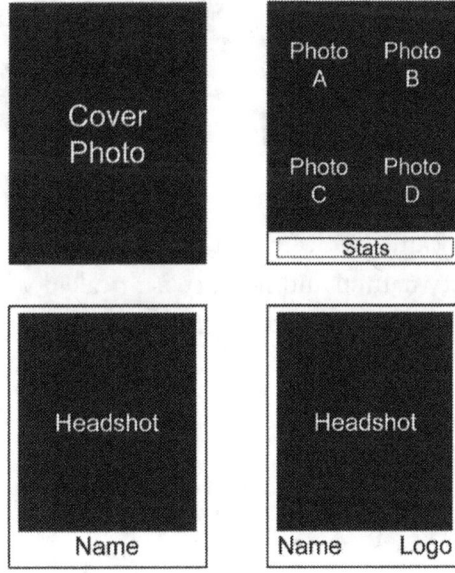

Jennifer Madison

Above is a sample zed card. Notice that there is no bright nail polish or jewelry on the model. Her pose looks very natural and her face isn't caked with makeup. The front of your zed card needs to have a headshot on it basically, a close up of your hair and face.

Height: 5'11" Bust: 36 Waist: 26 Hips: 36 Shoe: 11 Dress: 8-10 Hair: Blonde Eyes: Blue

One mistake many models make is putting on too much make-up. Remember, you want the picture to reflect the real you.

Study the zed card of Jennifer Madison. Take a few moments to look at the pictures. They have been arranged to draw your eyes back into the zed card as you study it.

#1. The first picture was placed on the top left-hand side of the zed card because we all read left to right, so this picture should catch your eyes first. The model is looking down and her sunglasses pull your eyes down toward the #3 picture.

#2. The second picture was placed on the top right-hand side because the model's long arms lead you back into the rest of the pictures. If it were placed on the bottom it would lead your eyes away from the zed card.

#3. The third picture was placed on the bottom left-hand corner because the model is looking up and her breast and arms lead your eyes to the picture on the bottom right-hand side.

#4. The fourth picture was placed on the bottom right hand side for two reasons. First, the model is looking up, which pulls your eyes back into the card, and second, because the model's arms are raised, which also leads your eyes back into the zed card.

If this sounds complex, don't panic. Just think about where in the zed card your pictures would be more effective. If you can't decide, then let the company that prints your zed card arrange the pictures for you.

Don't give all of your zed cards away to your family and friends. This is a common mistake and can get very expensive.

An easy and inexpensive way to please family and friends is to have laser jet copies made. Take a good quality photo or photos to any copy company and have them make copies for you.

Using the zed card format you can have four pictures made on one 8"x10" piece of paper.

Take in four pictures, have them reduced to a 4 x 5 inch size, then organize them next to each other like on the zed card shown on the previous page.

Each color copy should cost you between seventy-five cents and a dollar. That means your color pictures are only costing you twenty-five cents each.

If you don't have a zed card, color copies are a great inexpensive option. Cut the pictures up and put your name, address, phone number and stats on the back of each one.

This way you have a picture to give away if a job suddenly comes up or if you've run out of zed cards.

Color pictures are a good idea if you're just starting out in the modeling profession. They're inexpensive and you really need them. When you show up at a modeling interview and you don't have a picture, you've already lost the job. It doesn't matter how beautiful or perfect you are. The person that interviews you is rarely the casting agent. They are the middleman who collects pictures and summits them to the casting agent. The casting agent makes the decision on who is right for the job.

Never, ever go into an agency or to an interview with a photo from places like Glamour Shots. These pictures are great for family and friends but not for the real world of modeling. You're better off showing up empty handed then with a touched-up photo.

WHAT IS A PORTFOLIO?

A portfolio is a résumé of the modeling work you have done. If the only work you have done is paying a photographer for pictures to put on your zed card, then pick the best photos out and start your book.

There is a standard black portfolio case that zips open and is available at most stationary stores. It's pricey, and unless you've got an extensive portfolio, skip it.

A simple 3-ring black binder works very well. It only costs a few dollars and is a lot easier to carry.

You'll need also to buy non-glare 8 x11 sheet protectors. They cost about ten cents each.

As your portfolio grows your pictures will fit conveniently inside the plastic non-glare sheets. Your portfolio looks much more professional when it is full, even if full means only a page or two. As you get more work you add more plastic sheets. Having an agent flip through empty pages is embarrassing.

WHY DO I NEED A PORTFOLIO?

In the real world when you apply for a job a potential employer wants to see a résumé. Basically, they want to know what your experiences are. A portfolio is the same thing. In the world of modeling it's even more important because you have numerous employers. Each interview you go out on is a potential employer.

Sometimes you can go out once or twice a week on interviews, which means in a year you've seen more than one hundred employers!

Your most recent work (pictures) should appear in the front of the book. Never leave a page blank.

HOW MUCH DOES A PORTFOLIO COST?

You shouldn't be paying for a portfolio. You should be building it by the modeling jobs you complete. Always insist on a copy of one of the pictures at each photo shoot you get paid for.

This can be tricky. Some agents don't ask for copies, and at some photo shoots it is frowned upon to ask for anything since they are paying you.

These pictures are important and you have a right to have something from the shoot to add to your portfolio.

Always start with your agent. Ask them to get you a picture from each job they send you to. Sometimes you have to pay a small fee for a print.

Asking too many questions while on a job or getting argumentative with a photographer or coordinator can cost you not only the job but could end your modeling career.

HOW DO I BUILD MY PORTFOLIO?

One photo shoot at a time, even if it means working for a low wage and sometimes for free.

When you go to work for a new employer you don't start out at the top, right?

In modeling, getting your foot in the door is important. Waiting around for that one super job just doesn't happen. You need to work, build your portfolio, and build your experience. All models, including supermodels, started at the bottom.

SHOULD YOU WORK FOR FREE?

Local photographers and small-time magazines in your area are always looking for models to work for free.

You model for them and (in return,) they give you professional photographs of the shoot.

Volunteering your services for non-profit agencies that hold fashion shows is a wonderful way for you to gain experience, build your portfolio, and get exposure. Most everyone at these fashion shows are volunteers, and you will meet more real contacts here than most anywhere else.

Building up your portfolio and getting experience is very important, but you also need to know when it's time to ask for pay.

Don't underestimate yourself; your agent won't. Modeling is hard work and you should be paid for it.

HOW DO YOU FIND A GOOD PHOTOGRAPHER?

In chapter three we have an alphabetical listing, state by state, of thousands of photographers, along with their addresses, phone numbers, and (if available) e-mail addresses.

Do not run out and spend a lot of money on professional photographs. They may look good but they will not guarantee you work in the modeling profession.

Some photographers try to sell you expensive portfolio shots (pictures). They commonly tell you that you will not get an agent unless you have professional pictures to show them. This is not true. (See finding an agent in Chapter Four.)

To find a good photographer, you'll need to make sure they specialize in what you are looking for.

Every photographer has his or her own style and specialty, from weddings to portrait photography. This is why you need to know what to ask for, before hiring a photographer.

First you need to ask yourself, what type of pictures do I want the photographer to take?

If you want your baby or child photographed, then you need to find a photographer that specializes in baby or children photography.

Don't hire a photographer because they say they can shoot anything or because their fees are more reasonable. You will be disappointed with the results.

If you're uncomfortable talking with the photographer on the phone, you probably will be just as uncomfortable in front of their camera.

You need to feel a bond or instant rapport with them. It's not very hard to do. Be straightforward with them and tell them what you want.

With your direction their job becomes more focused and you get better results.

WHAT TYPE OF PICTURES DO I WANT?

You want a headshot, body shot and numerous indoor and outdoor shots to show your face, body, personality and versatility.

In other words "the real you" needs to be captured on film. If you don't know what the real you is, practice posing in front of a mirror.

Rummage through your closet and try on every outfit you own. Which one looks the best? Which one accents your long legs? Which one makes you look very sexy or handsome?

WHAT DO I BRING TO A PHOTO SHOOT?

Bring enough clothing for at least four complete changes, from head to toes (hats and shoes too). Don't bring jewelry. It normally is not used in a photo shoot.

For your body shot you'll need either a bathing suit or tight-fitting outfit. Remember, these pictures must reflect your physique, whether it is long and lean or short and round.

If you have a particular talent, bring props with you and let the photographer know about it. The more open you are with your photographer, the better your pictures will reflect "you."

If you play sports bring your sports equipment with you. Soccer balls, basketballs and volleyballs are all great props.

If you're a businessman, bring your glasses and briefcase with you.

Always get a good nights sleep the night before the photo shoot, and always arrive clean, dressed appropriately and never late.

HOW LONG ARE THE PHOTO SHOOTS?

Photo shoots last from two to three hours. Don't set your clocks or make appointments immediately before or after the photo shoot.

You need to be calm, relaxed and focused on what you are doing. I've seen horrible pictures taken by very good photographers. If the models aren't prepared mentally, or they are in a hurry, then even the best of photographers won't get good pictures.

HOW MUCH SHOULD I PAY THE PHOTOGRAPHER?

Fees always need to be negotiated before the photo shoot, never after it. A good rule of thumb is to spend about one hundred dollars per roll of film. Usually three rolls of film are shot at each photo shoot.

Some photographers have a flat fee between one hundred dollars and four hundred dollars. If they do, you need to know how many rolls of film their fee includes.

At a baby's photo shoot don't panic or feel guilty if your baby is fussy and it takes extra time to get good pictures. Photographers that specialize in baby photographs know what to expect.

Most photographers insist upon having a makeup artist and sometimes a hairstylist at their photo shoots. These people charge between fifty and one hundred and fifty dollars per each photo shoot (each.)

Makeup artists are worth their weight in gold, and even you men out there will need them.

They know what the modeling world is looking for. Don't argue or tell them that you do your own make up. Let them do their magic.

For a simple photo shoot a hairstylist really isn't necessary, unless you have limp, thin hair and really need help. Tell the photographer before the photo shoot. Trust their judgment. They're on your side, and if you don't look good, they don't look good.

WHO KEEPS THE NEGATIVES OR FILM?

If you are paying a photographer for a photo shoot you should get the film, although this isn't always what happens. Some photographers, especially in large metropolitan areas, insist upon making a contact sheet for you. Then they charge you for each picture you want blown up.

They insist that they don't make a profit off of the pictures. They are just doing it as a convenience for you.

For professional color enlargements the average fees are as follows:

4"x6" ($ 5–7)	5"x7" ($ 8–12)	8"x10" ($10–15)
9"x12" ($14–20)	11"x14" ($16–25)	

A contact sheet shows all of the photographs taken at your photo shoot. Each picture is small, usually 1–1/2"x1". You need to carefully study each picture before you have them blown up.

Photographers and agents have a trained eye and are much better at choosing them for you.

Study the contact sheet on the next page. Which pictures would you have blown up?

If you keep your film do not take it to your local store to be developed. Take it to a photo lab. You can find one in the yellow pages of your local phone book.

You've already spent a lot of time and money on this film; if it were lost or ruined it would be a terrible waste.

Have the photo lab make you a contact sheet.

Study the contact sheet and pick out a few shots you feel are the most flattering or that best represent you. Then ask the lab technician which of the pictures you picked out would look better blown up.

Start with a 4"x6"size. Don't blow up every picture; it's expensive and not necessary.

A headshot, full body shot, and one or two other favorites are all you need.

Keep your contact sheet and your negatives in a safe, dry place for future enlargements.

Don't give these photos away. Make color copies of them or use them to make your zed card.

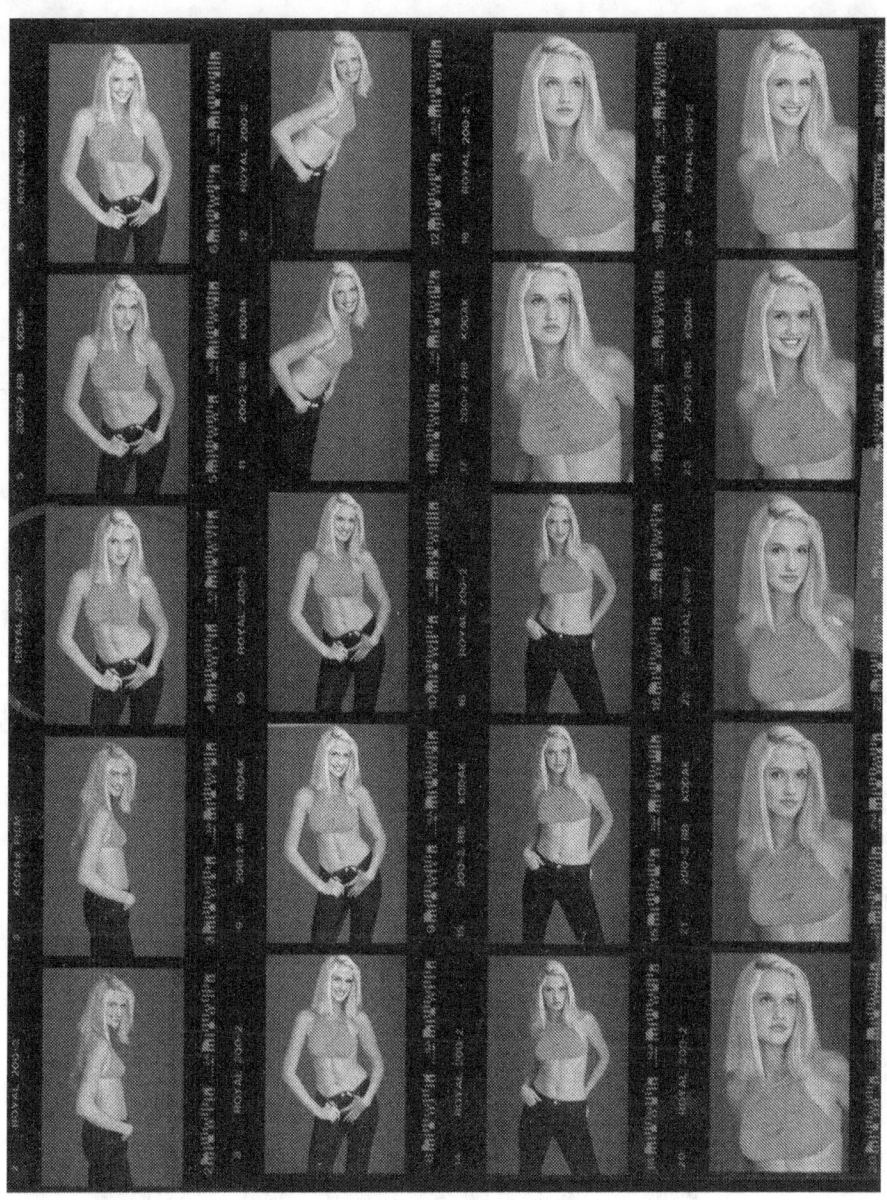

Study this contact sheet. Which picture would choose to enlarge?

3

PHOTOGRAPHERS &
PHOTOGRAPHY AGENCIES

There are tens of thousands of photographers in this country, and each one specializes in different parts or areas of the photography world.

In this chapter we have narrowed the list of photographers (from around the country) to professionals that have been in business for at least ten years and that have experience in both commercial and portrait photography.

The list is alphabetical, first by states and then by photographer.

Before you hire a photographer you need to ask yourself a few questions:

What kind of photographer should I hire?

What kind of pictures do I want taken?

How much should I pay for the photo shoot?

These important questions and others are all answered in chapter two.

Selecting a photographer from this list doesn't guarantee they will be the ideal photographer for you. Use this list as a guide to help you find an experienced photographer.

Start with your local phone book; it's a good source to find a professional photographer in your immediate area.

Cross-reference your local photographers with the list of photographers in this chapter.

This will help narrow your search for a professional who is right for you.

Finding the right photographer is an important step in all phases of your modeling career, whether you're just beginning the profession and/or when you're advancing to a higher level throughout your modeling career.

ALABAMA

ALABAMA AIR FOTO 120 Oxmoor Blvd #E Homewood, AL 35209 205-942-8777

ALABASTER PHOTO SVC 127 Main St. Alabaster, AL 35007 205-664-9261

AMERICAN COLOR STUDIOS 2541 6th Ave # 613 Haleyville, AL 33565 205-486-3072

BILL INGALLS PHOTOGRAPHY 853 S.Court St. Montgomery, AL 36104 334-264-3333

BILL RAPIER PHOTOGRAPHICS 811 Azalea Rd Mobile, AL 36693 334-661-6611

CARLETON PHOTOGRAPHY 5149 Carleton Ln Orange Beach, AL 36561 334-981-3888

CATHI LARSEN AGENCY 1675 Montclair Rd. #136 Birmingham, AL 35210 205-951-2445

CAYLOR PHOTOGRAPHY 514 DIXIE DR ENTERPRISE, AL 36330 334-393-1065

COLONIAL PHOTOGRAPHY 2411 Government St Mobile, AL 36606 334-478-5655

DENNIS KEIM STUDIOS 929 Willowbrook Dr Se #104 Huntsville, AL 35802 256-880-7898

DUNAWAYS STUDIO 625 Glover Ave Enterprise, AL 36330 334-347-1062

GALLERY 108 N Hoyle Ave Bay Minette, Al 36507 334-937-5130

HERB FORD PHOTOGRAPHY 2401 Rainbow Dr Gadsden, AL 35901 256-442-4372

HURT HOUSE OF PHOTOGRAPHY 130 Snow St Oxford, AL 36203 256-831-4261

JERNIGAN PHOTOGRAPHY 314 S 10th St Opelika, AL 36801 334-745-2334

JIM STOKES PHOTOGRAPHY INC 629 Azalea Rd Mobile, AL 36609 334-660-2833

LARRY WALDRUP PHOTOGRAPHY 728 Arcadia Cir NW Huntsville, AL 35801 256-539-8113

MICHAEL MASON PHOTOGRAPHY 1820 6th Ave Se #N Decatur, AL 35601 256-350-3037

MOSS PHOTOGRAPHY 8760 Madison Blvd #B Madison, AL 35758 256-830-9408

PALMER STUDIO 2008 Airport Blvd Mobile, AL 36606 334-417-3523

PHOTOGRAPHY BY GREG YOUNG 108 Main St Madison, AL 37758 256-772-8018

PHOTOGRAPHY BY MIKE MC KEMIE 11447 Lee Road 379 Valley, AL 36854 334-745-3202

PORTRAIT PALACE 744 Chestnut St Gadsden, AL 35901 256-547-8545

ROBERT NORRIS PHOTO 1433 Montgomery Hwy #C Vestavia Hills, AL 35216 205-979-7005

ROBERTSON PHOTOGRAPHY INC 2103 Eastern Blvd Montgomery, AL 36117 334-277-2228

S & S PHOTOGRAPHY 2365 Whitesburg Dr S Huntsville, AL 35801 256-533-0088

SAM BUCHANAN PHOTOGRAPHY 123 N Marion St Athens, AL 35611 256-232-1524

STATUS IMAGE PHOTOGRAPHY 618 Bradley St SW Decatur, AL 35601 256-355-5551

TERRY NIBLETT PHOTOGRAPHY 3381 Mccurdy Ave N Rainsville, AL 35986 256-638-3646

VAN BLANKENSHIP PHOTOGRAPHY 112 Coffee St E Talladega, AL 35160 256-362-3485

WILSON C-BLOUNT PHOTOGRAPHIC 28489 State Highway 75 Oneonta, AL 35121 1-800-628-6030

ZAP PROFESSIONAL PHOTOGRAPHY 307 Hargrove Rd #E Tuscaloosa, AL 35401 1-800-452-6687

ALASKA

ANCHORAGE PHOTOS 911 W 29th Ave Anchorage, AK 99503 907-561-5568

BRADY PHOTOGRAPHY 3939 Turnagain Blvd E Anchorage, AK 99517 907-248-7500

BYRNES PHOTO 7303 N Douglas Hwy Juneau, AK 99801 907-586-1273

DANNY DANIELS PHOTOGRAPHY 101 E 9th Ave #3a Anchorage, AK 99501 907-276-7755

FJORD PHOTOGRAPHY 158 Thomas St Ketchikan, AK 99901 907-225-6997

GREG MARTIN PHOTOGRAPHY 700 W 58th Sve #D Anchorage, AK 99518 907-563-6112

JEFF SCHULTZ PHOTOGRAPHY 2505 Fairbanks St Anchorage, AK 99503 907-279-2797

JIM DIEHL PHOTOGRAPHY Megeve Rd. Girdwood, AK 99587 907-783-2708

JUDY PATRICK PHOTOGRAPHY 600 Glenwood Ave Wasilla, AK 99654 907-376-4704

MARION STIRRUP PHOTOGRAPHY 1610 Ismailov St Kodiak, AK 99615 907-486-5079

MEMORY MAKERS PHOTOGRAPHY 3901 Old Seward Hwy Anchorage, AK 99503 907-563-2200

NELSONS PHOTOGRAPHY 606 Bentley Dr Fairbanks, AK 9701 907-452-3116

PHOTOGRAPHY BY DAVID GELOTTE 4500 Hillcrest Ave Juneau, AK 99801 907-780-6255

ROY MULLIN PHOTOGRAPHY 173 Redoubt Ave Soldotna, AK 99669 907-262-2727

THIRD EYE PHOTOGRAPHY Po Box 1010 Girdwood, AK 99587 907-783-2773

WORDS & PICTURES Po Box 190003 Anchorage, AK 99519 907-248-1974

ARIZONA

BOB WILCOX PHOTOGRAPHY 2907 N 2ND ST Phoenix, AZ 85012 602-264-2531

BRUCE BERMAN PHOTOGRAPHY 999 E Fry Blvd #216 Sierra Vista, AZ 85635 520-459-2619

DAVID BEAN PHOTOGRAPHY 4315 4th St Tucson, AZ 85711 520-323-0733

D I BARTOLOMEO PHOTOGRAPHY 16235 N 63rd St Scottsdale, AZ 85254 480-951-4162

FOREVER YOURS PHOTOGRAPHY 6943 5th Ave Scottsdale, AZ 85251 480-949-1695

HAL MARTIN FOGEL PHOTOGRAPHY 1715 N 16th Ave Phoenix, AZ 85007 602-258-2111

HASSAN PHOTOGRAPHY 311 W Camelback Rd Phoenix, AZ 85013 602-279-1199

JOHN HARRIS PHOTOGRAPHY 3210 S Fair Ln. Tempe, AZ 85282 602-437-8769

JUDY ANN BROWDER PHOTO 1964 Mesquite Ave Lake Havasu City, AZ 86403 520-855-1434

LOBECK'S FINE PHOTOGRAPHY 10 W 3rd St Yuma, AZ 85364 520-343-9878

MARTINEZ PHOTOGRAPHY 4576 11th Ave Tucson, AZ 85714 520-294-9404

PM PHOTOGRAPHIC 2506 N Stone Ave Tucson, AZ 85705 520-622-6238

PASSPORT ACTION PHOTO SVC 3375 N Campbell Ave Tucson, AZ 85719 520-323-9286

PORTRAITS BY REG 5450 S Lakeshore Dr #108 Tempe, AZ 85283 480-839-3709

RICK MUELLER PHOTOGRAPHY 14435 E Roosevelt St Phoenix, AZ 85006 602-267-8845

RODNEY BOYD PHOTOGRAPHY 14402 S 131st St Gilbert, AZ 85233 480-812-9209

SNYDER DANIEL 445 N 3rd Ave Tucson, AZ 85705 520-792-4828

STUDIO SEVEN PORTRAITURE 4500 Speedway Blvd #90 Tucson, AZ 85712 520-881-2406

THOMAS VENEKLASEN PHOTOGRAPHY 445 N 3rd Ave Tucson, AZ 85705 530-884-8143

WAYNE PEARCE PHOTOGRAPHY 11449 N Mandarin Ln Tucson, AZ 85373 520-575-8854

WEST STUDIOS 634 Schemmer Dr #303 Prescott, AZ 86305 520-776-1236

ARKANSAS

ARTISTRY PORTRAITS 1652 E Hammond St Fayetteville, AR 72701 501-253-9790

BARNETT'S STUDIO 3016 Jenny Lind Rd Fort Smith, AR 72901 501-783-7324

BOB MC CALL PHOTOGRAPHY 2722 E Nettleton Ave Jonesboro, AR 42401 870-932-5138

BOBS STUDIO OF PHOTOGRAPHY 109 N Block Ave Fayetteville, AR 72701 501-442-4782

BRYANT PHOTOGRAPHY 5515 Middle Warren Rd Pine Bluff, AR 71603 870-879-6551

CLIFTON EOFF PHOTOGRAPHER 1202 N 8th St Rogers, AR 72756 501-226-5184

GARY ALAN STRAIN PHOTOGRAPHY 1025 Parkway St Conway, AR 72032 501-329-6455

GARY'S STUDIO OF PHOTOGRAPHY 125 Albert Pike Rd Hot Springs, AR 71913 501-268-9304

GEORGE DILLON PHOTOGRAPHY INC 1407 E Moore Ave Searcy, AR 72143 501-268-9304

GRISHAM PHOTOGRAPHY 112 N Dudley Rd Magnolia, AR 71753 870-234-1380

HIGHLIGHTS PHOTOGRAPHY 812 N Thompson St #10 Springdale, AR 72764 501-756-3945

J K LLOYDS INC 2311 Biscayne Dr #140 Little Rock, AR 72227 501-224-7759

JOHN MILLER STUDIO 449 Washington St Camden, AR 71701 870-836-2479

JORDEN DAVIE PHOTOGRAPHY 1910 W 3rd St Little Rock, AR 77205-4410 501-372-3878

KEITH STURCH PHOTOGRAPHY 787 Rock St Batesville, AR 72501 870-793-6014

KIRKS PHOTOGRAPHY 1016 W South St #A Benton, AR 72015 501-778-8909

LITES PHOTOGRAPHY 1618 Brentwood Dr Pine Bluff, AR 71601 870-535-2210

MATTHEWS PHOTOGRAPHY 770 S Saint Louis St Batesville, AR 72501 870-698-1566

PLUMLEE PHOTOGRAPHY 2233 County Road 612 Green Forest, AR 72638 870-749-2588

RALPH ARMSTRONG PHOTOGRAPHERS 1105 W 33rd Dr. Little Rock, AR 72206 501-521-1718

ROBERT JENKINS PHOTOGRAPHY 501 Falls Blvd N Wynne, AR 72369 870-238-8648

ROBERT O SEAT PHOTOGRAPHY 2295 White Dr Batesville, AR 72501 870-793-3291

SCHLOSSER PHOTOGRAPHY 820 E Main St Blytheville, AR 72315 870-763-3326

TOM CLOWERS HOUSE OF PORTRAITS 515 Holcomb St Springdale, AR 72210 501-821-0901

WATTS-CATES PHOTOGRAPHY 910 Lyledale Rd Benton, AR 72015 501-228-5040

CALIFORNIA

A-1 BROADWAY FOTO 536 W Vista, CA 92083 760-724-0840

A-OFFICAL PASSPORT PHOTO 2353 Midway Dr San Diego, CA 92110 619-223-1661

ABTEY WEDDING PHOTOGRAPHY 234 Los Alamos Ave Santa Barbara, CA 93109 805-962-4331

ARBOR PHOTOGRAPHIC 6880 Archibald #49 Alta Loma, CA 91701 909-948-0790

ARTHUR MINTZ PHOTOGRAPHY 20490 Saratoga Los Gatos Rd Saratoga, CA 95070 408-867-4077

AUSTIN'S UPTOWN STUDIO 1709 Del Paso Blvd Sacramento, CA 95815 916-925-2310

BAIN PHOTOGRAPHY 3843 E Colorado Blvd Pasadena, CA 91107 626-449-8180

BARBER PHOTOGRAPHY 34085 Pacific Coast Hwy #117 Dana Point, CA 92629 949-493-5840

BARROS CREATIVE IMAGES 1357 Buchanan Rd Pittsburg, CA 94565 925-432-8000

BEATIE PHOTOGRAPHY 15185 Sun Valley LN Del Mar, CA 92014 858-755-7707

BEAUTIFUL DAY PHOTOGRAPHY 5608 E 2nd St Long Beach, CA 90803 562-439-6826

BELLE N BEAU PHOTOGRAPHY 310 S 1st Ave Arcadia, CA 91006 626-446-6000

BERNARD PHOTOGRAPHER 166 Geary St #500 San Francisco, CA 94108 415-421-3248

BEST OF TIMES PHOTOGRAPHY 512 Polk St Monterey, CA 93940 813-375-7131

BILL FOX SPORTS PHOTOS 22 Commercial Blvd #F Novato, CA 94949 415-883-4437

BILL NUNES PHOTOGRAPHER 443 5th Gustine, CA 95322 209-854-680

BILL SMITH PHOTOGRAPHY 3711 Sacramento, CA 95816 916-452-4992

BLEVINS PHOTOGRAPHY 15566 Cornuta Ave Bellflower, CA 90760 562-925-6469

BONNIE'S PHOTOGRAPHY & VIDEO 1532 W Yale Ave Orange, CA 92867 714-998-2666

BOUDOIR PHOTOGRAPHY-STAHLBERG 620 Main St Martinez, CA 94553 925-229-2939

BUD WHITE SCHOOL PORTRAITS Po Box 723 Cupertino, Ca 95015 408-866-5144

CAM LEN STUDIO 7466 N Fresno St Fresno, Ca 93720 559-439-0162

CARLA GILBERT PHOTOGRAPHY 628 Glencrest Pl Solana Beach, Ca 92075 858-755-3804

CASTRO COLOR STUDIOS 1056 W Gardena, CA 90247 310-329-4653

CAUCHI PHOTOGRAPHY 1019 Edwards Rd Burlingame, Ca 94010 650-342-5178

CHRISTOPHER MICHAEL PHOTO 434 W Arrow Hwy Claremont, CA 91711 909-621-0591

CHRYSALIS PHOTOGRAPHY 66 Punta Perdido Monterey, CA 93940 831-372-0567

CLASSIC WEDDING CAMERA 6747 Citronell Ave Pico Rivera, CA 90660 562-949-1967

CLEO'S PHOTOGRAPHY 630 20th St #202 Oakland, CA 94612 510-839-3095

COASTSIDE PHOTOGRAPHY 731 Main St Half Moon Bay, CA 94019 650-726-1412

COOK'S PHOTOGRAPHY 504 Mars Ave Lompoc, CA 93436 805-733-3736

COOKE'S FINE PHOTOGRAPHY 80 Running Iron Rd Bishop, CA 93514 760-872-2345

CREATIVE CAMERA 2222 2nd St #21 Livermore, CA 94550 925-455-9763

CREATIVE IMAGE By Raymond 1060 Lynwood Dr San Bernardino, Ca 92404 909-882-3922

CREATIVE IMAGES 1403 W Arrow Hwy San Dimas, CA 91733 626-963-7884

CREATIVE LIGHT PRODUCTIONS 5701 State Farm Dr #120 Rohnert Park, CA 9492 707-795-0388

CRISTIANO PHOTOGRAPHY 1617 Alum Rock Ave #A San Jose, CA 95116 408-258-1717

DAVID BRANTLEY PHOTOGRAPHY 1344 W 24th St Merced, CA 95340 209-383-1756

DAVID EARHART PHOTOGRAPHY 1277 N D St San Bernardino, CA 92405 909-889-2888

DEAN LESTER PHOTOGRAPHY 2801 Junipero Ave #212 Long Beach, CA 90806 562-426-3960

DEBBI DE MONT PHOTOGRAPHY 3736 7th St Long Beach, CA 90804 562-433-1087

DENNIS COLEMAN PHOTOGRAPHY New Castle, CA 95658 916-663-1214

DESERT PHOTO 104 E Fredricks St Barstow, CA 92311 760-256-7141

DON HAGOPIAN PRO PHOTO 4415 Coldwater Canyon Ave Studio City, CA 91604 818-980-3320

DON HUGHES PHOTOGRAPHY 927 6th St Los Banos, CA 93635 209-826-6284

DORE STUDIO 2442 Mission St San Francisco, CA 94110 415-282-3321

DOUGLAS BLIVEN MASTER OF PHOTO 126 S 5th St El Centro, CA 92243 760-352-5954

DOWSING PHOTOGRAPHY STUDIOS 22533 Hawthorne Blvd Torrance, CA 90505 310-373-6111

ED AVILA PHOTOGRAPHY 47 San Miguel Ave #3 Salinas, CA 93901 831-757-1777

EDDIE BARRON PHOTOGRAPHY 239 S Robertson Blvd #8 Beverly Hills, CA 92011 310-652-8034

EUGENE PHOTO & VIDEO INC 4738 Woodman Ave Sherman Oaks, CA 91423 818-907-8169

FAST FOTO 317 Oak St Brentwood, CA 94513 925-634-9914

FICARRA STUDIOS 704 E Olive Ave Fresno, CA 93728 559-266-0624

FICHERA STUDIO 1629 Paramount Blvd Montebello, CA 90640 323-721-1163

FILMWORKS SUPERIOR PHOTOGRAPHY 1226 Lincoln Way Auburn, CA 95603 530-823-1134

FINE PHOTOGRAPHY BY WOLFE 4845 Kenneth Ave Orcutt, CA 93455 805-934-3358

FIRESTONE PHOTOGRAPHY 139 Washington Blvd Fremont, CA 94539 510-490-6789

FLASHBACKS PHOTOGRAPHY 222 Central Ct Stockton, CA 95204 209-948-2748

FOCAL POINT PRODUCTIONS 2559 San Anselmo St San Diego, CA 92109 858-581-3352

FOTO ESTUDIO MORENO 309 W 2nd St Calexico, CA 92231 760-357-4971

FOX'S SCHOOL PORTRAITS 212 Goodman St Bakersfield, CA 93305 661-324-3697

G PAUL BISHOP PORTRAITURE 2125 Durant Ave Berkeley, CA 94704 510-841-2079

GAINSBOROUGH STUDIO 227 E Kern Ave Tulare, CA 93274 559-686-4838

GARY WIGDAHL PHOTOGRAPHY 132 E Main St El Cajon, CA 92020 919-440-6069

GENESIS PHOTOGRAPHY 185 Moffett Blvd Mountain View, CA 94043 650-967-2301

GLENN NAKAMICHI PHOTOGRAPHY 3400 McCall Ave #112 Selma, CA 93662 559-896-5240

GLENN WILLIAMS PHOTOGRAPHY 1006 W Benjamin Holt Dr Stockton, CA 95207 209-477-3636

GOLDEN IMAGES 748 Woodside Rd Redwood City, CA 94061 650-365-4230

HALL, NORMAN C 55 New Montgomery St San Francisco, CA 94105 925-952-4902

HALVERSON'S PHOTOGRAPHY 493 N La Cadena Dr Colton, CA 92324 909-825-0123

HEIMLICH PHOTOGRAPHY 791 Kevenaire Dr Milpitas, CA 95035 408-945-6446

HELDERS PHOTOGRAPHY 527 6th St Marysville, CA 95901 530-743-6539

HOUSE OF PHOTOGRAPHIC ARTS 5815 Gibbons Dr Carmichael, CA 95608 916-487-1005

HUDSON PHOTOGRAPHY 1188 River Ave Oakdale, CA 95361 209-847-0540

IMAGES 824 S Broadway Santa Maria, CA 93454 805-922-2932

INSTANT PHOTO SVC 7324 Reseda, CA 91355 818-996-6296

INTERFACE VISUAL 607 Charles Ave #C Seaside, CA 93955 831-899-8830

J & M PHOTOGRAPHY 16727 Bear Valley Rd #270 Hesperia, CA 92345 760-244-4767

JACK WILSON PHOTOGRAPHY 1302 Monte Vista Ave Upland, CA 91786 909-985-5454

JADWINS 2540 La France Dr Bakersfield, CA 93304 661-832-0677

JAMES FIDELIBUS PHOTOGRAPHY 1727 Bonanza St Walnut Creek, CA 94596 925-938-3999

JAMES HYNES PHOTOGRAPHY 31926 Quartz LN Castaic, CA 91384 661-295-0057

JEANNINE'S PHOTOGRAPHY 4505 Tokay Dr Oakley, CA 94561 925-625-3403

JERRY BRYAN PHOTOGRAPHY 2890 Pio Pico Dr Carlsbad, CA 92008 760-434-3318

JIM WOODS PHOTOGRAPHY 360 Mobil Ave Camarillo, CA 93010 805-482-3840

JOHANSEN PHOTOGRAPHY GALLERY 1125 J St Sacramento, CA 95814 916-442-6080

JOHN S GRAVES PHOTOGRAPHY P.O.Box 808 Laguna Beach, CA 92652 949-497-2091

JOSEPH CARROLL PHOTOGRAPHY 27715 Jefferson Ave #205 Temecula, CA 92590 909-676-8170

JUDY ANN BROWDER PHOTOGRAPHY 263 Victory Dr Needles, CA 92363 760-326-2067

K C PHOTOGRAPHIC SVC 427 Center St Taft, CA 93268 661-763-5429

KAHL PHOTOGRAPHY INC 300 E Yosemite Ave #101 Manteca, CA 95336 209-239-1022

KATHLEEN AHERN PHOTOGRAPHY 2155 Las Positas Ct #C Livermore, CA 94550 925-606-8800

KELLOGG PHOTOGRAPHY 26 Medway Rd #5 San Rafael, CA 94901 415-459-4415

LARRY'S PHOTOGRAPHY 1612 Mission St Santa Cruz, CA 95060 831-423-2815

LAVOUX PHOTOGRAPHY 9455 Carmelita Ave Atascadero, CA 93422 805-466-9363

LENSART STUDIO 1537 Solano Ave Berkeley, CA 94707 510-526-2140

LES FOSTER PHOTOGRAPHY 39056 Foxholm Dr Palmdale, CA 93551 661-947-6790

LIGHTWORKS PHOTOGRAPHY 1725 3rd St Napa, CA 94559 707-252-4172

MARC GLASSMAN PHOTOGRAPHY P.O. Box 1997 Palm Desert, CA 92261 760-568-1635

MC CARTNEY PHOTOGRAPHICS 74 Harper Canyon Rd Salinas, CA 831-375-3533

MC GILL PHOTOGRAPHY 8366 Montana Dr Paradise, CA 95969 530-877-9785

METCALF PHOTOGRAPHY 1922 S Nevada St Oceanside, CA 92054 760-722-0678

MICHAEL ANTONE PHOTOGRAPHY 35223 Wycombe Pl Newark, CA 94560 510-796-5802

MICHAEL J ELDERMAN PHOTO 1860 Chicago Ave #113 Riverside, CA 92507 909-682-0834

MICHAEL VAN AUKEN PHOTOGRAPHY 3449 Misty LN Concord, CA 94519 925-687-3686

MILLENER PRODUCTIONS PHOTO 685 Pine Knot Ave Big Bear Lake, CA 92315 909-866-3054

MILLS PHOTO STUDIO 126 Mill St Grass Valley, CA 95945 530-273-6818

MOMENTS TO REMEMBER 22151 Clarendon St Woodland Hills, CA 91367 818-713-9433

NEW IMAGE STUDIO OF PHOTOGRAPHY 2655 Park Marina Dr Redding, CA 96001 530-243-4301

NOEL GRADY PHOTOGRAPHY 277 Rodney Ave Encinitas, CA 92024 760-753-8630

NOLTE PHOTOGRAPHY DESIGN 913 San Pablo Ave Albany, CA 94706 510-526-4671

O'CONNOR PHOTOGRAPHY 26752 Oak Ave #D Canyon Country, CA 91351 661-251-8000

OMAR NOOR PHOTOGRAPHY 2797 Walnut Creek, CA 94596 925-945-8381

OSCAR'S PHOTOGRAPHY & VIDEO 649 S Oxnard, CA 93030 805-487-5154

PAUL BACOSA STUDIO 1274 Benton St Santa Clara, CA 95050 408-296-1016

PHOTOGRAPHICS MEMORIES 2340 Fairfield St Eureka, Ca 95501 707-443-2639

PHOTOGRAPHY BY ALAIN TOMATIS 6294 Skyway Paradise, CA 95969 530-877-2134

PHOTO BY FORREST 1414 E Thousand Oaks Blvd #218 Thousand Oaks, CA 91362 805-496-2255

PHOTOGRAPHY BY MARK 121 W Empire St Grass Valley, CA 95945 530-272-4590

PHOTOGRAPHY BY RICHARD 121 W Jones St Santa Maria, CA 93458 805-925-7430

PORTRAITS BY MAC 931 Tennessee St Vallejo, CA 94590 707-552-1008

PRO IMAGE 17800 Hesperian Blvd San Lorenzo, CA 94580 510-276-6250

RAMIREZ PHOTOGRAPHY 6205 Santa Ynez Ave Atascadero, CA 93422 805-466-3278

RICHARD'S PHOTOGRAPHY 7540 Westlawn Ave Los Angeles, CA 90045 310-306-4945

ROBERT PIERCE STUDIOS 2474 W 3rd St Santa Rosa, CA 95401 707-528-0850

ROBERT THOMAS PHOTOGRAPHY 18481 Carolyn Dr Castro Valley, CA 945 46 925-846-4446

ROLAND HILTSCHER PHOTO 906 E Commonwealth Ave Fullerton, CA 92831 714-738-1171

ROMERO PHOTOGRAPHY 1999 S Coast Hwy Laguna Beach, CA 92651 949-494-5828

ROSS STANDEL PHOTOGRAPHY 17200 Ventura Blvd #118 Encino, CA 91316 818-907-0107

SAN MATEO PHOTOGRAPHY 329 S Ellsworth Ave San Mateo, CA 94401 650-342-1757

SANFORD STUDIO INC 14106 Whittier Blvd Whittier, CA 90605 562-698-0071

SCHENCK & SCHENCK PHOTOGRAPHY P.O. Box 526 Claremont, CA 91711 909-624-3963

SCOTT MC CUE PHOTOGRAPHY 19 Orinda Way #H Orinda, CA 94563 925-253-1719

SHARAGA STUDIOS 18319 Delano St Reseda, CA 91335 818-881-8180

SHELBY STOVER PHOTOGRAPHY 129 Chorro St San Luis Obispo, CA 93405 805-541-1120

SHELDON OF LOS ALTOS 380 Main St Los Altos, CA 94022 650-948-3823

SHOOT ON SITE PHOTO STUDIOS 555 San Mateo Ave San Bruno, CA 94066 650-952-8470

STEVE RUBIOLO PHOTOGRAPHY 1022 B St Hayward, CA 94541 510-538-2212

SUNNY SEKI PHOTOGRAPHY 8907 Valley Blvd Rosemead, CA 91770 626-285-7700

SUTTON PHOTOGRAPHY 44803 Beech Ave Lancaster, CA 93534 661-942-4813

TINA'S PHOTOGRAPHY 529 F St Eureka, CA 95501 707-442-0914

TONY GRANT PHOTOGRAPHY 926 Soquel Ave #A Santa Cruz, CA 95062 831-425-7868

TOYO MIYATAKE STUDIO 235 W Fairview Ave San Gabriel, CA 91776 626-289-5674

VAN'S STUDIO OF PHOTOGRAPHY 600 N D St Madera, CA 93638 559-673-8400

VILLAGE STUDIO 8215 La Mesa Blvd La Mesa, CA 91941 619-466-6708

VISUAL IMAGE PRODUCTIONS 217 W Main St Visalia, CA 93291 559-734-1465

WAYNE BANKS PHOTOGRAPHY P.O. Box 261 Alta Loma, CA 91701 909-982-5499

WAYNE COATS PHOTOS 14919 Clement Dr Clearlake, CA 95422 707-994-2881

WAYNE SMITH PHOTOGRAPHY 4882 McGrath St #280 Ventura, CA 93003 805-658-2761

WESTCHESTER PHOTOGRAPHY 2002 E Woodlyn Rd Pasadena, CA 91104 310-670-2364

WILLIAM F GEORGE PHOTOGRAPHY 1207 Union St Alameda, CA 94501 510-521-0402

WOLVERINE PHOTOGRAPHY 8926 Benson Ave #K Montclair, CA 91763 909-985-2899

WOOD PHOTOGRAPHY 36559 Fremont, CA 94536 510-793-1891

YOUNGBLOOD PHOTOGRAPHY 406 Sherman St Healdsburg, CA 95448 707-431-2955

Z STUDIOS 2085 Sperry Ave # A Ventura, CA 93003 805-644-5554

COLORADO

A LENSMAN 1013 W Chatfield Ave Littleton CO 80127 303-933-1935

ABDOO STUDIO 2422 E 6th Ave Denver, CO 80206 303-388-6453

ARNOLD'S STUDIO 713 S Fir St Yuma, CO 80759 970-848-2326

AVALON PHOTOGRAPHY 10970 S Parker Rd # A1 Parker, CO 80134 303-840-1324

AVALOS PHOTOGRAPHY 511 W Northern Ave Pueblo, CO 81004 719-542-0188

BETTINGER PHOTOGRAPHY 2431 S University Blvd Denver, CO 80210 303-7336076

BIRLAUF & STEEN PHOTO 401 Delaware St Denver, CO 80204 303-629-0415

BLACK MOUNTAIN PHOTOGRAPHY Po Box 588 Monte Vista, CO 81144 719-852-2520

BOB SWERER PHOTOGRAPHY 2440 S College Ave Fort Collins, CO 80525 970-493-0239

BROOMFIELD PHOTOGRAPHY INC 60 Garden Ctr #101 Broomfield, CO 80020 303-469-1251

CHINN PHOTOGRAPHY STUDIO 106 Colorado Ave Pueblo, CO 81004 719-542-7127

CLARKE PHOTOGRAPHY 1535 Remington St Fort Collins, CO 80524 970-482-0724

COLORADO IMAGES BY JIM CLARK 2511 29th Ave Greeley, CO 80634 970-330-5315

COLORADO PHOTOGRAPHICS 304 E Mulberry St # 2 Fort Collins, CO 80524 970-493-4673

CREATIVE PHOTOGRAPHY 308 E Main St Montrose, CO 81401 970-249-9809

DAVID SCHLATTER PHOTOGRAPHY 1855 S Pitkin Ave Louisville, CO 80027 303-494-2200

FAMILY ALBUM PHOTOGRAPHY 1701 Santa Fe TRL # 50 Trinidad, CO 81082 719-846-9366

GENE PHOTOGRAPHY 1030 MONTROSE AVE COLORADO SPRINGS, CO 80906 719-389-0575

GRAND MESA PHOTOGRAPHY 637 ½ Karen Ct Grand Junction, CO 81504 970-245-6976

HASKELL PHOTOGRAPHY INC 1620 Platte St Denver, CO 80202 303-455-0933

JEFF ANDREW PHOTOGRAPHY 718 Hunters Cir Frisco, CO 80443 970-668-3399

JIM P GARRISON PHOTOGRAPHY Po Box 1104 Gunnison, CO 81230 970-641-5520

JOE COCA PHOTOGRAPHY 429 E Magnolia St Fort Collins, Co 80524 970-482-0858

JONSSON ENTERPRISES INC 904 Highway 133 Carbondale, CO 81623 970-963-9532

KELLY JOHN P 140 E Homestead Dr Basalt, CO 81621 970-927-4197

LIGHT SOURCE PHOTOGRAPHY 444 E College Dr Durango, CO 81301 970-259-0744

MARONA PHOTOGRAPHY 695 Animas View Dr Durango, CO 81301 970-247-2415

MASAMORI PHOTOGRAPHY 2010 Lamar St Denver, CO 80214 303-237-3041

MICK WEBSTER PHOTOGRAPHER 3505 S Taft Ave Loveland, CO 80537 970-663-2974

MORRIS PHOTOGRAPHY 624 Coffman St Longmont, CO 80501 303-776-5311

PHOTOEVENTS 391 S Race St Denver, CO 80209 303-778-7154

PHOTOFOLIO PHOTOGRAPHICS SVC 8411 N 73rd St Longmont, CO 80503 303-440-4418

PHOTOGRAPHY BY DINA 2313 Silver Trails Dr Fort Collins, CO 80526 970-407-1849

PHOTOGRAPHY BY FULKS 12794 Us Highways 285 Conifer, CO 80433 303-838-4848

PHOTOS ON LOCATION 2200 Kearney St Denver, CO 80207 303-751-5582

PORTFOLIO COLLECTION 1016 Oak St Steamboat Springs, CO 80487 970-879-3718

PORTRAITS BY LESLIE 228 S Union Ave Pueblo, CO 81003 719-544-5834

RANDALL'S PHOTOGRAPHY 7400 Indiana St. Arvada, CO 80007 303-425-6077

RON MASAMORI PHOTOGRAPHY 5051 Garrison St Wheat Ridge, CO 80033 303-399-5885

SILVER SCENE PHOTOGRAPHY 322 Silver St Lake City, CO 81235 970-944-2603

STEVE MUNINGER PHOTOGRAPHY 210 #A N Aspen, CO 81611 970-925-4510

STRINGHAM PHOTOGRAPHY 732 Cooper Ave Glenwood Springs, CO 81601 970-945-2931

STUDIO MANOR PHOTOGRAPHY 840 N Lincoln Ave Loveland, CO 80537 970667-3341

TED SPRING PHOTOGRAPHY 15 S Wilcox St Castle Rock, CO 80104 303-668-4994

THOMAS ROSHKIND PHOTOGRAPHY 663 Boulder St Minturn, CO 81645 970-827-5917

THOMPSON PHOTOGRAPHY 226 W 3rd St Rifle, CO 81650 970-625-2572

TODD POWELL PHOTOGRAPHY 410 Galena St Frisco, CO 80433 970-668-2280

WEST LIGHT GRAPHICS 814 N 8th St Montrose, CO 81401 970-249-5929

CONNECTICUT

A/1 PHOTO-STUDIO 79 Orchard Hill LN Middletown, CT 06457 860-632-0808

ALVAREZ PHOTOGRAPHY 79 Twitchgrass Rd Trumbull, CT 06611 203-261-8802

ART RICH PHOTOGRAPHY 500 N Main St Southington, CT 06489 860-621-6711

ARTPHOTO BY PIETRO 156 N Main St Norwich, CT 06360 860-886-2388

AUTUMN STUDIOS 3 Terre Haute Rd Danbury, CT 06810 203-794-0016

BACCHIOCHI PHOTO Svc 32 Gilbert St Ridgefield, CT 06877 203-438-8588

BILL KOZMA PHOTOGRAPHY 5 Main St Norwalk, CT 06851 203-853-4755

BUD TRENKA PHOTOGRAPHERS 960 Hope St Stamford, CT 06907 203-323-7506

CHILDREN FAMILIES-KATE MERCER 1225 Pequot TRL Stonington, CT 06378 860-536-0095

CORBIT STUDIO 2 Elm St Bridgeport, CT 06604 203-333-2149

CURTIS STUDIOS 216 Main St Durham, CT 06422 860-349-8679

D C LA COURSE PHOTOGRAPHER 6 Colonial Dr Deep River, CT 06417 860-526-3788

DAKILLE STUDIO 299 Main St New Britain, CT 06051 860-223-3572

DENNIS BOGART PHOTOGRAPHY 66 Pistapaug Rd Northford, CT 06472 203-484-9193

FALLON PHOTOS 576 Rubber Ave Naugatuck, CT 06770 203-729-8357

GANNON PHOTOGRAPHY 38 Schnoor Rd Killingworth, CT 06419 860-663-1386

GHC PHOTOGRAPHY 6 Post Office LN Greens Farms, CT 06436 203-259-7398

GULINO PHOTOGRAPHY 68 Asher Ave Pawcatuck, CT 06379 860-599-3984

GUY H GRUBE MASTER-PHOTOGRAPHY 80 Abington Rd Eastford, CT 06242 860-974-0033

IMAGES BY DAVID 60 Redmont Rd Stamford, CT 06903 203-324-9311

IMAGES STUDIO 578 W Main St Norwich, CT 06360 860-887-5589

IRA NOZIK PHOTOGRAPHERS 37 Jerome Ave Bloomfield, CT 06002 860-243-2800

JOHN LESTER PHOTOGRAPHY 19 Old Mill Rd Avon, CT 06001 860-673-5960

LARAMIE PHOTOGRAPHY 98 Windham St. Willimantic, CT 06226 860-423-1402

MINARDI PHOTOGRAPHY STUDIO 53 Ridgeway Rd Easton, CT 06612 203-374-8578

MOLETTO PHOTOGRAPHY 2420 Main St #6 Stratford, CT 06615 203-375-0008

MOTTA STUDIO PHOTOGRAPHY 169 Center St Wallingford, CT 06492 203-269-3540

MULDOON PHOTOGRAPHY 41 Trout Brook Rd Bristol, CT 06010 860-582-5259

NGM PHOTOGRAPHY 310 Rd Windham, CT 06280 860-456-3377

PASSPORT PHOTO IMMEDIATE 351 ATLANTIC ST STAMFORD, CT 06901 203-323-9902

PHOTOGRAPHY BY HEIDI JOHNSON 70 east St. New Milford, CT 06776 860-350-6446

PHOTOGRAPHY BY JOSEPH 14 Dunbar Rd. Milford, CT 06460 203-878-1666

PHOTOGRAPHY-ROBT SATTER 6 post office lane Greens Farms, CT 06436 203-259-1334

RICK CIABURRI STUDIO 205 Maple Ave Cheshire, CT 06410 203-272-5054

ROGER SALLS PHOTOGRAPHY 80 Ferry Blvd Stratford, CT 00615 203-375-1258

RUSSELL STUDIO 16 Brentford Berwick Ledyard, CT 06339 860-536-4646

RYAN PHOTOGRAPHY 139 HAZARD AVE #1 ENFIELD, CT 06082 860-763-2590

S M COOPER PHOTOGRAPHY 205 Research Dr Milford, CT 06460 203-878-6825

STEFAN'S PHOTOGRAPHY 83 Loubier Dr Somers, CT 06071 760-749-0529

STEFAN'S PHOTOGRAPHY 38 Poquonock Ave Windsor, CT 06095 860-688-7727

TRACEY STUDIO 634 Old Waterbury Rd Southbury, CT 06488 203-264-9498
UNIQUELY YOURS 48 Macnamara St Waterbury, CT 06708 203-596-7226
WOODSTOCK STUDIO STUART WALLS 24 Broad St Milford, CT 06460 206-878-8119

WASHINGTON DC

CENTRAL PHOTO CO 709 G St Se Washington, DC 20003 202-544-6065
DUNN PHOTOGRAPHIC ASSOC 2126 P St NW Washington, DC 20037 202-955-6066
DUPONT PHOTOGRAPHERS 1828 Jefferson Pl NW Washington, DC 20036 202-659-1535
FITZ-PATRICK PHOTOGRAPHY 3609 Jenifer St NW Washington, DC 20015 202-364-1985
HIGHSMITH, CAROL M 6856 Eastern Ave NW Washington, DC 20012 202-347-0910
LAMBERT, KATHERINE 6856 Eastern Ave NW Washington, DC 20012 202-882-8383
LAUTMAN PHOTOGRAPHY 4906 41st St NW Washington, DC 20016 202-966-2800
MARVIN T JONES & ASSOC 5203 14th St NW Washington, DC 20011 202-726-4066
MAX HIRSCHFRLD STUDIO 1027 33rd St NW #2 Washington, DC 20007 202-333-7450
SCL NEW YORK Washington, DC 20002 202-635-0200
VASQUEZ CLAUDIO 516 8th St Se Washington, DC 20003 202-543-7782
VEERASARN, JAKRARAT 443 I St NW Washington, DC 20001 202-387-8667
VINCE FINNIGAN & ASSOC 806 Maryland Ave Be Washington, DC 20002 202-544-2945
Z TARAN PHOTOGRAPHY 5060 Macarthur Blvd NW Washington, DC 20016 202-543-5322

DELAWARE

AMALFI STUDIO 307 Stahl Ave New Castle, DE 19720 302-328-1895
CARLOS ALEJANDRO PHOTOGRAPHY Hockessin, DE 19707 302-234-1100
COUNTRY STUDIO 499 Ponderosa Dr Magnolia, DE 19962 302-697-2062
DEAN FLOYD INC 2 S Poplar St #B Wilmington, DE 19801 302-655-7193

FIRST STATE PHOTO SVC 216 Rehoboth Ave Rehoboth Beach, DE 19971 302-227-6145

INGO FOTOGRAFIE 3101 Skyline Dr Wilmington, DE 19808 302-737-2508

JIM DALLAS 1613 Temple Ter Wilmington, DE 19805 302-654-4995

JOHN LOY PHOTOGRAPHY 1611 Shipley Td Wilmington, DE 19803 3 02-762-3812

MATEJA ASSOCIATES 2104 Anson Rd Wilmington, DE 19810 302-475-5874

MC CLAIN IMAGERY 1244 E 14th St Wilmington, DE 19802 302-427-2467

NA VAR STUDIO RT 24 E Millsboro, DE 19966 302-934-9366

NEWELL JR, JOHN D 406 W 13th St Wilmington, DE 19801 302-654-2292

RAY'S PHOTOGRAPHIC SVC 3 Harborview Rd Lewes, DE 19958 302-645-7960

RON DUBICK STUDIO 4 Bowie Dr Wilmington, DE 19808 302-234-6680

RUSTY RISTINE INC N1800 W 11th St #A Wilmington, DE 19805 302-652-7886

SRT PHOTOGRAPHY 1910 ½ Lancaster Ave Wilmington, DE 19805 302-656-2562

TERENCE ROBERTS PHOTOGRAPHY 1909 N Market St Wilmington, DE 19802 302-658-8854

VAN RIPER, FLOYD W 200 W 10th St Wilmington, DE 19801 302-654-3248

WILLIAM HENRY ASSOC 953 Boggs Dr Dover, DE 19901 302-736-9918

YOUNG'S STUDIO 134 W Loockerman St Dover, DE 19904 302-734-2447

ZULLINGER, CARSON T 1909 N Market St Wilmington, DE 19802 302-654-3905

FLORIDA

ALAN FERGUSON PHOTOGRAPHY 1234 2nd St Sarasota, FL 34236 941-366-4288

ALLEN CHEUVRONT STUDIOS 4607 NW 6th St #H Gainesville, FL 32609 352-378-4671

ALLEN'S STUDIO 12986 SW 89th Ave Miami, FL 33176 305-945-5003

APPLE PHOTOGRAPHIES 3032 49th St N St Petersburg, FL 33710 727-522-7557

ARTISTIC WEDDINGS 4988 Clarcona Ocoee Rd Orlando, FL 32810 407-298-7753

BECKER STUDIO 511 N Harbor City Blvd #A Melbourne, FL 32935 321-254-4600

BEER'S PHOTOGRAPHY 110 E Pace Dr Perry, FL 32347 850-584-4422

BILL KELLEY PHOTOGRAPHIES Inv 3281 E Marcia St Inverness, FL 34453 352-344-0241

BOB BAGGETT PHOTOGRAPHY Inc 3110 W Azeele St Tampa, FL 33609 813-870-0349

BOUDROT'S CUSTOM WEDDING PHOTO 320 10th Ave Vero Beach, FL 32962 561-567-8398

BRAD MILLS PHOTOGRAPHY 1716 Nebraska Ave Palm Harbor, FL 34683 727-787-8611

BRANAN PHOTOGRAPHY 1523 Se Fort King St Ocala, FL 34471 352-351-1405

BRYN-ALAN PHOTOGRAPHY Studio 7406 N Tamiami Trl Sarasota, FL 34243 941-351-2891

BRYN-ALAN STUDIO 3914 Beach Blvd Jacksonville, FL 32207 904-398-0993

BRYN ALAN STUDIO 3055 1st Ave S St Petersburg, FL 33712 727-327-3316

BURG PHOTOGRAPHIX INC 932 N Maitland Ave Maitland, FL 32751 407-628-9705

CARRIAGE HOUSE STUDIO 630 Kingsley Ave Orange Park, FL 32073 904-264-5111

CARTER PHOTOGRAPHY 5649 Sunflower Ave Milton, FL 32570 850-623-8317

COLONIAL PHOTOGRAPHY 118 Parshley St Se Live Oak, FL 32060 904-362-2223

DAVE EICHER PHOTOGRAPHY 1770 Oakhurst Ave Winter Park, FL 32789 407-647-3147

DAVID EWART PHOTOGRAPHY 125 N Arcturas Ave Clearwater, FL 33765 727-441-4249

DAVID HANKO PHOTOGRAPHY 5150 4th St N St Petersburg, FL 33703 727-526-7084

DAVIDOFF STUDIOS 223 Sunset Ave Palm Beach, FL 33480 561-655-1164

DON RHODES PHOTOGRAPHY 204 Washington Ave Homestead, FL 33030 305-245-7042

FADGEN'S OF PLANTATION PHOTO 21 Acre Dr Plantation, FL 33317 954-584-0404

FINE ARTS PHOTOGRAPHERS 1556 Venera Ave Coral Gables, FL 33146 305-661-1685

FLASH PHOTO 903 NW 6th St Gainesville, FL 32601 352-373-6001

HAYES PHOTOGRAPHY 1921 Kudza Rd West Palm Beach, FL 33415 561-969-0262

HIME PHOTOGRAPHY 3900 Clark Rd #3 Sarasota, FL 34233 941-924-9287

IMAGES BU ALISON PHOTOGRAPHY 1440 Kennedy Dr Key West, FL 33040 305-294-9455

ISLAND PHOTOGRAPHIES 101 W Venice Ave #6 Venice, FL 34285 941-485-0699

JILL KAHN PHOTO 2089 NE 123rd St Miami, FL 33181 305-891-7833

JIM JERNIGAN'S PHOTOGRAPHY 1820 E Silver Springs Blvd Ocala, FL 34470 352-732-7927

JIM ROBERTS PHOTOGRAPHER 2112 N Orange Ave Orlando, FL 32804 407-898-4652

L A BREWER PHOTOGRAPHY Po Box 314 Lake City, FL 32056 901-755-6629

LASTING IMPRESSIONS 997 Appaloosa Rd Tarpon Springs, FL 34689 727-934-4456

MADDOCK PHOTOGRAPHERS 3941 5th Ave N St Petersburg, FL 33713 727-321-7093

MC DONALD STUDIO 2929 Ave G NW Winter Haven, FL 33880 863-294-1795

MEDIA IMAGE PHOTOGRAPHY 21 Se 2nd Pl Gainesville, FL 32601 352-375-1911

MURNOR STUDIO 264 Andalusia Ave Coral Gables, FL 33134 305-444-3143

NEWHALL PHOTOGRAPHY 305 N Main St Havana, FL 32333 850-224-3824

NICK'S QUALITY PHOTO STUDIO 8212 NE 2nd Ave Miami, FL 33138 305-754-3362

O Y THOMAS PHOTOGRAPHY 11902 Little Rd New Port Richey, FL 34654 727-868-3669

PETER GORMAN PHOTOGRAPHER 3456 Se Dixie Hwy Stuart, FL 34997 561-287-3972

PHIL HINES PHOTOGRAPHY 298 Avenue O Se Winter Haven, FL 33880 863-294-8884

PHOTOGRAPHIC ASSOCIATES INC 55 Royal Palm Pt Vero Beach, FL 32960 561-562-5411

PHOTOGRAPHY 35 5201 SW 13th St Gainesville, FL 34652 727-849-2401

PHOTOGRAPHY UNLIMITED 9735 Hollowbrook Dr Pensacola, FL 32514 850-479-8230

RENAUD PHOTOGRAPHY 6490 NW 150th St Chiefland, FL 32626 352-493-0976

RICHARD'S PHOTOGRAPHY 1410 Market St #B Tallahassee, FL 32312 850-890 0511

RON BERNARD PHOTOGRAPHY 714 43rd St W Bradenton, FL 34209 941-745-3112

STERLING PHOTO 2460 Minton Rd West Melbourne, FL 32904 321-725-9210

STONE'S STUDIO INC 2503 N 12th Ave Pensacola, FL 32503 850-432-2351

TIM ALLEN & ASSOC PHOTOGRAPHY 1118 Jenks Ave Panama City, FL 32401 850-763-5795

TOM REYNOLDS 968 SW 9th Ave Boca Raton, FL 33486 561-394-3636

TOOTSIE'S PHOTOGRAPHY 4675 SW Country Pl Palm City, FL 34990 561-287-0998

GEORGIA

ALPHA STUDIO 111 Keystone Ct Athens, GA 30605 706-543-4883

AMERICAN FAST PHOTO & CAMERA 126 Bankhead Hwy Carrollton, GA 30117 770-830-9595

ARMSTRONG'S PHOTOGRAPHY 200 Little Creek Rd Jesup, GA 31546 912-427-8081

BOB SHAPIRO PHOTOGRAPHY 15 Lagrange St Newnan, GA 30263 770-253-4821

CAMERA ONE 3105 Cross Country Hl Columbus, GA 31906 706-569-4390

CHARLES HUGULEY PHOTOGRAPHY 865 Clifton Rd NE Atlanta, GA 30307 404-377-0950

CLAYTON CAMERA CRAFT PHOTO 28 N Main St Alpharetta, GA 30004 770-475-0022

CLAYTON ONE HOUR PHOTO Po Box 773 Clayton, GA 30525 706-782-6429

CONNELL STUDIOS 1108 Lakeview Dr. Valdosta, GA 31602 229-244-7200

D B HARRELL PHOTOGRAPHY 215 Sherman Dr Brunswick, GA 31523 912-265-8636

DANNY LEE PHOTOGRAPHY 917 Center St NE Conyers, GA 30012 770-922-9628

DYESS-TIDWELL STUDIO 135 E Jackson St Thomasville, GA 31792 229-226-1600

FITZ-SYMMS 1552 Walton Way Augusta, GA 30904 706-724-7759

FORWELL STUDIO INC 210 N Glenwood Ave Dalton, GA 30721 706-226-2208

FRANK CHRISTIAN STUDIO 2150 Central Ave Augusta, GA 30904 706-737-9290

GARNER WALKER PHOTOGRAPHY 2236 Bemiss Rd Valdosta, GA 31602 229-244-6226

GARRISON'S PHOTOGRAPHY 8667 Hospital Dr Douglasville, GA 30134 770-949-2600

GERALD POLLACK & ASSOC 111e 34th St Savannah, GA 31401 912-133-0248

GORDON ADAMS PHOTOGRAPHY 1642 Arden Dr SW Marietta, GA 30008 770-428-1391

H & R PHOTOGRAPHY 4285 Memorial Dr # A Decatur, GA 30032 404-296-7057

HALL STUDIO 1940 Rollingwoods Way SW Marietta, GA 30064 770-423-0689

J JACKSON PHOTOGRAPHY 211 Broad St Rome, GA 30161 706-291-8164

JIM HOLMES PHOTOGRAPHY 12 Margatha Dr Savannah, GA 31406 912-354-8234

JOHN JONES PHOTOGRAPHY Highway 441 BYP Cornelia, GA 30531 706-778-9000

LEE F MC DAVID PHOTOGRAPHY 3880 Lake St Macon, GA 31204 478-746-4750

MARK WILLIAMS PHOTOGRAPHY 706 Highway 1—S Swainsboro, GA 30401 478-237-3692

MARKLE STUDIO 1280 Rolling Green Drive, Acworth, GA 30102 770-928-1256

MEMORIES PHOTOGRAPHY 108 Sandy Way Statesboro, GA 30461 912-764-2357

MICHAEL'S PHOTOGRAPHY 1 Galleria Pkwy Se Atlanta, GA 30339 770-984-2446

MILLER PHOTOGRAPHY 1802 Frederica Rd St Simons Island, GA 31522 912-638-8558

PHOTOGRAPHY BY DAVID 1094 Green St Roswell, GA 30075 770-992-3383

PHOTOS BY SEBO INC 7879 N Main St Jonesboro, GA 30236 770-477-7304

RICK MILTON PHOTOGRAPHY 3830 Washington Rd Martinez, GA 30907 706-860-3612

ROBERSON ADVERTISING PHOTO 2322 Lumpkin Rd Augusta, GA 30906 706-793-3289

SEA ISLAND PHOTOGRAPHY 4th St Sea Island, GA 31561 912-638-5123

SMITH'S STUDIO & CAMERA SHOP 208 W Center St Carrollton, GA 30117 770-832-8958

WARREN L BOND PHOTOGRAPHY 6326 Highway 85 #A Riverdale, GA 30274 770-997-6406

HAWAII

ACE PORTRAIT STUDIO 1157 S King St Honolulu, HI 96814 808-591-9220

ALOHA PHOTO 660 Ala Moana Blvd #206 Honolulu, HI 96813 808-537-9835

CLAUDE'S PHOTOGRAPHY 94-981 Alali St Waipahu, HI 96797 808-677-5943

HOUSE OF PHOTOGRAPHY 1107 S King St Honolulu, HI 96814 808-596-0440

JERRY GRIGORY PHOTOGRAPHY 312 Lakau Pl Kihei, HI 96753 808-874-3089

JOHN PIERRE'S STUDIO 143 Dickenson St #201 Lahaina, HI I96761 808-667-7988

MARIO PEREZ PHOTOGRAPHICS 4-1552 Kuhio Hwy #A Kapaa, HI 96746 808-822-7958

PANA ENTERPRISES INC 120 Kaiulani Ave Honolulu, HI 96815 808-922-4927

PHOTO SPECTRUM 3122 Kuhio Hwy #A7 Lihue, HI 96766 808-245-7667

PHOTOGRAPHY BY IRVIN 1721 Wili Pa Loop # 101 Wailuku, HI 96793 808-242-9447

ROGER'S OF KAILUA 350 Hahani St Kailua, HI 96734 808-261-0381

IOWA

ALEXANDER'S GALLERY 486 w 4th St Dubuque, IA 52001 319-584-2346

APGAR PHOTOGRAPHY STUDIO 18 w Main St Marshalltown, IA 50703 641-752-5314

BIG ED'S PHOTOS 23553 200th Ave Davenport, IA 52804 319-285-4368

BOYD-FITZGERALD INC 4038 Utica Ridge Rd Bettendorf, IA 52722 319-359-9010

BUCKROYD STUDIO 1222 Central Ave Fort Dodge, IA 50501 515-576-4481

CAMEO PHOTOGRAPHY 1914 Main St Keokuk, IA 52632 319-524-2671

CLARK STUDIOS 112 1st S t SW Orange City, IA 51041 712-737-2020

CLIFF STOCK PHOTOGRAPHY 1420 Central Ave Dubuque, IA 52001 319-556-2235

COTECOLOR 11 Allamakee St Waukon, IA 52172 319-568-2253

DOES PHOTOGRAPHY 402 Lakeside Dr Fairbank, IA 50629 319-635-2268

DON PETERSON PHOTOS INC 117 N St # A Fort Dodge, IA 50501 515-576-6391

DREASLER PHOTOGRAPHY 302 Fulton St. Keokuk, IA 52632 319-524-2035

ELDEN'S PHOTOGRAPHY & FRAMING 201 13th Ave SW Waverly, IA 50677 319-532-4673

FREDRICK'S PHOTOGRAPHY 1401 e 7th St Atlantic, IA 50022 712-243-5512

FULLHEART PHOTOGRAPHY 1502 39th St Fort Madison, IA 52627 319-372-6073

HALL'S PHOTO 434 7th Ave Marion, IA 5230 319-377-3129

ILLUSIONS FINE PORTRAITURE 1221 1st Ave SE Cedar Rapids, IA 52402 319-364-1856

IMAGES & MORE PHOTOGRAPHY 2601 Summer St Burlington, IA 52601 319-753-0690

JACK HANSON PHOTOGRAPHY 200 Kingsridge Dr Council Bluffs, IA 51503 712-322-7585

JOHN DAVID KING PHOTO DESIGNS 1702 State St Bettendoref, IA 52722 319-359-6544

MUELLER STUDIO 404 N Main St Clarion, IA 50525 515-532-2869

NATIONAL STUDIO 700 Oak St Burlington, IA 52601 319-852-3035

NICESWANGER PHOTOGRAPHY 1707 N Carroll St Carroll, IA 51401 712-792-1267

PHOTOGRAPHY BY WILSON 203 1st St e Independence, IA 50644 319-334-3748

PORTRAITS BY SARA 213 1st Ave W Newton, IA 50208 641-792-7786

SAUL STUDIO 605 Sumner Ave Humboldt, IA 50548 515-332-1776

TAYLOR-MORTENSEN STUDIOS 700 Reed St Akron, IA 51001 712-568-2874
VANDER WERF PHOTO 3146 Logan Ave Waterloo, IA 50703 319-232-5576
VORLAND PHOTOGRAPHY 2609 Rainbow Dr Cedar Falls, IA 50613 319-277-7141
WAYNE MAKEEFF PHOTOGRAPHY 4410 44th Pl Des Moines, IA 50310 515-278-5055
WILLIAM LUSE PHOTOGRAPHY 814 6th Ave De Witt, IA 52742 319-659-5221

IDAHO

ASPENWOOD PHOTOGRAPHY 2369 Addison Ave E Twin Falls, ID 83301 208-734-0342
BRAUN STUDIOS 106 S Kimball Ave Caldwell, ID 83605 208-459-1555
BRAUN STUDIOS PHOTOGRAPHERS 317 12th Ave S Nampa, ID 83651 208-466-7873
DAVIS PHOTO 12 College Ave Rexburg, ID 83440 208-356-4800
HOLDEN PHOTOGRAPHY 7236 Ustick RD Boise, ID 83704 208-322-1980
KEN FIREBAUGH PHOTOGRAPHY 1780 Gwen Dr Pocatello, ID 83204 208-233-9449
PHOTOGRAPHY BY BOB KEMPE 731 Hopkins Ln Soda Springs, ID 83276 208-547-3544
QUICKSILVER STUDIOS 319 E Front Ave Coeur D Alene, ID 83814 208-765-4099
RAINER'S PORTRAIT STUDIO 825 N Mountain View Rd Moscow, ID 83843 208-882-7372
SIM'S STUDIO 705 W Bannock St Boise, ID 83702 208-344-1113
STODDARD PHOTOGRAPHY 577 D St Idaho Falls, ID 83402 208-523-5910
THOMAS PHOTOGRAPHY 1235 Oakley Ave Burley, ID 83318 208-378-3134

ILLINOIS

ACCENT PHOTOGRAPHY 507 N Main St Edwardsville, IL 62025 618-656-3335
B & W PHOTO CORLEY 118 N Walnut St Champaign, IL 61820 217-351-6222
BONITA'S PORTRAITS 151 W Dodds St Divernon, IL 62530 217-628-3863
CEDARLEAF PHOTOGRAPHY 1921 W Main St Belleville, IL 62226 618-234-9700
CHIP ZELLET & ASSOC 466 Central Ave # 37 Northfield, IL 60093 847-441-9161

CLASS ACT PHOTOGRAPHY 3112 S Park Ave Springfield, IL 62704 217-787-4947
COLLINS PHOTOGRAPHY 101 E Riverside Blvd Loves Park, IL 61111 815-877-8884
CREATIVE IMAGES Old Highway 59 E Lawrenceville, IL 62439 618-943-4361
DE PAUL PHOTOGRAPHY 120 N Walkup Ave Crystal Lake, IL 60014 815-459-1540
DON WEAVER PHOTOGRAPHY 213 N 7th St De Kalb, IL 60115 815-856-5556
HAURY COLOR STUDIO 2103 Vandalia St Collinsville, IL 62234 618-344-2117
J PHILIP PAILLE PHOTOGRAPHER 114 W 3Rd s St Mt Carmel, IL 62863 618-262-7826
JAY LEE STUDIOS 6211 N Milwaukee Ave Chicago, IL 60646 773-775-5100
JET ONE HOUR PHOTO 1057 N Roselle Rd Hoffman Estates, IL 60195 847-310-8660
KEN MEADE STUDIOS 275 Springfield Rd Hillsboro, IL 62025 217-532-9494
KRANTZ PHOTOGRAPHY 180 Marsh Ave Montgomery, IL 60538 630-897-6282
LORANNE STUDIO 107 Westgate Plz Streator, IL 61364 815-672-2037
MAXWELL & BELLIS PHOTOGRAPHERS 1032 Maine St Quincy, IL 62301 217-222-2405
PEARSON PHOTOGRAPHY 12323 S Wolf Rd Palos Park, IL 60464 708-448-4050
PHOTO'S BY RICK 17244 Oak Park Ave Tinley Park, IL 60477 708-429-7555
PORTRAITS BY THOMAS 557N Hough ST # C Barrington, IL 60010 847-381-7710
RICHARD KLEIN PHOTOGRAPHY 1352 Logsdon Ln Buffalo Grove IL 60089 847-634-9390
RUSS BERKMAN PHOTOGRAPHY INC 5244 Greenwood St Skokie, IL 60077 847-967-0300
SOMMER PHOTO SVC 1220 E Wood ST Decatur, IL 62521 217-428-2747
SPIKE POWERS PHOTOGRAPHY 325 Monroe Ave Charleston, IL 61920 217-345-4151
STUDIO WEST 512 N Milwaukee Ave Libertyville, IL 60048 847-362-9060
SUGGS PHOTOGRAPHY 2105 Robert Dr Champaign, IL 61821 217-356-4793
TERRY'S PHOTOGRAPHY 106 George St Morris, IL 60450 815-942-0110
TINTYPE 233 S Walnut St Arthur, IL 31911 217-543-2233
UNIVERSAL PHOTOGRAPHY 15129 Cicero Ave Oak Forest, IL 60452 708-687-3765
VIC BEAUTY STUDIO 5330 W Ardmore Ave Chicago, IL 60646 773-631-3420
VIERNUM PHOTOGRAPHY & VIDEO 1629 Mandel Ave Westchester, IL 60154 708-562-4143
VOEGELE'S STUDIO 1012 Laurel St Highland, IL 62249 618-654-7291

WOODS PHOTOGRAPHICS 7 Apache Dr Springfield, IL 62707 217-546-4777

INDIANA

A-1 HOUR PHOTO & PORTRAITS 10 S 18th St Lafayette, IN 904 765-448-1314

AL GREEN STUDIO INC 249 N Madison Ave Greenwood, IN 46142 317-888-7105

ASPEN IMAGES PHOTOGRAPHY 418 e Lincoln Way La Porte, IN 46350 219-324-2220

BARRY'S PHOTOGRAPHY 1006 Monroe St La Porte, IN 46350 219-362-1315

BARRY'S PHOTOGRAPHY 58 Lincoln Way Valparaiso, IN 46383 219-462-9755

BOB STRAUB PHOTOGRAPHY 12820 Cynthiana Rd Evansville, IN 47720 812-963-5014

BOCKOVER PHOTOGRAPHY PO Box 2134 Michigan City, IN 46361 219-879-6071

CAMERA CRAFTSMEN STUDIOS 101 N 6th St Lafayette, IN 47901 765-742-9002

CAMPBELL'S CREATIVE PHOTOGRAPHERS 2725 17th St Columbus, IN 47201 812-372-9971

CLIQUE CREATIVE SVC 422 E 4th St Marion, IN 46952 765-664-230

DAVE FERGUSON PHOTO ART STUDIO 1620 KOSSUTH ST LAFAYETTE, IN 47905 765-742-1829

DE FABIS PHOTOGRAPHY 3901 Kessler Blvd Indianapolis, IN 16228 317-291-8111

DON HARDESTY PHOTOGRAPHY 1224 Washington Sq Evansville, IN 47715 812-476-4569

DON J PARKER PHOTOGRAPHY 219 W Broadway St Princeton, IN 47670 812-385-2077

DOUGLAS STUDIOS PHOTOGRAPHY 1538 Main St Lafayette, IN 47901 765-447-7341

ED MOSS PHOTOGRAPHER 5701 N Meridian St Indianapolis, IN 46208 317-255-5592

EDDA TAYLOR PHOTOGRAPHY Courthouse Sq # 304 Crown Point, IN 46307 219-662-9500

ELLISON PHOTOGRAPHY 1205 N Central Ave Connersville, IN 47331 765-825-0609

FEDERSPIEL PHOTOGRAPHY 319 Broadway St New Haven, IN 46774 219-749-2662

GALLERY PORTRAITS 755 S 100 W Bluffton, IN 16714 219-824-5470

GIOLAS PHOTOGRAPHERS INC 7994 Broadway Merrillville, IN 46410 219-769-7934

HIRSCH STUDIO 4504 Wozniak Rd Michigan City, IN 46360 219-874-7747

HOOSIER AIR PHOTO INC 3432 W 16th St Indianapolis, IN 46222 317-632-4115

HOTSHOE PHOTOGRAPHY 1821 E 100 N Kokomo, IN 46901 765-452-6612

JAMES PHOTOGRAPHY 3100 98th Pl Highland, IN 46322 219-844-8118

MC GRATH PHOTOGRAPHY 1004 W Oak St Zionsville, IN 46077 317-873-4935

MC KOWN STUDIO & GALLERIES 417 S 14th St New Castle, IN 47362 765-521-3686

MICHAEL GRAY PHOTOGRAPHY 1466 Bellemeade Ave Evansville, IN 47714 812-473-0645

PATTERSON STUDIOS 9 E Flora St Washington, IN 47501 812-254-2752

PHOTOGRAPHY BY JILDA 1708 I St Bedford, IN 47421 812-275-4541

PHOTOS BY DON WOOD 404 W 3rd St Madison, IN 47250 812-265-3080

PICTURE PERFECT PHOTOGRAPHY 212 E 5th St Jasper, IN 47546 812-482-6099

PORTRAITS BY JOLENE 544 N Jefferson St Huntington, IN 46750 219-356-2660

PORTRAITS BY SHARON 2416 E Morgan Ave Evansville, IN 47711 812-474-1991

PYLE PHOTOGRAPHY 33 N 8th ST Richmond, IN 47374 765-962-4753

RIVER PARK PHOTO 1209 Mishawaka Ave South Bend, IN 46615 219-287-3855

ROBERT MC CARTY PHOTO 2815 Market St Jasper, IN 47546 812-4822-5542

RUTH CHIN-PHOTOGRAPHY 1007 N Tillotson Ave Muncie, IN 47304 765-284-4582

SIMS PHOTOGRAPHIC 1810 Pine St Michigan City, IN 46360 219-872-7496

STEVE SHELDON PHOTOGRAPHY 311 S Swain Ave Bloomington, IN 47401 812-336-8661

TOM STEELE PHOTOGRAPHY State Road 54 W Linton, IN 47441 812-847-8389

VOORHEES STUDIO INC 1100 E Broadway Logansport, IN 16947 219-753-2200

WILCOX PHOTOGRAPHIC SVC 4320 W Orland Rd Angola, IN 46703 219-833-3605

YEAGLEY PHOTOGRAPHY 1546 Ohio Ave Anderson, IN 46016 765-642-9133

KANSAS

ANDRADE PHOTOGRAPHY INC 18 E 2nd St Liberal, KS 67901 620-624-6492

ATTIG PHOTOGRAPHY STUDIO 130 E Park St Olathe, KS 66061 913-782-1948

AZIM STUDIOS 422 S Oliver St Wichita, KS 67218 316-686-6262

DAVID MENCL PHOTOGRAPHY 924 N Main St Hutchinson, KS 67501 620-662-7781

DONALDSON'S STUDIO 1317 Arrowhead St Wichita, KS 67203 316-943-2393

DONNERT PHOTOGRAPHY 3950 Eagle Rd Manhattan, KS 66503 785-539-6032

DOUGLAS PHOTOGRAPHIC IMAGING 2300 E Douglas Ave Wichita, KS 67214 316-264-3013

EVELAND-SMITH PHOTOGRAPHY INC 24 W 12th Ave Hutchinson, KS 67501 620-662-2031

EXPRESSIVE IMAGES 22655 139TH St Basehor, KS 66007 913-724-3242

FRANK PHOTOGRAPHY INC 2305 Orchard Ln Lawrence, KS 66049 785-743-5119

FULMER STUDIO 113 S Main St El Dorado, KS 67042 316-321-9130

GREENWOOD PHOTOGRAPHY 623 S Main ST Hugoton, KS 67951 620-544-2106

HARRY'S PHOTOGRAPHY 403 David Ave Holcomb, Ks 67851 620-277-2043

KENNEY PHOTOGRAPHY 117 S Main St Mc Pherson, KS 67460 620-241-7930

LEON'S PHOTOGRAPHY 1301 Central St Leavenworth, KS 66048 913-651-2785

LUTHER'S PHOTOGRAPHY 5601 E Central Ave Wichita, KS 67208 316-686-8591

MANN'S STUDIO & CAMERA SHOP 212 N Main St Mc Pherson, KS 67460 620-241-3714

MARCOM PHOTOGRAPHY 107 S Main St Ed Dorado, KS 67042 316-321-1441

MORSE STUDIO PHOTOGRAPHY 715 N Plum St Newton, KS 67114 316-283-6662

PHOTOGRAPHY BY LE 1186 US Highway 77 Marysville, KS 66508 785-562-5540

PORTRAITS BY SHANE 1415 Main St Great Bend, KS 67530 620-793-3247

PRISM PHOTOGRAPHY 3430 E Central Ave Wichita, KS 67208 316-683-4586

RANIERI PROFESSIONAL ONE HOUR 413 Main St Seneca, KS 66538 785-336-3719

STEPHEN'S COMMERCIAL 931 S Kansas Ave Topeka, KS 66612 785-354-7153

STUDIO DE LARI 119 Gunsmoke St Dodge City, KS 67801 620-227-3831

TREASURED IMAGES-DON RUNYON 311 N Walnut St Pittsburg, KS 66762 620-231-3350

TROY'S PHOTOGRAPHY 214 ½ W Wyatt Earp Blvd Dodge City, KS 67801 620-225-2929

TURNER PHOTOGRAPHY 104 N 2nd St Lindsborg, KS 67456 785-227-2112

WALLACE PHOTOGRAPHY 1940 NW Central Ave Topeka, KS 66608 785-232-6625

KENTUCKY

ALLISON PHOTOGRAPHY 607 S 4th St Murray, KY 42071 270-753-8809

BEL MENDOZA PHOTOGRAPHER 3411 Calais Dr Jeffersontown, KY 40299 502-267-7060

CAPTURED ART STUDIO INC 868 E 4th St London, KY 40741 606-878-8154

DARWIN'S PHOTOGRAPHY 2620 Bardstown Rd Louisville, KY 40205 502-451-8886

EXPRESS IMAGE PHOTO 101 E Central St Harlan, KY 40831 606-573-3138

GENE BOAZ PHOTOGRAPHY 709 Bleich Rd Paducah, KY 42003 270-554-2642

GENTRY PHOTOGRAPHY 701 Philadelphia St Covington, KY 41011 859-291-3358

HOWARD WELLS PHOTOGRAPHY 1401 Triplett ST # B Owensboro, KY 42303 270-685-4020

JEUNESSE OF LOUISVILLE 6007 Colebrooke Ln Okolona, KY 40219 502-968-3033

LOGUE PHOTOGRAPHY 318 E Lexington Ave Danville, KY 40422 859-236-3905

LOU ELLIS PHOTOGRAPHY 143 N Public Sq Glasgow, KY 42141 270-651-8009

MARK KIDD STUDIOS OF KENTUCKY 125 Clay Ave Lexington, KY 40502 859-255-8088

MARTIN STUDIO OF PHOTOGRAPHY 23 S Main ST Henderson, KY 42420 270-826-4453

MGM PHOTOGRAPHY 140 N 4th St Louisville, KY 40202 502-585-4042

MICHAEL ROBERTSON PHOTOGRAPHY 100 S Spring St Louisville, KY 40206 502-581-1081

MICHAEL'S PHOTOGRAPHY INC 701 Ford ST Corbin, KY 40701 606-528-7760

PHOTOS FOREVER 7706 Stevens School Rd Whitesville, KY 42378 270-233-4454

RODGERS STUDIO 224 W Main St Frankfort, KY 40601 502-223-3173

SHUTTERBUG PHOTO 1207 Broadway Ave Bowling Green, KY 42104 270-781-3315

THARP'S PHOTOGRAPHY 1507 Glenrock Rd Louisville, KY 40216 502-368-0095

WAINSCOTT GALLERY 9700 Bunsen Pkwy Louisville, KY 40299 502-493-0806

WALT ROYCRAFT PHOTOGRAPHY 160 Carolyn Ln Nicholasville, KY 40356 859-887-1891

LOUISIANA

ALLEN BREAUX STUDIO 110 Energy Pkwy Lafayette, LA 70508 337-235-6364

ARDOIN PHOTO GALLERY 4025 Louisiana Ave Lake Charles, LA 70607 337-477-0772

ARTISTIC IMAGES PHOTOGRAPHY 1006 Clausel St Mandeville, LA 70448 985-626-8385

BARBERITO PHOTOGRAPHERS 3206 Taft Park Metairie, LA 70002 504-455-6818

BERT BURR'S PROFESSIONAL PHOTO 1018 W 5th St Bogalusa, LA 70427 985-735-3671

BOB BRADFORD PHOTOGRAPHY 2214 Milton St New Orleans, LA 70122 504-943-2622

BREAUX'S PORTRAIT STUDIO 730 W Laurel Ave Eunice, LA 70535 337-457-2416

BURT TIETJE PHOTOGRAPHY 307 N Main St Jennings, LA 70546 337-824-6084

C F WEBER PHOTOGRAPHY 516 Natchez St New Orleans, LA 70130 504-522-7503

COMPLETE PHOTO CTR 4720 Jackson St Ext Alexandria, LA 71303 318-445-4658

CREATIVE PHOTOGRAPHY 206 Mississippi Ave Ferriday, LA 71334 318-575-2904

DARBY PHOTOGRAPHY 675 Old Spanish Trail Slidell, LA 70458 985-641-4177

DON & JAN STUDIOS 234 S Main St Opelousas, LA 70570 337-948-6096

ED BROUSSARD PHOTOGRAPHY 3601 Johnston St #1 Lafayette, LA 70503 337-981-2304

GLENN LUTTRELL PHOTOGRAPHY 1717 N 7th St West Monroe, LA 71291 318-323-3724

JAY FAUGOT PHOTOGRAPHY 1334 Jefferson St Lafayette, LA 70501 337-233-4333

JIM BABIN PHOTOGRAPHY 734 Wood St Houma, LA 70360 985-868-6934

JOHN H WILLIAMS PHOTOGRAPHER 315 E Blvd Baton Rouge, LA 70802 225-387-4468

JOHN SHAW PHOTOGRAPHY 926 3rd St Natchitoches, La 71457 318-357-1238

JOHNSON STUDIO 1409 Washington St Monroe, LA 71201 318-388-3027

KEEPSAKE PHOTOGRAPHY 410 N Main ST Jennings, LA 70546 337-824-8825

LANDRY STUDIO 300 N Michaud St Carencro, LA 70520 337-896-6842

LAYNE PHOTOGRAPHY 7620 Goodwood Blvd Baton Rouge, LA 70806 225-928-2986

LE BOEUF, CARL L 1031 Hagan Ave New Orleans, LA 70119 504-524-9253

MARK'S STUDIO INC CPP 316 Ruth St Houma, LA 70364 985-873-8312

MICHAEL'S PHOTOGRAPHY 116 Lobdell Ave Baton Rouge, LA 70806 225-926-6412

MIGUEZ PHOTOGRAPHY 824 Main St Franklin, LA 70538 337-828-0650

MIKE POSEY PHOTOGRAPHY 3524 Canal St New Orleans, LA 70119 504-488-8000

MONSOUR'S PHOTOGRAPHY 929 Broad St Lake Charles, LA 70601 337-433-2333
PATTY STEWART'S PHOTOGRAPHY 131 Davis Ln West Monroe, LA 71291 318-396-5312
PUCKETT'S PHOTOGRAPHY 2814 Tupelo St Lake Charles, LA 70601 337-433-2069
RAPID PHOTO 4520 S Sherwood Forest Blvd Baton Rouge, LA 70816 225-292-6279
RON E DOBBS PHOTOGRAPHIC SVC 235 Antibes St W Mandeville, LA 70448 985-674-0698
SMITH PHOTOGRAPHIC SVC INC 643 Stoner Ave Shreveport, LA 71101 318-424-4402
THURMAN C SMITH PHOTOGRAPHY 2020 Market St Shreveport, LA 71101 318-425-8767
UNIVERSAL PHOTOGRAPHY 429 Florida Blvd New Orleans, LA 70124 504-482-6624
VERNON ROGERS PHOTOGRAPHY 104 Stevenson Dr Monroe, LA 71203 318-322-

MAINE

BLACK COW PHOTO INC 222 Saint Johns St # 235 Portland, ME 04102 207-772-7791
CHRETIEN STUDIO 95 Glenwood Ave Westbrook, ME 04092 207-856-6298
DAN GAIR PHOTOGRAPHIC 72 Route 236 Kittery, ME 03904 207-439-9622
KLYNE STUDIO 212 Howard ST Bangor, ME 04401 207-942-3190
KUCINE PHOTOGRAPHY INC 273 Presumpscot St Portland, ME 04103 207-773-2568
LUCE STUDIO 158 Lower Main St Farmington, ME 04938 207-778-4920
NINA FULLER PHOTOGRAPHY 446 Sowler Rd Cape Elizabeth, ME 04107 207-767-4400
PAT MICHAUD PHOTOGRAPHY 341 Water ST Augusta, ME 04330 207-623-2027
PHOTOGRAPHY ASSOCIATES 228 N Main St Old Town, ME 04468 207-827-4550
PHOTOGRAPHY BY BROWN INC 530 Methodist Rd Westbrook, ME 04092 308-854-2098
PICTORIAL STUDIO Academy Hill Dr Newcastle, ME 04553 207-563-3305
RAND RAABE PHOTOGRAPHY 22 Robinson Rd Scarborough, ME 04074 207-883-3003

STEPHEN FAZIO PHOTOGRAPHY 25 W Kidder St Portland, ME 04103 207-871-7031

STRETCH TUEMMLER STUDIO 45 Casco ST Portland, ME 04101 207-871-0350

STUDIO 1 PHOTOGRAPHY 48 Town Landing Rd Dresden, ME 04342 207-737-8636

TANNERY HILL STUDIOS INC 25 Park DR Topsham, ME 04086 507-725-5689

TOM MC PHERSON PHOTOGRAPHY 141 Kennebec St Portland, ME 04101 207-774-1318

VOSCAR THE MAINE PHOTOGRAPHER 93 Hardy ST Presque Isle, ME 04769 207-769-5911

MARYLAND

BEL AIR STUDIO 13 N Main St Bel Air, MD 21014 410-838-1586

CAMERA ONE PO BOX 823 Cambridge, MD 21613 410-228-5818

CHASE STUDIOS INC 4815 Saint Elmo Ave Bethesda, MD 20814 301-986-1050

CLASSIC PHOTOGRAPHY 6900 Laurel Bowie Rd Bowie, MD 20715 301-809-2500

CLEMENT D REHEARD JR PHOTOGRAPHY 8218 Burnley Rd Baltimore, MD 21204 410-828-8811

COMPETITION PHOTOS INC 35 E Dover St Easton, MD 21601 410-822-8880

DELAINE HOBBS STUDIO 205 N Main St Mt Airy, MD 21771 301-829-1380

DOEHRER PHOTOGRAPHY 2807 Armacost Ave Finksburg, MD 21048 410-861-8025

DORE PORTRAIT STUDIO 7917 Liberty Rd Baltimore, MD 21244 410-655-1974

GLOGAU STUDIO 5110 Ridgefield Rd #204 Bethesda, MD 20816 301-652-9577

GUILL PHOTO 1320 Reisterstown Rd Pikesville, MD 21208 410-486-6161

HARVEY & HARVEY PHOTOGRAPHY 27966 Marlboro Rd Edgewater, MD 21037 410-956-4159

IMAGES 21614 Great Mills Rd Lexington Park, MD 20653 301-862-1203

LAWRENCE FITTON PHOTOGRAPHY 2029 Maryland Ave Baltimore, MD 21218 410-727-0092

LIGHTNER PHOTOGRAPHY 9504 Deereco Rd Lutherville, MD 21093 410-252-0201

MICHAEL B KRESS PHOTOGRAPHY 4710 Bethesda, MD 20814 301-654-0909

MURRILL PHOTOGRAPHY 328 Cranbrook Rd Cockysvl Hnt Vly, MD 21060 410-666-7611

PARAGON LIGHT 401 Brookletts Ave Easton, MD 21601 410-820-7738

PERCEPTIVE EYE 903 Whitaker Mill Rd Joppa, MD 21085 410 877-8102

PHOTOGRAPHY BY DALE 1309 Pennsylvania Ave Hagerstown, MD 21742 301-733-2320

PHOTOGRAPHY BY JEANNINE 88 E Main St Frostburg, MD 21532 301-689-2156

POINT OF VIEW PHOTOGRAPHY 7002 Carroll Ave Takoma Park, MD 20912 301-270-2340

RO JAY PHOTOGRAPHERS 5540 Randolph Rd #B Rockville, MD 20852 301-881-0041

RUHL STUDIOS 36 N Centre St Cumberland, MD 21502 301-724-1303

STONE PHOTOGRAPHY 5110 Ridgefield Rd #208 Bethesda, MD 20816 301-654-3185

STUART POHOST PHOTOGRAPHY 810 Caddington Ave Silver Spring, MD 20901 301-593-6200

STUDIO ONE 8216 Wisconsin Ave Bethesda, MD 20814 301-652-1345

VALLEY STUDIO 11000 Bower Ave #4 Hagerstown, MD 21740 301-582-1499

MASSACHUSETTS

ALBERT'S PHOTO STUDIO 409 Moody ST Waltham, MA 02453 781-894-0082

ATLANTIC PHOTO SVC 100 Southampton St Boston, MA 02118 617-427-8300

CAPRICORN STUDIOS 315 Pleasant St Fall River, MA 02721 508-672-6460

CREATIVE STUDIO OF PHOTOGRAPHY 454 Main St Fitchburg, MA 01420 978-343-3017

EASEL PHOTOGRAPHY BY DUGGAN 79 Prospect St Greenfield, MA 01301 413-774-9929

FINKLE PHOTOGRAPHY 246 Merriam Ave Leominster, MA 01453 978-537-1934

FORBES CAMERA SHOP 300 Main St Greenfield, MA 01301 413-773-9898

FREELANCE PHOTOIMAGES 483 Water St Framingham, MA 01701 508-877-7700

HARDING-GLIDDEN INC 217 Washington St Westwood, MA 02090 781-326-8182

HIGGINS & ROSS 200 Market St Lowell, MA 01852 978-454-4248

HUDSON PHOTOGRAPHY 105 Washington St North Easton, MA 02356 508-230-2844

HYZEN PHOTOGRAPHY & VIDEO 621 Boston Post Rd Sudbury, MA 01776 978-443-5308

J GEIGER IND PHOTOGRAPHY 20 Millbrook DR Plainville, MA 02762 508-695-0467

JAMES A LANGONE PHOTOGRAPHER 36 Loring St Springfield, MA 01105 413-732-1174

KEVIN DOWNEY PHOTOGRAPHY 21 Massasoit St Northampton, MA 01060 413-584-0670

KORDAY STUDIO 50 Franklin St Framingham, MA 01702 508-87-6323

BECKER PHOTOGRAPHY 1 Chevalier Ave Greenfield, MA 01301 413-773-8437

MICHAEL ZIDE PHOTOGRAPHY 320 Riverside Dr Florence, MA 01062 413-585-5888

MILLER STUDIO 17 Foster St Quincy, MA 02169 617-472-2330

NASH STUDIO INC 100 Grove St Worcester, MA 01605 508-791-5530

PETER NOEL PHOTOGRAPHY 99 Washington St Melrose, MA 02176 781-665-8381

PHOTOGRAPHY BY R RUSCANSKY 44 Mechanic St Boston, MA 02113 617-964-4848

ROBERT MAYER PHOTOGRAPHY 51 Exchange St Athol, MA 01331 978-249-7995

SAMUELS STUDIO INC 8 Waltham St Maynard, MA 01754 978-897-7901

STUDIO OF MARK RICHARDS 58 Falcon St Needham, MA 02492 781-449-7135

STUDIO ONE PHOTOGRAPHY 2083 Acushnet Ave New Bedford, MA 02745 508-995-8920

STUDIO SERGEI 181 Dory Cir West Springfield, MA 01089 413-733-3530

SUNSHINE PHOTOGRAPHICS 20 McKay St Pittsfield, MA 01201 413-443-5050

TIM SYLVIA PHOTOGRAPHER 38 Bethel St New Bedford, MA 02740 508-992-6711

VISUAL ARTS 134 Water St Wakefield, MA 01880 781-246-2939

XENOPHON BEAKE PHOTOGRAPHY 934 Glendale Rd Wilbraham, MA 01095 413-596

MICHIGAN

ALAN LOWY PHOTOGRAPHY 28830 W 8 Mile Rd Farmington Hills, MI 48336 248-471-7299

ALDERMAN PHOTOGRAPHIC ARTS 700 E Maple Rd Birmingham, MI 48009 248-644-0422

ALLEN BROOKS STUDIO 6811 Deerhurst Dr Westland, MI 48185 834-525-3930

ANDREWS PHOTOGRAPHY 612 N State St Big Rapids, MI 49307 231-796-8393

ANNE I TRAHAN PHOTOGRAPHY 512 Lincoln St # 308 Bay City, MI 48708 517-894-4800

ARELLA STUDI S 22801 Newman St Dearborn, MI 48124 313-274-0732

ASHFORD O PHOTOGRAPHY 5130 Old Haverhill Rd Grand Blanc, MI 48439 810-694-6012

BEEHR, RICHARD 305 Wilson Dr Midland, MI 48642 517-631-0856

BILL PLUS JEAN PHOTOGRAPHY 2342 Shadowlane Dr NE Grand Rapids, MI 49505 616-363-6964

BIRDS EYE VIEW PHOTOGRAPHY 3322 Southgate Dr Flint, MI 48507 810-234-9708

BOB MOUSTAKAS PHOTOGRAPHY 601 N 5th Ave Ann Arbor, MI 48104 734-717-6890

BOYNTON PHOTOGRAPHY 1600 E Michigan Ave Lansing, MI 48912 517-487-1600

BRECKENRIDGE STUDIO OF PHOTO 42000 Grand River Ave Novi, MI 48375 248-344-1511

BROCKWAY PHOTOGRAPHY 614 Shelden Ave Houghton, MI 49931 906-482-1900

BUBLITZ PHOTOGRAPHY 101 S Mason St Saginaw, MI 48602 517-792-1600

BUZ HOLZMAN PHOTOGRAPHY 29655 W 14 Mile Rd Farmington Hills, MI 48334 248-932-1780

CARROLL'S PHOTOGRAPHY 17543 Fort St Riverview, MI 48192 734-285-2350

CLASSIC PHOTOGRAPHY 29959 Northwestern Hwy Southfield, MI 48034 248-350-2420

CLASSIC PHOTOGRAPHY 4331 3 Mile Rd Traverse City, MI 49686 231-947-6655

CORY'S PHOTOGRAPHY STUDIO 11620 S Saginaw St Grand Blanc, MI 48439 810-694-3500

CREATIVE IMAGES BY MARISSA 4286 Pheasant Dr Flint, MI 48506 810-736-1041

CURT FROOK PHOTOGRAPHY 10441 S West Bay Shore Dr Traverse City, MI 49684 231-946-8544

DALE R HAGEN PHOTOGRAPHY 201 N 3rd St Grand Haven, MI 49417 616-846-5000

DAVID ROBERTS PHOTOGRAPHY 1200 E Avon Rd Rochester, MI 48307 248-652-2131

DENNY'S STUDIO OF PHOTOGRAPHY 1577 Holton Rd North Muskegon, MI 49445 231-744-3354

DONALD N PENNINGTON PHOTO 5427 Pine View Dr Ypsilanti, MI 48197 734-485-0820

EIGHTH STREET PHOTOGRAPHY 439 8th St Calumet, MI 49913 906-337-2205

FOX PORTRAIT STUDIO INC 22934 Woodward Ave Ferndale, MI 48220 248-544-1110

GOLDEN MEADOWS PHOTOGRAPHY 1509 S Lapeer Rd Lake Orion, MI 48360 248-693-3303

GRAHAM PHOTOGRAPHY 2000 Walton Rd Niles, MI 49120 616-683-2274

GUARINO STUDIOS PHOTOGRAPHY 1210 S Westnedge Ave Kalamazoo, MI 49008 616-381-7316

GUYS & DOLLS PHOTOGRAPHY 105 E State St Clare, MI 48617 517-386-9361

HAFER PHOTOGRAPHY 2907 Division St #102 ST Joseph, MI 49085 616-983-5670

HARRISON'S CREATIVE PHOTO 3353 N Jennings Rd Flint, MI 48504 810-238-4445

HICKS STUDIO 1982 Hemmeter Rd Saginaw, MI 48603 517-792-1171

HOLLAND PHOTOGRAPHY 950 Central Ave Holland, MI 49423 616-392-4972

IMAGES BY JULIA 4400 Mechanic Rd Hillsdale, MI 49242 517-439-9961

JERRY LEWIS PHOTOGRAPHERS INC 342 River St Manistee, MI 49660 231-723-2422

JOHN MARTIN PHOTOGRAPHY 725 S Adams Rd Birmingham, MI 48009 248-646-3831

KENNY'S STUDIO 227 E Aurora St Ironwood, MI 49938 906-932-3620

KGT PHOTOGRAPHY INC 660 Bellevue Milford, MI 48381 248-684-6482

KRUZ PHOTOGRAPHICS 1309 Broadway St Ann Arbor, MI 48105 734-668-6988

LAPORTE STUDIO 1610 Ludington St Escanaba, MI 49829 906-786-6653

LIGHTS ON STUDIO 5400 S Pennsylvania Ave Lansing, MI 48911 517-393-1161

MARION'S STUDIO 66900 Gratiot Ave Richmond, Mi 48062 810-727-9906

MARK 1 PHOTOGRAPHY 1201 S Euclid Ave Bay City, MI 48706 517-686-6917

PAULA CHRISTENSEN PHOTOGRAPHY 2354 Delaware Dr Ann Arbor, MI 48103 734-995-8880

PERKINS PHOTOGRAPHY 4940 24th Ave Fort Gratiot, MI 48059 810-385-3200

PHOTO CENTER 29207 Southfield Rd Southfield, MI 48076 248-443-1808

PHOTOGRAPHY BY DAVID 216 N Maple St Traverse City, MI 49684 231-946-1392

PHOTOGRAPHS BY LYLE 1652 S Shore Dr Holland, MI 49423 616-335-3210

PIERONEK STUDIOS 11633 Joseph Campau St Detroit, MI 48212 313-365-8070

RAYMOND D KOPEN PHOTOGRAPHY 825 W Lake Lansing Rd, MI 48823 517-332-4018

ROCHELEAU PHOTOGRAPHY 6948 N Black River Rd Cheboygan, MI 49721 231-625-9957

RUMMEL PORTRAIT STUDIOS 2141 Warwick St Saginaw, MI 48602 517-793-6930

SIELOFF STUDIO 36366 Groesbeck Hwy Clinton Twp, MI 48035 810-791-5000

SUNSET STUDIOS 2211 10TH St Port Huron, MI 48060 810-984-3794

TALBOT STUDIOS 320 S Main St Ann Arbor, MI 48104 734-668-7701

WEED PATCH PHOTOGRAPHY STUDIO 732 W Grand River Ave Howell, MI 48843 517-546-1759

WHIPPLE PHOTO SVC 111 N Forest St Standish, MI 48658 517-846-4151

WHITE'S PHOTOGRAPHY 131 W State St Hastings, MI 49058 616-945-3967

MINNESOTA

ALP PHOTOGRAPHY 69 E. 4th St. Winona, MN 55987 507-452-2936

BARNES PHOTOGRAPHY 540 Benson Ave. SW. Willmar, MN 56201 320-235-1313

BREUTZMAN PHOTOGRAPHY 1503 14th St. NW. Rochester, MN 55901 507-282-9176

CHAMPA STUDIOS 403 9th Ave. N. St. Cloud, MN 56303 320-251-1550

CROSBY STUDIO 1105 W. Lincoln Ave. Olivia, MN 56277 320-523-1040

DAN MAGNUSON STUDIOS 31 Water St. Excelsior, MN 55331 952-470-0663

DAN ROTHER PHOTOGRAPHY 1505 Brooke Ct. Hastings, MN 55033 651-437-8828

ELLIS PHOTOGRAPHY 637 Snelling Ave. N. ST. Paul, MN 55104 651-644-0121

ENSTROM STUDIO 302 2nd Ave. Bovey, MN 55709 218-245-1330

G W TUCKER PHOTOGRAPHIC STUDIO 526 Chestnut St. Virginia, MN 55792 218-741-7464

GRANDMAISON PHOTOGRAPHIC 4271 Haines Rd. Hermantown, MN 55811 218-727-4000

JOHN PETERSON PHOTOGRAPHY 316 E. Howard ST. Hibbing, MN 55746 218-263-7312

LA BAW'S PHOTOGRAPHY 104 6th Ave. SE Rochester, MN 55904 507-288-6579

LARSON PHOTOGRAPHY 315 C. St. NE. Brainerd, MN 56401 218-829-1269

LASTING MEMORIES PHOTOGRAPHY 149 Lime Valley Ln. Mankato, MN 56001 507-625-1481

LOCY STUDIO 1301 E. College Dr. Marshall, MN 56258 507-532-4901

LOWER PHOTOGRAPHY 3509 9th Ave. NW. Rochester, MN 55901 507-282-2534

MARCUS PHOTOGRAPHY 7031 Glenwood Ave. Golden Valley, MN 55427 763-545-0051

MC MAHON STUDIO PHOTOGRAPHY 900 S. 3rd. St. Minneapolis MN 55415 612-339-9709

MEYER STUDIO 520 Minnesota Ave. St. Peter, MN 56083 507-931-4200

NEALLY PHOTOGRAPHY 17 E. Wabasha St. Duluth, MN 55803 218-724-0443

NEIL KVEBERG PHOTOGRAPHY 1590 McCarthy Rd. Eagan, MN 55121 651-454-4007

PEOPLE PHOTOGRAPHY 2134 Highland Ave. Albert Lea, MN 56007 507-373-6180

PHOTOGRAPHERS GUILD 161 Snelling Ave. N. St. Paul, MN 55104 651-646-3239

PHOTOGRAPHY BY MARK MIRANDA 63 W. 3rd St. Winona, MN 55987 507-464-4588

REGAN PHOTOGRAPHY 1459 W. 5th St. Winona, MN 55987 507-542-2163

RICKERS PHOTOGRAPHY STUDIO 918 3rd Ave. Worthington MN 56187 507-376-3555

SIEBOLD PHOTOGRAPHY 50 7th St. Cloquet, MN. 55720 218-879-9574

SILVER LIGHT PHOTOGRAPHY 11550 Stillwater Blvd. N. Lake Elmo, MN 55042 651-439-9107

STASSEN'S PHOTOGRAPHY 130 3RD St. Tracy, MN 56175 507-629-3540

TEXLEY PHOTOGRAPHICS 1912 7th St. SW. Willmar, MN 56201 320-214-8622

THOMAS-LEONARD PHOTOGRAPHY 419 Pierce St. Eveleth, MN 55734 218-744-1021

ZAHLER PHOTOGRAPHY 112 Central Ave. E. St. Michael, MN 55376 763-497-2603

MISSISSIPPI

ADVANCED PHOTOGRAPHY 832 Ridgewood Rd. Ridgeland, MS 39157 601-956-7277

BOB HUBBARD'S VISTA STUDIOS 2009 Oak Grove Rd. Hattiesburg, MS 39402 601-264-4444

CHRIS GRILLIS PHOTOGRAPHY 2727 Old Canton Rd. Jackson, MS 39216 601-362-9975

D-RAWLS PHOTOGRAPHY 1910 Hardy St. #B Hattiesburg, MS 39401 601-544-2293

GIL FORD PHOTOGRAPHY INC. 1048 Greymont Ave. Jackson, MS 39202 601-353-9675

HAWKINS PHOTOGRAPHY 3724 N. State St. Jackson, MS 39216 601-982-3262

HORRELL PHOTOGRAPHY 720 North St. Jackson, MS 39202 601-969-1919

IMAGE PLACE INC. 780 Poplarville St. Tupelo, MS 38801 662-842-0676

JOE MC KEWEN STUDIO 411 Cruise St. Corinth, MS 38834 662-286-2067

JOHN KEEN PHOTOGRAPHY 612 Highway 1 South Greenville, M. 38701 662-334-1467

JOHNSON PHOTOGRAPHY 624 Highway 51 #A Ridgeland, MS 39157 601-856-7946

KAY HOLLOWAY PHOTOGRAPHY 147 Millsaps Ave. # C Jackson, MS 39202 601-353-8865

LARSON PHOTOGRAPHERS 1017 Washington Ave. Greenville, MS 38701 662-332-8422

LONNIE KEES PHOTOGRAPHY 1491 Canton Mart Rd. Jackson, MS 39221 601-977-9830

ORIGINAL SOUTHERN IMAGES 3528 Debbie Drive Olive Branch MS 38654 662-393-3063

PHOTOGRAPHY BY CHARLES 107 W. Front St. Iuka, MS 38852 662-423-3359

PHOTOGRAPHY UNLIMITED 4189 Chesterville Rd. Tupelo, MS 38801 662-844-4544

PHOTOSOURCE 1518 Bienville Blvd. #B Ocean Springs, MS 39564 228-872-7229

PICKET PHOTOGRAPHY 1617 Monroe St. Vicksburg, MS 39180 601-636-7451

SHIRWOOD PHOTOGRAPHY 1920 Highway 45 N. Columbus, MS 39705 662-328-5067

STEWART'S PHOTOGRAPHY 2305 Bluecutt Rd. Columbus, MS 39705 662-327-4617

SUNSET PHOTOGRAPHY 15520 Lemoyne Blvd. Biloxi, MS 39532 228-392-7755

WALLACE REEVES STUDIOS 1611 Ingalls Ave. Pascagoula, MS 39567 228-762-3802

MISSOURI

BARTH PHOTOGRAPHY 3700 S. Crysler Ave. Independence, MO 64055 81`6-252-9429

CLASSIC STUDIO 600 Osage Ave. Sedalia, MO 65301 660-826-8888

DON BESS STUDIO INC. 107 Strauss Dr. Flat River, MO 63601 573-431-7686

EDGE PHOTOGRAPHY 2656 E. Lombard St. Springfield, MO 65802 417-864-7553

F-STOP OF ST. LOUIS 3150 N. Lindbergh Blvd. St. Ann, MO 63074 314-298-1727

HAL WAGNER STUDIO 11214 Natural Bridge Rd. Bridgeton, MO 63044 314-731-2231

HAMMOND PHOTOGRAPHY INC. 301 Mid Rivers Dr. St. Peters, MO 63376 636-926-0967

J KENT BIXLER PHOTOGRAPHY 6651 N. Oak Tree FY Kansas City MO 64118 816-453-3051

JEAN'S STUDIO 110 Country Line Rd. Sikeston, MO 63801 573-471-3800

LINDA'S STUDIO 2003 Southridge Dr. Jefferson City MO 65109 573-636-5575

LUCAS PHOTOGRAPHY RR 4 Box 45J Moberly, MO 65270 263-7835

MARTIN SCHWEIG STUDIO 329 N. Euclid Ave. St. Louis, MO 63108 314-361-3000

MATSON PHOTOGRAPHY INC. 5976 Howdershell Dr. #202 Hazelwood, MO 63042 314-895-1800

MAX PHOTOGRAPHIC SVC. 1918 Missouri Blvd. Jefferson City, MO 65109 573-635-6622

McCARTHY PHOTOGRAPHY INC. 8901 Saint Charles Rock Rd. Overland, MO 63114 314-428-5090

McCARTHY PHOTOGRAPHY INC. 11200 Olive Blvd. Creve Coeur, MO 63141 314-432-1221

MICHAEL GOODWIN PHOTOGRAPHY 2769 W. Lark St. Springfield, MO 65810 417-881-5855

MIGNARD PHOTOGRAPHY 1950 S. Glenstone Ave. #R Springfield, MO 65804 417-881-7422

PAT PATTERSON PHOTOGRAPHY 2700 Bloomfield Rd. Cape Girardeau, MO 63703 573-335-5197

PHILLIP'S PHOTOGRAPHY 2417 Barron Rd. Poplar Bluff, MO 63901 573-686-4343

PHOENIX PHOTOGRAPHY 9950 Kennerly Rd. Sappington, M. 63128 314-843-5998

PHOENIX PHOTOGRAPHY 13418 Clayton Rd. St. Louis, MO 63131 314-275-8338
PHOTOGRAPHY BY DE WEESE 424 W. Reed St. Moberly, MO 65270 660-263-6543
PICTURE THIS PHOTOGRAPHY 1728 SE Silkwood Ct. Lees Summit MO 64063 816-524-4266
RAINBOW PHOTOGRAPHY STUDIO 115 E. Long St. Branson, MO 65616 417-334-4271
RALPH POKORNY PHOTOGRAPHY 221 E. Pacific St. Nevada, MO 64772 417-667-2112
ROBERT MIDDENDORF PHOTOGRAPHY 826 Westrun Dr. Ballwin, MO 63021 636-256-3757
ROBERTSON'S CREATIVE PHOTO 605 Broadway St. Cape Girardeau, MO. 63701 573-651-3999
SCHLOMER PHOTOGRAPHY 304 S. Ohio Ave. Sedalia, MO 65301 660-827-2900
STRAUSS PEYTON INC. 515 N. Lindbergh Blvd. St. Louis, M. 63141 314-997-8966
STRIKE A POSE 1628 W. 3rd. St. Joplin, MO 64801 417-782-3811
STUDIO THREE PHOTOGRAPHY 119 w. Lexington Ave. Independence, MO 64050 816-461-6829
SUMMERLIN STUDIO 1531 E. 32nd St. Joplin, MO 64804 417-623-6233
TANNER STUDIO 4401 S. Grand Blvd. St. Louis, MO 63111 314-353-4000
THOMAS SCHWARTZ STUDIO 7290 Manchester Rd. St. Louis, MO 63143 314-644-1166
THOMPSON PHOTOGRAPHICS 244 Indacom Dr. St. Peters, MO 63376 636-447-2396
TODD STUDIOS INC. 701 N. 15th St. #412W. St. Louis, MO. 63103 314-231-0565
TROTTER PHOTO 14231 Manchester Rd. Ballwin, MO 63011 636-394-7689
WILBORN & ASSOC. PHOTOGRAPHERS 3101 Mercier St. Kansas City, MO 64111 816-531-9000

MONTANA

ALSA PHOTOGRAPHY 422 Grand Ave. Billings, MT 59101 406-252-4276
ANDERSON PHOTOGRAPHY 1337 Janie St. Billings, MT 59105 406-252-5100
BELMONT STUDIO 629 Grand Ave. Billings, MT 59101 406-245-5168

BRUCE PITCHER PHOTOGRAPHY 9410 Forest Creek Dr. Bozeman, MT 59718 406-587-0949

BRYANT PORTRAIT DESIGN 817 S. Higgins Ave. Missoula, MT 59801 721-2414

CENTENNIAL PORTRAITS 101 Central Ave. Great Falls MT 59401 406-452-6300

CLARK MARTEN PHOTOGRAPHY 354 Upper Flat Rd. Columbus, MT 59019 406-322-5554

CLARKSON'S STUDIO 401 n. Hoback St. Helena, MT 59601 406-442-2046

CURTISS JAY FLECK PHOTOGRAPHY 801 N. Haggin St. Red Lodge, MT 59068 406-446-2455

HADNAGY PHOTOGRAPHY 833 W. Quartz St. Butte, MT 59701 406-723-5439

HELMBRECHT STUDIO 224 4th Ave. Havre, MT 59501 406-265-4252

IMAGES BY STEPHEN 306 S. 2nd Street Hamilton, MT 59840 406-363-2622

KASPER'S PHOTO SHOPS 1603 Grand Ave. Billings, MT 59102 406-252-7600

LYNN SCHEELER PHOTOGRAPHY 1011 Alder Ave. Laurel, MT 59044 406-628-8876

MARC HEFTY PHOTOGRAPHER 2021 S. Higgins Ave. Missoula, MT 59801 406-543-5075

MC MILLAN STUDIO 322 Central Ave. Great Falls, MT 59401 406-452-2202

NOICE STUDIO & GALLERY 127 Main St. Kalispell, MT 59901 406-755-5321

RIKSHOTS PHOTOGRAPHY 411 W. Mendenhall St. Bozeman, MT. 59715 406-586-6767

SCHWARTZ PHOTOGRAPHY 103 E. Main St. Sidney, MT 59270 406-482-1236

SCOTT BREUM PHOTOGRAPHY 1639 South Ave. W. Missoula, MT 59801 406-728-6277

SCOTT PHOTOGRAPHY 1400 2nd Ave. N. Great Falls MT 59401 406-761-2059

SHARP FOCUS 11 Wathena Dr. Butte, MT 59701 406-494-6033

THIRD EYE PHOTOGRAPHICS 58 N. Last Chance Gulch St. Helena, M. 59601 406-443-4668

TIM RICE DÉCOR PORTRAITS 310 Wisconsin Ave. Whitefish, MT 59937 406-862-5416

TONY SMITH PHOTOGRAPHY 134 Grand Ave. Billings, MT 59101 406-252-7905

WINSLOW STUDIO & GALLERY 16 S. Tracy Ave. Bozeman, MT 59715 406-587-8826

NEBRASKA

APPLE STUDIOS 621 Court St. Beatrice, NE 68310 402-223-3456

BAILEY PHOTOGRAPHY 218 W. 2nd St. Grand Island, NE 68801 308-382-4195

BELL'S COUNTRY STYLE PHOTO 1303 1st Corso Nebraska City, NE 68410 402-873-5320

BOBIER PORTRAIT STUDIO 2515 Dakota Ave. South Sioux City, NE 68776 402-494-5192

BROWN-HARANO PHOTOGRAPHY 412 N. Dewey St. North Platte, NE 69101 308-532-4792

CERAOLO PHOTOGRAPHY 4120 Van Dorn St. Lincoln, NE 68506 402-489-2339

CHRISTIAN PHOTOGRAPHY 1906 Broadway Scottsbluff, NE 69361 308-632-3121

CONNIE SWANSON PHOTOGRAPHY 209 W. 3rd. St. Grand Island, NE 68801 308-382-1117

CRAIG FULKERSON PHOTOGRAPHY 4909 S. 118th St. Omaha, NE 68137 402-895-6082

DAVID DALE PHOTOGRAPHY 1621 A. Street Lincoln, NE 68502 402-477-2824

DOWNEY'S FINE PHOTOGRAPHY 17 E. 16th St. Scottsbluff, NE 69361 308-632-4832

EVANS STUDIO 1124 N. Cotner Blvd. Lincoln, NE. 68505 402-467-3569

HAL MAGGIORE PHOTOGRAPHY 722 N. Eddy St. Grand Island, NE 68801 308-381-7603

HAMILTON'S STUDIO 3530 J. Street Lincoln, NE 68501 402-475-0121

HOUSE OF PHOTOGRAPHY 401 Emerson Ave. Alliance, NE 69301 308-762-1291

IMAGES BY RJ 1009 N. Broad St. Fremont, NE 68025 402-721-8321

J R WURTZ PHOTOGRAPHY 1250 Aldrich Rd. Lincoln, NE 68510 402-488-0271

JENSEN PHOTOGRAPHY 12 e. 22ND St. Kearney, NE 68847 308-234-2681

LAD PHOTOGRAPHY 2517 W. Lincoln Hwy Grand Island, NE 68803 308-382-8811

MARK'S PHOTOGRAPHY 2105 E. US Hwy 30 Grand Island, NE 68801 308-382-1566

MC CLELLAND PHOTOGRAPHERS 14706 California St. Omaha, NE. 68154 402-493-6250

ORTHMANN'S PHOTOGRAPHY STUDIO 709 W. 1st St. Hastings, NE 68901 402-463-5802

PICTURE MAN 4230 Progressive Ave. Lincoln, NE 68504 402-467-2577

RADER PHOTOGRAPHY 1039 N. Main St. Fremont NE 68025 402-721-7975
REGAL PHOTOGRAPHY 1417 S. 133rd. St. Omaha, NE 68144 402-330-7649
RICK BILLINGS PHOTOGRAPHY 13132 Davenport St. Omaha, NE 68154 402-333-5508
STUDIO 5 611 Elmwood Ave. Lincoln, NE 68510 402-475-3971
STUDIO B PHOTOGRAPHY MAIN STREET CHAMBERS, NE 68725 402-482-5765
TOM STERBA PHOTOGRAPHY 5726 A Street Omaha, NE 68106 402-551-3456
VAN ALLAN CLASSIC PORTRAITS 2801 E. Omaha Ave. Norfolk, NE 68701 402-379-2025
WEBER'S STUDIO 817 W. 2nd St. Hastings NE 68901 402-462-9839
WINKELBAUER PHOTOGRAPHY 900 W. 2nd St Hastings, NE 68901 402-462-4171
WORLEY STUDIO 508 Box Butte Ave. Alliance, NE 69301 308-762-3335

NEW HAMPSHIRE

ANDREW EDGAR PHOTOGRAPHY 135 McDonough St. Portsmouth, NH 03801 603-436-4221
ANDRUSKEVICH PHOTOGRAPHY 96 Main Street Nashua, NH 03060 603-880-8558
AUREL STUART PHOTOGRAPHY 22 Russell Street Manchester, NH 03104 603-623-4193
B ST. PIERRE STUDIO 68 Tinker Rd. Merrimack, NH 03054 603-883-2517
BOB RAICHE PHOTOGRAPHY 305 Stark Ln. Manchester, NH 03102 603-623-7912
BOB SHEVETT PHOTOGRAPHY 199 Pleasant View Rd. Newbury, NH 03255
CARL AUSTIN HYATT PHOTO 855 Islington St. #319 Portsmouth, NH 03801 603-436-8161
CHARLES HAMPE PHOTOGRAPHER 43 Shaker Rd. Belmont, N. 03220 603-267-7186
KAREVY PHOTOGRAPHY 312-Marlboro St. Keene, NH 03431 603-357-2644
LES MAC DONALD PHOTOGRAPHY 111 Jack Frost Ln. Conway, NH 03818 603-447-5028
LIGHTWORKS PHOTOGRAPHY 769 State St. Portsmouth, N. 03801 603-431-6889
MEMORIES STUDIO 101 Lafayette Dr. Rye, NH 03870 603-964-6551
MULTI-MEDIA CREATIONS 8 Gemini Dr. Keene, NH 03431 603-352-8366
PEAK IMAGES 13 Barefoot Pl. Gilford, NH 03249 603-293-8107

R B CROTEAU PHOTOGRAPHY 92 W. Pearl St. Nashua, NH 03060 603-889-1101
RARE IMAGES PHOTOGRAPHY 9 Woodburn Dr. Litchfield, NH 03052 603-882-0641
RHEAULT PHOTOGRAPHERS INC. 72 Hanover St. Manchester, NH 03101
ROY STUDIOS 1657 Brown Ave. Manchester, NH 03103 603-625-6011
STUDIO ONE 50 Bridge Street # 301 Manchester, NH. 03101 603-622-2738
VISUAL REFLECTIONS 17 Knight Ave. Littleton, NH 03561 603-444-6881

NEW JERSEY

A J CONNECTION 1455 Ferrell Rd. Monroeville, NJ 08343 856-478-2455
ACKERMAN STUDIO INC. 169 Ackerman Ave. Clifton, NJ 07011 973-546-3309
ACME STUDIO OF PHOTOGRAPHY 75 Smith St. Perch Amboy, NJ 08861 732-826-1099
ALAN BROOKER PHOTOGRAPHY 118 Pond Dr. Freehold, NJ 07728 732-780-2451
ALLAMUCHY STUDIO Johnson Rd. Allamuchy, NJ 07820 908-852-6334
BAITER STUDIO 12 Mine Brook Rd. Bernardsville, NJ 07924 908-221-9226
BASSETTI PHOTO 110 South Ave. Minotola NJ. 08341 856-967-0770
BOGARD STUDIO 326 Morris Ave. Elizabeth, NJ 07208 908-354-7466
CAMERA HAVEN & STUDIO 530 State Rd. 515 Vernon, NJ 07462 973-764-4848
CARRIAGE HOUSE STUDIO 203 E. willow St. Wenonah, NJ 08090 856-468-6119
CHARLES ANTHONY STUDIO 1973 Springfield Ave. Maplewood, NJ 07040 973-763-2333
CREATIVE IMAGE PHOTOGRAPHY 325 Valley Rd. West Orange, NJ 07052 973-325-2352
CREATIVE IMAGE STUDIO 209 Spring St. Newton NJ 07860 973-579-2038
CRESENT PHOTO LAB 5032 Route 70 Merchantville, NJ 08109 856-665-3363
DAMIEN STUDIO 106 Broadway Denville, NJ 07834 973-627-1751
DENNIS STUDIO INC. 45 E. Main St. Bergenfield, NJ 07621 201-384-3155
DU PREE STUDIOS 1 Bethany commons # 15 Hazlet, NJ 07730 732-264-8855
FORTE PHOTOGRAPHY 22 Ridge Rd. Hackettstown, NJ 07840 908-852-9578
GLEN ROC PHOTOGRAPHY STUDIO 192 Scotch Rd. West Trenton, NJ. 086298 609-883-5553

HARLAN PHOTOGRAPHERS INC. 22 S. Broad St. Ridgewood, NJ 07450 201-445-2119

IMAGE ONE PHOTOGRAPHERS 308 High St. Hackettstown, NJ 07840 908-852-5409

IRVINGTON PHOTO STUDIO 2 Union Ave. # 2 Irvington, NJ 07111 973-374-6856

JAMES YOUNG PHOTOGRAPHER 460 Bloomfield Ave. Caldwell, NJ 07006 973-226-7276

JANET STUDIOS 2104 Kings Hwy Ocean, NJ 07712 732-531-8848

JOHN ULISSI STUDIO 174 N. Broadway Pennsville, NJ 08070 856-678-8050

KLEIN & ULMES INC. 549 Lincoln Blvd. Middlesex NJ 08846 732-356-2900

LANE STUDIOS 590 Main Ave. Passaic, NJ 07055 973-777-6814

MARTINO STUDIO OF PHOTOGRAPHY 10 S. Michigan Ave. Kenilworth, NJ 07033 908-245-5110

MICHAEL FOXSON PHOTOGRAPHY 13 Ames Blvd. Hamburg, NJ 07419 973-827-5217

PETER WALLBURG STUDIOS 15 Beechwood Rd. Summit, NJ 07901 908-277-2078

PHOTOGRAPHY BY RALPH LOEWY 30 S. Doughty Ave, Somerville, NJ 08876 908-526-3340

RICHARD ZOSCHAK PHOTOGRAPHY 559 Wills Rd. Landing, NJ 07850 973-398-0061

STEVEN WASKOW PHOTOGRAPHY 1 Westfield Ct. Princeton, NJ 08540 609-921-3982

TED ROBINSON PHOTOGRAPHY 53 Morris Ave. Neptune City, NJ 07753 732-775-6370

WONDERLAND STUDIO 666 Franklin Ave. Nutley, NJ 07110 973-667-3683

ZUGCIC PHOTOGRAPHERS INC. 424 Union Hill Rd. Morganville, NJ 07751 732-536-3288

NEVADA

ALLEN PHOTOGRAPHERS INC. 3223 Industrial Rd. Las Vegas, NV 89109 702-735-2222

ANFINSON UNLIMITED 2270 Aquila Ave. Reno, NV 89509 775-323-1182

ANTHONY PAUL PHOTOGRAPHY 1060 Telegraph St. #2 Reno, NV 89502 775-322-2515

BERNHARD & WILLIAMS PHOTO 3075 S. Valley View Bl. Las Vegas, NV 89102 702-251-3040

COMSTOCK PHOTOGRAPHIC 1620 Mill St. Reno, NV 89502 775-882-4333

FRANK VALERI PHOTOGRAPHY 5108 Forrest Hill Ln. Las Vegas, NV 89108 702-878-0341

HARTUNG & DICKMAN PHOTOGRAPHIC 5401 Longley Ln. # 8 Reno, NV 89511 775-825-3080

JANI MAE PRO PHOTOGRAPHERS 1800 S. Eastern Ave. Las Vegas NV 89104 702-641-1800

JAY ALDRICH PHOTOGRAPHY P.O. Box 1807 Minden, NV 89423 775-782-4383

JERRY NEWTON PHOTOGRAPHY 3365 Meridian Ln. Reno, NV 89509 775-786-4546

JOHN MARK'S PHOTOGRAPHY STUDIO 876 S. Virginia St. Reno, NV 89502 775-323-1008

LAS VEGAS PHOTO SVE 3305 Spring Mountain Rd. # 60 Las Vegas, NV 89102 702-364-0950

LIFETOUCH NATIONAL STUDIO 80 E. Patriot Blvd. Reno NV 89511 775-851-0444

LUDWICK'S PHOTOGRAPHY 126 S. Taylor St. Fallon, NV 89406 775-423-3700

MATHIS PHOTOGRAPHY STUDIO 211 E. Plumb Ln. Upper Level Reno, NV 89502 775-348-7606

NEW VIEW PHOTO STUDIO 2912 S. Highland Dr. #G Las Vegas, NV 89101 702-732-2349

PATRICE BINGHAM PHOTOGRAPHY 3545 Airway Dr. # 103 Reno, NV 89511 775-851-3566

PHOTOGRAPHY BY BRET HOFMANN 606 Mount Rose St. Reno, NV 89509 775-329-1284

PHOTOGRAPHY BY VAN 2511 W. Bonanza Rd. Las Vegas, NV 89107 702-646-4441

PHOTOGRAPHY WITH LOVE 558 Valley Dr. Incline Village, NV 89451 775-831-8593

PHOTOMANIA 1300 W. Sunset Rd. #2729 Henderson, NV 89014 702-436-3459

ROSS PHOTO STUDIO 1845 Prater Way Sparks NV 89431 775-358-8485

SAMPSEL & PRESTON PHOTOGRAPHY 3111 S. Valley View Blvd. #W116 Las Vegas, NV 89102
SHARON THORNE PHOTOGRAPHY 3 Panavista Circle Yerington, NV 89447 775-463-7007
SPICER PHOTOGRAPHY 4145 Plateau Rd. Reno, NV 89509 775-746-5151
TIME CAST P.O. Box 1626 Carson City, NV 89702 775-883-6427
VALERIE CLARK PHOTOGRAPHY 35 Martin St. Reno, NV 89509 775-329-8292
WELLS PHOTOGRAPHY 6629 Gazelle Dr. Las Vegas NV 89108 702-656-6991

NEW MEXICO

AARDVARK PHOTOS 900 Gold Ave. SW Albuquerque, NM 87102 505-243-0812
AMADOR STUDIO 13 BELL OF ALBUQ2 Wyatt Dr. # B. Las Cruces, NM 88005 505-524-3527
BILL UERQUE 351 Washington St. SE. Albuquerque, NM 87108 505-265-8755
DAN MORGAN PHOTOGRAPHY 640 Coors Blvd. NW. #4 Albuquerque, NM 87121 505-831-6638
FOREVER IMAGES PHOTOGRAPHY 1109 Michigan Ave. Alamogordo, NM 88310 505-434-1117
HAWTHORNE STUDIO 1526 Pacheco St. Santa Fe, NM 87505 505-471-6128
JACK DIVEN PHOTOGRAPHY 1864 Amis Ave. Las Cruces, NM 88005 505-524-0092
JACK NEWSOM PHOTO 3529 Constitution Ave. NE. Albuquerque, NM 87106 505-265-7595
JAMES HART PHOTOGRAPHY 1410 2nd St. Santa Fe, NM 87505 505-983-7945
KENNETH BROWN PHOTOGRAPHY 1200 Lobo Canyon Rd. Grants, NM 87020 505-287-3716
LARSEN'S STUDIO 300 N. Downtown Mall Las Cruces, NM. 88001 505-523-0624
LIGHT LANGUAGE PHOTO STUDIO 106 W. Coal Ave. Gallup, NM. 87301 505-722-5850
LOZOYA STUDIOS 1205 Broadway Blvd SE. Albuquerque, NM 87102 505-243-1007
M C PHOTOGRAPHIC 2400 N. Prince St. Clovis, NM 88101 505-762-9856
MEMORY MAKER PORTRAITS 1370 Central Ave. #A Los Alamos, NM 87544 505-662-9329

NORM JOHNSON PHOTOGRAPHY 4310 Paseo Del Norte NE #B Albuquerque, NM 87113

PHOTO IMAGERY-ROY WALSTON 3640 High St. NE Albuquerque, NM 87107 505-344-8986

PHOTOGRAPHY STUDIO 720 Saint Michaels Dr. #N Santa Fe, NM 87505 505-471-3212

PHOTOGRAPHY-MARY FREDENBURGH 1304 Maclovia St. Santa Fe, NM 87505 505-473-0700

RON FOWLER PHOTOGRAPHY 514 Pile St. Clovis, NM 88101 505-769-3270

SATURDAY'S CHILD 1701 Valdez Rd. NE Albuquerque, NM 87112 505-271-9500

STUDIO 7 COMM. PHOTO 517 Central Ave. NW. # B Albuquerque, NM 87101 505-268-4582

TOM BRAHL PHOTO 132 Pinon Trl. Cedar Crest NM 87008 505-281-2450

TORRES PHOTOGRAPHY 1860 Lester Ave. Las Cruces, NM 88001 505-524-0700

UNIQUE PHOTOGRAPHY 129 Westerfield Pl. Clovis, N. 88101 505-763-3368

NEW YORK

A BECK'S PHOTOGRAPHY STUDIO 3744 82nd St. Flushing, NY 11372 718-424-8751

ACE OF HEARTS PHOTOGRAPHY 172 Avondale Dr. Centereach, NY 11720 631-698-3309

ALDO'S PHOTO STUDIO 6108 18th Ave. Brooklyn, NY 11204 718-236-6300

ARMAND D'ARIENZO-MASTER 1112 Post Rd. Scarsdale, NY 10583 914-472-3489

BARBARA BOARDMAN STUDIO 11 S. Main St. Wayland, NY 14572 716-728-2090

CAMPBELL PHOTO & IMAGE CTR. 4779 Boston Post Rd. Pelham, NY 10803 914-738-2901

CASCADILLA PHOTOGRAPHY 618 Elmira Rd Ithaca, NY 14850 607-272-7386

CHENANGO STUDIOS 21 Main St Binghamton, NY 13905 607-722-0428

CLICK STUDIOS 75 Bruso Rd. Malone, NY 12953 518-483-1705

COLOUR PORTRAITS INC. 117 Boyle Rd. Selden, NY 11784 631-732-3579

CORPORATE PHOTOGRAPHIC SVE 200 Mamaroneck Ave #LL3 White Plains, NY 10601

COSTA PHOTOGRAPHY STUDIO 7 Grand St. Oneonta, NY 13820 607-432-5861

CREATIVE PHOTOGRAPHY 47 W. Main St. Babylon, NY 11702 631-422-1048

DE VITO STUDIOS 438 Sunrise Hwy. Rockville Centre, NY 11570 516-764-7371

DEDE HATCH PHOTOGRAPHY 1251 Trumansburg Rd. #1 Ithaca, NY 14850 607-273-0244

DUNCAN STUDIO 38 State St. Pittsford, NY 14534 716-586-3350

FERLISE PHOTOGRAPH STUDIO 24 Tailor Ln. Levittown, NY 11756 516-796-0712

GIL PHOTOGRAPHERS 19015 Linden Blvd. Jamaica, NY 11412 718-525-5440

GLENN CHILDS PHOTOGRAPHY 4932 Sheridan Dr. Williamsville, NY 14221 716-632-4227

GORDON JAMES IMAGE MAKER 871 Niagara Falls Blvd. Amherst, NY 14226 716-837-5665

HILITE PHOTO STUDIO 206 Commack Rd. Commack, NY 11725 631-499-6338

HILLCREST PHOTOGRAPHERS 18516 Union Tpke Flushing NY 11366 718-454-2190

JON ELDER PRODUCTIONS 21 w. 3RD St. Jamestown, NY 14701 716-488-0813

LANE PHOTOGRAPHY STUDIO 109 Somerstown Dr. Ossining, NY 10562 914-762-5335

LASTING IMPRESSIONS 3196 Westchester Ave. Bronx, NY 10461 718-792-4014

LIFETOUCH NATIONAL SCHOOL 11 Jericho Rd. Glenmont, NY 12077 518-767-9947

LLOYD STUDIO LTD. EAGLE TROY, NY 12180 518-272-5902

MALIS PHOTOGRAPHY 1837 Stuyvesant Ave. East Meadow, NY 11554 516-794-5275

MIKE SAPORITO PHOTOGRAPHY 48 Market St. Saugerties, NY 12477 845-246-3380

NICOLETTI PHOTOGRAPHICS 154 W. Lincoln Ave. Mt.Vernon, NY 10550 914-668-2199

PARKER II STONE 6622 Temple Dr. East Syracuse, NY 13057 315-463-0577

PHOTOS-N-MOTION 199 W. 1st St. # 2 Oswego, NY 13126 315-342-3198

PRECIOUS MOMENTS PHOTO 1 Central Ave. #314 Tarrytown, NY 10591 914-631-8555

RAYMOND KOSTYN PHOTOGRAPHER 137 S. Main St. New City, NY 10956 845-634-6666

SALZMAN-ASHLEY STUDIO 45 Cuttermill Rd. Great Neck, NY 11021 516-829-6330

SHERWOOD TRIART STUDIOS 79 Broadway Hicksville, NY 11801 516-931-5400

STUDIO ELEVEN PRODUCTIONS 11 S. Highland Ave. Nyack, NY 10960 845-353-0220

TAROLLI STUDIO 8530 Morgan Rd. Clay, NY 13041 315-622-2344

TEDESCO PHOTOGRAPHERS 85 Shaber Rd. Patchogue, NY 11772 631-654-5059

TOM LA BARBERA PHOTOGRAPHY 11 Randall Middletown, NY 10940 845-342-6709

TWO MORROW'S PHOTOGRAPHERS 39 Jackson St. Batavia, NY 14020 716-343-5100

NORTH CAROLINA

BOB BOYD PHOTOGRAPHY 2613 Carver St. Durham, NC 27705 919-477-1209

BRASWELL PHOTOGRAPHY 4520 Fountain Dr. Wilmington, NC 28403 910-791-5670

BURNIE BATCHELOR STUDIO 619 Oberlin Rd. Raleigh, NC 27605 919-833-7527

CHARLES GRAHAM PHOTOGRAPHY 302 Pomona Dr. #G Greensboro, NC 27407 336-852-6026

CHARLES HARE STUDIO 1821 Skyway Dr. #B Monroe, NC 28110 704-283-6695

CHARLOTTE IMAGE PHOTOGRAPHY 4832 Park Rd. #H Charlotte, NC 28209 704-525-2968

CONWAY PHOTO & PRINT SHOP HIGHWAY 158 W J. Conway, NC 27820 252-585-0394

COTSWOLD PHOTOGRAPHERS 1419 East Blvd. #E. Charlotte, NC 28203 704-358-1700

CREATIVE PHOTOGRAPHY 704-Longview St. Greensboro, NC 27403 336-294-2152

CUSTOM CREATIONS 5539 W. Market St. Greensboro, NC 27409 336-294-8100

DANIELS PHOTOGRAPHY 1504 Falls Church Rd. Raleigh, NC 27609 919-954-7391

DAVID STALLINGS JR. PHOTO 615 Peyton Ave. Durham, NC 27703 919-596-2407

DON EARLEY PHOTOGRAPHY 1241 Fort Bragg Rd. Fayetteville, NC 28305 910-485-6660

EDISON'S PHOTOGRAPHICS 3530 N. Tyron St. Charlotte, NC 28206 704-333-0123

ELMS AERIAL PHOTOGRAPHY 111 Bartow Dr. Manteo, NC 27954 252-473-1309

EVELYN GRAHAM PHOTOGRAPHY 231 Church Rd. Fairview, NC 28730 828-628-1831

FAMILY STUDIO 126 ½ E. Innes St. Salisbury, NC 28144 704-633-1751

FRANCIS PHOTOGRAPHY 605 Washington St. Eden, NC 27288 336-623-2760

G & G PORTRAIT SHOP 35 Market St. SW Concord, NC 28025 704-786-6020

GARY HINSHAW PHOTOGRAPHY 136 S. Main St. Randleman, NC 27317 336-498-3514

JIM DRUM PHOTOGRAPHY 501 E. Main St. Yadkinville, NC 27055 336-679-2256

JOHN ELKINS PHOTOGRAPHY 1058 W. Club Blvd. #223 Durham, NC. 27701 919-286-4049

JOHN ROSENTHAL PHOTOGRAPHY 67 Burris Pl. Chapel Hill, NC 27516 919-929-5212

LANCE RICHARDSON PHOTOGRAPHY 1600 E. Franklin St. Chapel Hill, NC 27514 919-942-4044

LESTER'S PHOTOGRAPHY STUDIO 2739 Bragg Blvd. Fayetteville, NC 28303 910-484-0055

MARTY PRICE PHOTOGRAPHY 109 Edgewater Dr. Concord, NC 28027 704-786-4604

MAURICE PLEMMONS PHOTOGRAPHY 849 Sand Hill Rd. Asheville, NC 28806 828-667-8754

MIXON PHOTOGRAPHY 803 Baker Rd. High Point, NC 27632 336-434-6796

OVERBEE STUDIO 2712 E. Ash St. Goldsboro, NC 27534 919-778-5400

PHOTOGRAPHY BY FRYE & ASSOC. 107 Government Ave. SW Hickory, NC 28602 828-322-9474

PINEAPPLE PHOTOGRAPHY STUDIO 501 New Bridge St. Jacksonville, NC 28540 910-346-4111

RAINES & COX 315 Nash St. E. Wilson, NC 27893 252-237-3935

SEIVERS STUDIO Hwy 52 Mt. Airy, NC 27030 336-786-6868

SNYDER PHOTOGRAPHY INC. 6269 Arden Forest Cir. Clemmons, NC 27012 336-766-6792

STAR STRUCK PHOTOGRAPHY 213 N. Aspen St. Lincolnton, NC 28092 704-732-1169

STUDIO ONE 126 W. Main St. Elkin, NC 28621 336-835-1976

SUPERIEUR PHOTOGRAPHICS 122 Griffith Plaza Dr. #B Winston Salem, NC 27103 336-765-1116

TIM TALLEY PHOTOGRAPHY 2738 US Highway 158 Reidsville, NC 27320 336-349-9489

UNIVERSAL ARTIST 205 Avery Ave. Morganton, NC 28655 828-433-1511

VPS-VINTAGE PHOTO STUDIOS 2315 Geddie Pl. High Point, NC 27260 336-885-2000

WARNER PHOTOGRAPHY 60 Biltmore Ave. #B Asheville NC 28801 828-254-0346

WESTBROOK STUDIOS INC. 1236 S. Church St. Burlington, NC 27215 336-226-6474

NORTH DAKOTA

ALLEN ROSS PHOTOGRAPHY 1291 13th Ave. E. West Fargo, ND 58078 701-282-6966

ARVID REIMANN PHOTOGRAPHY 1609 31st. St. SW. Minot, ND 58701 701-839-3940

BEHL'S PHOTOGRAPHY 802 Demers Ave. Grand Forks, ND 58201 701-772-9431

CAULFIELD STUDIO INC. 13 N. 3rd. St. Grand Forks, ND 58203 701 746-0078

FOWLER PHOTOGRAPHY 120 N. 5th St. Bismarck, ND 58501 701-222-3040

JIM ERICKSON PHOTOGRAPHY 521 6TH St. Devils Lake, ND 58301 701-662-2719

JMO PHOTOGRAPHY 510 10TH Ave. N. Fargo, ND 58102 701-293-7319

LILJA PHOTOGRAPHY 1768 35TH St. NE Larimore, ND 58251 701-343-2676

MAHAR PHOTOGRAPHY 219 9th Ave. W. Williston, ND 58801 701-572-6074

MATSON'S STUDIO 449 w. main St. Valley City, ND 58072 701-845-2581

MICHAEL MOORE PHOTOGRAPHY 1427 12 Ave. S. Fargo, ND 58103 701-293-7017

MONARCH PHOTO-PORTRAIT STUDIO 1302 Main Ave. Fargo, ND 58103 701-235-0105

ROBIDEAU PHOTOGRAPHY 1462 I 94 Business Loop E. Dickinson, ND 58601 701-227-4748

SCHERLING PHOTOGRAPHY 2801 13th Ave. SW Fargo, ND 58103 701-237-3157

TWETEN'S PHOTOGRAPHY 524 Hill Ave. Grafton, ND 58237 701-352-1513

ZIELSDORF STUDIO 56 1st Ave SE Beach, ND 58621 701-872-4371

OHIO

ACCENT PHOTOGRAPHY Wolf Rd. Cleveland, OH 44140 440-892-9111

ARBOGAST PHOTOGRAPHY 503 Pittsburgh St. Columbiana, OH 44408 330-482-9551

BERAN'S STUDIO 14417 Detroit Ave. Cleveland, OH 44107 216-521-9923

BILL COST JR. PHOTOGRAPHY 786 W. Main St. Newark, OH 43055 740-345-0001

BILL'S LIGHT PHOTOGRAPHY 902 s. 7TH St. Ironton, OH 45638 740-533-0592

BUELL-KRAFT STUDIO 262 Marion Ave. Mansfield, OH 44903 419-524-2261

CHILDRESS PHOTO STUDIO 2012 W. 25th St. #617 Cleveland, OH 44113 216-781-1247

COCKRILL'S STUDIO 131 W. State St. Alliance, OH 44601 330-821-8303

CREATIVE PHOTOGRAPHY-MAXMILLAN 6210 Belmont Ave. Girard, OH 44420 330-539-5006

DON POUND STUDIO 13 W. Main St. Newark, OH 43055 740-345-9818

EASTERLING STUDIOS 431 Wayne Ave. Dayton, OH 45410 937-222-8410

ED TILLEY PHOTOGRAPHER 3423 Cleveland Ave. NW Canton, OH 44709 330-493-7777

FALLS PHOTOGRAPHY 15 ½ N. Franklin St. Chagrin Falls, OH 44022 440-247-8970

FREEZE FRAME 111 N. Grant St. Wooster, OH 44691 330-263-6925

GREAT AMERICAN PHOTOGRAPHY 3409 Maryland Ave. Cleveland, OH 44122 216-765-8250

HARLAN HOOVER PHOTOGRAPHY 8375 Patterson Rd. Hilliard, OH 43026 614-876-6968

JEFF SPRANG PHOTOGRAPHY 141 State Route 603 W. Shiloh, OH 44878 419-895-1955

JOE FRIEDMAN & ASSOC. 3300 N. Dixie Dr. Dayton, OH 45415 937-275-4277

LIBERTY STUDIOS 1344 Heyl Rd. Wooster, OH 44691 330-264-8309

MARK HORNING PHOTOGRAPHY 68 W. Bagley Rd. Berea, OH 44017 440-826-3120

MEARS PHOTOGRAPHY 159 e. water St. Chillicothe, OH 45601 740-774-4120

OLIVER PHOTOGRAPHY 314 Broadway St. Greenville, OH 45331 937-548-1983

OSBORNE'S KEEPSAKE PORTRAITS 2119 Northridge Rd. Findlay, OH 45840 419-422-4121

P J PHOTOGRAPHY INC. 4316 Park Ave. Ashtabula, OH 44004 440-998-2265

PHOTO CREATIONS BY MARK HAND 11720 Fort Laramie Swanders Rd. Anna, OH 45302

PHOTO WORKS 659 Dewitt Dr. Cleveland, OH 44143 440-449-2985

PRESTIGE SENIOR PORTRAITS 922 Springville Ave. Fostoria, OH 44830 419-435-9049

QUAYLE'S PHOTOGRAPHY 303 Firwood Rd. Huron, OH 44839 419-433-5682

REFLECTIONS-TIME PHOTOGRAPHY 3825 Dillon Falls Rd. Zanesville, OH 43701 740-452-6843

ROBERT CLAYTON PHOTOGRAPHY 2375 Monroe Concord Rd. Troy, OH 45373 937-890-3488

ROBERT BARBIAN PHOTOGRAPHY 146 w. 46TH St. Ashtabula, OH 44004 440-998-0200

SCOTT GALLOWAY PHOTOGRAPHY 2772 Copley Rd. Copley OH 44321 330-666-4477

SUNBURST PHOTOGRAPHY STUDIO 4808 n. summit St. Toledo, OH 43611 419-726-0234

VIKTOR'S PORTRAIT STUDIO 4074 Park Ave. W. Mansfield, OH 44903 419-529-2666

W & B PRODUCTIONS 441 Melrose Ave. Toledo, OH 43610 419-241-1164

WAGNER PHOTOGRAPHIC SVE 1812 w. State St. Alliance, OH 44601 330-821-7166

WOODARD PHOTOGRAPHIC INC. 3401 Woodville Rd. #H Northwood, OH 43619 419-693-1490

WOOFTER PHOTOGRAPHY 2996 State Route 5 #B Cortland, OH 44410 330-638-5500

OKLAHOMA

ANTHONY HART PHOTOGRAPHER 911 s. Main St. Stillwater, OK 74074 405-377-0911

BLUNCK STUDIOS 228 W. Main St. Moore, OK 73160 405-794-7748

BOB MC CORMACK STUDIOS 1610 S. Carson Ave. Tulsa, OK 74119 918-587-2628

CARL'S STUDIO INC. 322 W. Chickasha Ave. Chickasha, OK 73018 495-224-2716

CONNAWAY PHOTO 6600 N. Meridian Ave. #100 Oklahoma City, OK 73116 405-843-4749

CREATIVE IMAGE 518 W. Chickasha Ave Chickasha, OK 73018 405-222-0599

GORDON DINSMORE STUDIO 3621 NW 50th St. Oklahoma City, OK 73112 405-942-5135

GROOMERS PORTRAIT STUDIO 602 W. Main St Ardmore, OK 73401 580-226-1834

HARRY MYERS STUDIOS 829 Pershing Dr. W. Ardmore, OK 73401 580-223-6063

HEIL PHOTOGRAPHY 600 NE Washington Blvd Bartlesville, OK 74006 918-335-2770

JACK HARDY PHOTOGRAPHY 18 N. Vann St. Pryor, OK 74361 918-825-5358

JAMES PHOTOGRAPHICS 1402 22nd. St. Woodward, OK 73801 580-256-4314

JIM FOWLER STUDIO 521 W. Broadway St. Muskogee, OK 74401 918-683-2222

JOHN WILLIAMS PHOTOGRAPHY 6 W. Main St. Ardmore, OK 73401 580-223-7230

KILLAM PHOTOGRAPHY 1702 W. Oklahoma Ave. Enid, OK 73703 580-233-9766

LACKEY PHOTOGRAPHY 819 N. Hudson Ave. Tulsa, OK 74115 918-835-4082

MARK EMMONS PHOTOGRAPHY 504 Wyandotte Ave MC Alester, OK 74501 918-423-7488

MOTO PHOTO 3323 S. Boulevard St. Edmond OK 73013 405-340-5006

MOTO PHOTO 220 S. Van Buren St. Enid, OK 73703 580-242-1755

PHOTOGRAPHY BY SHERRY 3720 Lincoln Rd. Bartlesville, OK 74006 918-335-1980

PORTRAITS BY JESS ANDERSON 9 S. Mill St. Pryor, OK 74361 918-825-7966

RUTH KELLY STUDIO 201 W. Broadway St. Muskogee, OK 74401 918-687-7311

SHOEMAKER'S PHOTOGRAPHY 208 N. Main St. Sand Springs, OK 74063 918-241-1511

STRATFORD PHOTOGRAPHY 603 N. 24th St. Muskogee, OK 74401 918-683-5193

T K'S PORTRAIT STUDIO 100 W. Main St. Ringling, OK 73456 580-662-2520

TED WEST PHOTOGRAPHY 220 NW 59th St. Oklahoma City, OK 73118 405-843-9920

TOM FLORA PHOTOGRAPHY 601 W. Independence St. Shawnee, OK 74804 405-273-8631

TOURIAN'S STUDIO 120 W. College Ave. Weatherford, OK 73096 580-772-7175

VAN DYKE STUDIO 4709 N. Macarthur Blvd. Oklahoma City, OK 73122 405-787-3262

WARREN'S STUDIO 207 Rock Island Ave. El Reno, OK 73036 405-262-0285

OREGON

AUKER PHOTOGRAPHY 1506 SE Ramona St. Portland, OR 97202 503-233-5610

BALL STUDIO 564 SW Adams Ave. Corvallis, OR 97333 541-753-5721

BILL MARTIN PHOTOGRAPHY 13015 SW Pacific Hwy Tigard, OR 97223 503-639-2266

BROWN'S STUDIO & CAMERA SHOP 2020 Sherman Ave. North Bend, OR 97459 541-756-5611

CHRIS ANDERSON PHOTOGRAPHY 3315 SE Pinehurst Ave Portland, OR 97267 503-659-4565

COHEN & PARK PORTRAIT STUDIO 111 SE Douglas St #A Newport, OR 97365 541-265-5419

CONTEMPORARY IMAGES PHOTO 3405 SE Harrison St. Milwaukee, OR 97222 503-654-2463

EASTMAN PHOTOGRAPHY 61592 SE Quay Ct. Bend, OR 97702 541-389-4481

EDMUND KEENE PHOTOGRAPHERS 920 SW 13th Ave. Portland, OR 97205 503-224-3581

ERICKSON PHOTOGRAPHY 6 S. Main St. Pendleton, OR 97801 541-276-7261

EYE OF THE LADY 410 NE 3rd St. #4 Mc Minnville, OR 97128 503-472-9243

GEMINI PHOTOGRAPHY 993 Robin Hood Ave Eugene, OR 97401 541-484-5572

HAWLEYWOOD PHOTOGRAPHY 733 Lyon St. S Albany, OR 97321 541-928-8663

HERITAGE STUDIO 21 S. 6th St. Cottage Grove, OR 97424 541-942-4053

HOWDYSHELL PHOTOS 625 NW 8th St. Pendleton, OR 97801 541-276-7491

JE T' PHOTOGRAPHY 12353 SE Lusted Rd. Sandy, OR 97055 503-668-6911

KEN JUBB PHOTOGRAPHY 1321 NE 69th Ave Portland, OR 97213 503-253-1410

KNIGHT PHOTOGRAPHY 1410 E. Powell Blvd. Gresham, OR 97030 503-667-0937

LEIF STUDIOS 516 SE Jackson St. Roseburg, OR 97470 541-673-9865

LUZADER PHOTOGRAPHY 910 NE South Shore Rd. Portland, OR 97211 503-286-6073

MAHONEY PHOTOGRAPHY 5605 River St. West Linn, OR 97068 503-655-3044

MAJESTIC ART & PHOTO'S 39761 McDowell Creek Dr. Lebanon, OR 97355 541-451-1077

MICHAEL JAMES PHOTOGRAPHY 663 Jackson St. Roseburg, OR 97470 541-672-8929

MIKE BALTEAU PHOTOGRAPHY 33387 Stone Rd. Warren, OR 97053 503-397-1207
MODERNE BRIGGS STUDIOS 112 E 13th Ave Eugene, OR 97401 541-683-4574
PAUL RANDALL PHOTOGRAPHY 505 Eugene St. Hood River, OR 97031 541-386-3748
PHOTOGRAPHY BY KAY CALDWELL 1420 SE Roberts Dr. Gresham, OR 97080 503-667-4644
PICTUREMAN PHOTOGRAPHY 1037 NE Keel Ave Lincoln City, OR 97367 541-994-5120
R J STUDIO 405 NE 3rd St. #8 Mc Minnville, OR 97128 503-472-0840
RICE'S PHOTOGRAPHY 8145 SW Canyon Dr. Portland, OR 97225 503-292-0734
ROBERT JAFFE PHOTOGRAPHY 140 Nursery St. Ashland, OR 97520 541-734-0677
ROCHON PHOTOGRAPHY 1234 N. Rhododendron Dr Florence, OR 97439 541-997-8055
ROCHON PHOTOGRAPHY 117 3rd St. Reedsport, OR 97467 541-271-2686
SPENCER STUDIO 540 E. Villas Rd. #A Medford, OR 97502 541-779-1743
STEWART HARVEY PHOTOGRAPHY 2405 NW Thurman St. Portland, OR 97210 503-274-9711
STRO'S PHOTOGRAPHY INC 319 W. Washington St. Stayton, OR 97383 503-769-5044
TERRY DAY NATURAL IMAGES 1257 W. Harvard Ave. Roseburg, OR 97470 541-672-4615
WALTERS PHOTOGRAPHERS 405 NW Despain Ave Pendleton, OR 97801 541-278-0115
WILLIAM MILLER PHOTOGRAPHY 1722 E. Mcandrews Rd. #B Medford, OR 97504 541-779-7997

PENNSYLVANIA

A J ESPOSITO STUDIO 228 York Rd. Warminster, PA 18974 215-674-1716
ACCRA PHOTOGRAPHY 2803 Belmont Ave. Norristown, PA 19403 610-631-5237
ACE HOFFMAN STUDIOS 222 W. Main St. Plymouth, PA 18651 570-779-5327
ALAN KING PHOTOGRAPHY 3722 Mount Royal Blvd Glenshaw, PA 15116 412-486-7007
ALGOE STUDIO 2740 E. State St. Hermitage, PA 16148 724-342-0667

ANTHONY'S PHOTO STUDIO 837 Alter St. Hazleton, PA 18201 570-455-1269

ART OF PHOTOGRAPHY 28 Essex Circle Dr. Shrewsbury, PA 17361 717-235-2491

BARGERON PHOTOGRAPHY 66 W. Plumstead Ave. Lansdowne, PA 19050 610-626-1056

BERNARD KADISH PHOTOGRAPHY 125 Hughes St. Kingston, PA 18704 570-288-1620

BIEVENOUR PHOTOGRAPHY CTR. 620 W. Market St. York, PA 17404 717-843-3231

BIXBY PHOTO STUDIO 63 Central Ave. Wellsboro, PA 16901 570-724-1484

BOB LAMBERT PHOTOGRAPHY 238 S. Corl St. State College, PA 16801 814-237-9660

BRIAN HEMMIS PHOTOGRAPHY 7575 Hamot Rd. Erie, PA 16509 814-866-2585

BRISTOL PHOTOGRAPHERS OF PA 310 Mill St. Bristol, PA 19007 215-788-5544

BUCHMAN STUDIO 204 6th Ave McKeesport, PA 15132 412-672-4396

C R MOLTON PHOTOGRAPHY 1420 W. Liberty Ave. Pittsburgh, PA 15226 412-561-4650

CAPRISTO STUDIOS 320 S. Pennsylvania Blvd. #313 Wilkes Barre, PA 18701 570-826-6842

CARRIAGE STUDIO OF PHOTOGRAPHY 99 Hedgerow Dr. Morrisville, PA 19067 215-736-3636

COVER STUDIO PORTRAIT 504 Main St. Johnstown, PA 15901 814-536-5189

D & D PHOTOGRAPHY 455 Shenango Rd. Beaver Falls, PA 15010 724-846-0891

DANCE OF LIGHT PHOTOGRAPHY RR 6 Box 223 Altoona, PA 16601 814-949-9220

DIANA PHOTO GRAPHICS 232 E. 9th St. Hazleton, PA 18201 570-455-8657

E J VENISH PHOTOGRAPHY 35 W. Dutton Mill Rd. Aston, PA 19014 610-494-7005

EARL & SEDOR PHOTOGRAPHER 239 Schuyler Ave. #117 Kingston, PA 18704 570-283-5055

EASTBURN PHOTOGRAPHY 2215 E. Lincoln Hwy Coatesville, PA 19320 610-384-5555

FLORY STUDIO OF PHOTOGRAPHY 551 N. Chestnut St. Palmyra, PA 17078 717-838-9087

FRAMUS STUDIOS P.O.Box 984 Pottstown, PA 19464 610-326-2147

GLENN TAYLOR PHOTOGRAPHY 437 N. Main St. Red Lion, PA 17356 717-244-0672

H & H PHOTO 118 Carlisle St. # 107 Hanover, PA 17331 717-632-0706
JONATHAN NAKLES PHOTOGRAPHY 142 E. Otterman St. # 2 Greensburg, PA 15601 724-838-7740
LASTING IMPRESSIONS PHOTO RR 6 Stroudsburg, PA 18360 570-992-5305
MARTIN'S STUDIO 948 Route 519 Eighty Four, PA 15330 724-228-2067
MARTIN-PRATT PHOTOGRAPHY 313 Park St. Honesdale, PA 18431 570-253-0491
ORLANDO'S PHOTO SVC 1539 Hilltop Rd. Pottstown, PA 19464 610-327-2018
PHOTO SPECIALISTS 3714 Beale Ave. Altoona, PA 16601 814-942-6133
REFLECTIONS 1808 Lincoln Way White Oak, PA 15131 412-678-7223
REVELATION PHOTOGRAPHY 11145 Route 954 Hwy N Creekside, PA 15732 724-397-8555
RON BENNETT STUDIO 130 S. Main St. Butler, PA 16001 724-282-4440
RUSCHEL STUDIO 120 N. Main St. Washington PA 15301 724-225-7400
SEAVY'S STUDIO 11 E. Wallace Ave New Castle, PA 16101 724-652-7311
SPELLMAN'S PHOTOGRAPHIC STUDIO 245 Mcclellandtown Rd. Uniontown, PA 15401
STUDIO TEN PHOTOGRAPHY 553 Clever Rd. McKees Rocks, PA 15136 412-788-1040
WESTERMAN PHOTOGRAPHY 316 Preston Ave Pittsburgh, PA 15214 412-931-6233

RHODE ISLAND

CORBETT PHOTOGRAPHY 928 W. Main Rd. Middletown, RI 02842 401-846-4861
DAVID SILVERMAN PHOTOGRAPHY 51 Debbie Drive Cranston, RI 02921 401-944-1835
FULLER, KIM 150 Forest Ave. Middletown, RI 02842 401-849-3211
HOT SHOTS PHOTOGRAPHY 31 Graystone St. Warwick, RI 02886 401-739-6171
RIC MURRAY 232 W Exchange St. Providence, RI 02903 401-751-8806
TEBO PHOTOGRAPHY 54 High St. Westerly, RI 02891 401-596-5880

SOUTH CAROLINA

ADAMSON STUDIO 269 W. Laurens St. Laurens SC 29360 864-984-7013

ALLEN GIBSON PHOTOGRAPHY 1510 S. Langley Dr. Florence, SC 29501 843-661-2600

ALT LEE INC. 2710 Gervais St. #C Columbia, SC 29204 803-799-2604

CAROLINA CUSTOM PHOTOGRAPHICS 929 Gervais St. Columbia SC 29201 803-771-6341

CHARLES DAVIS PHOTOGRAPHY 1 Broken Prop Rd. Garnett, SC 29922 803-625-3768

CRAFT'S PHOTOGRAPHY 114 Anderson Ave. Anderson, SC 29625 864-226-0828

DRIGGERS PHOTOGRAPHY 6291 Saint Andrews Rd. Columbia, SC 29212 803-798-8547

DWAIN PATRICK PHOTOGRAPHY 5083 Wesley Rd. Murrells Inlet, SC 29576 843-651-6700

FAMILY PHOTOGRAPHER 246 E. Blackstock Rd. #7 Spartanburg, SC 29301 864-574-1081

GARRISON PHOTOGRAPHY 1505 Charleston Hwy West Columbia, SC 29169 803-796-0697

H GORDON HUMPHRIES GALLERY 1507 Gervais St. Columbia, SC 29201 803-929-1901

HOUSE OF PORTRAITS 1251 S. 5th St. Easley, SC 29642 864-859-1500

HOWARD STUDIOS 768 Anderson St. Belton, SC 29627 864-338-7130

JACK OWEN PHOTOGRAPHY 6046 N. Trenholm Rd. Columbia, SC 29206 803-782-5789

JERRY HATLEY PHOTOGRAPHY 3110 Wade Hampton Blvd. #6 Taylors, SC 29687 864-268-0567

KIRK PROUTY PHOTOGRAPHY 310 Broad St. Charleston, SC 29401 843-571-5222

LACKEY'S STUDIOS 766 John Calhoun Dr. SE Orangeburg, SC 29115 803-534-3122

LANCELOT PHOTOGRAPHY STUDIO 502 S. Prospect St. Columbia, SC 29205 803-779-5554

LIMELITE PHOTOGRAPHY 465 Rast St. Sumter, SC 29150 803-773-7545

LISTA'S STUDIO OF PHOTOGRAPHY 203 Laurens St. SW Aiken, SC 29801 803-481-3686

MELANIE BLOUNT PHOTOGRAPHY P.O.Box 22592 Hilton Head Isle, SC 29925 843-681-2462

OLAN MILLS PORTRAIT STUDIO 1034 Sunnybrook Dr. Johns Island, SC 29445 843-216-0802

PHOTOGRAPHY BY SKIP MEACHEN 39 Scarborough Head Dr. Hilton Head Isle, SC 29928

PHOTOGRAPHY BY SQUIRE 6621 Cartwright Dr. Columbia, SC 29223 803-786-9155

PHOTOS UNLIMITED 655 Bultman St. Sumter, SC 29150 803-773-4451

RANDY SMITH PHOTOGRAPHY 4 E Fieldsparrow Ct. Greenville, SC 29615 864-297-0889

RICKY STRICKLAND PHOTOGRAPHY 1506 2nd Loop Rd. # C Florence, SC 29505 843-669-1354

RODNEY DODSON PHOTOGRAPHY 5909 N. Kings Hwy Myrtle Beach, SC 29577 843-449-3528

RUSSELL LOWERY PHOTOGRAPHY 117 Cleveland St. Greenville, SC 29601 864-271-7804

SHERWOOD STUDIO 638 Old Chapin Rd. Lexington, SC 29072 803-359-6831

SMITH STUDIOS 202 S. Limestone St. Gaffney, SC 29340 864-489-4747

SOUTH DAKOTA

D BREMER PHOTOGRAPHY 834 S. Park St. Aberdeen, SD 57401 605-229-0363

GENE'S STUDIO 519 W. 22nd St. Sioux Falls, SD 57105 605-332-7651

GENELLI FINE PHOTOGRAPHY 600 N. West Ave. Sioux Falls SD 57104 605-335-8333

HARDIN'S PHOTOGRAPHY 717 S. Main St. Aberdeen, SD 57401 605-225-5344

HERITAGE O'Neill studio 1508 Mount Rushmore Rd. Rapid City, SD 57701 605-348-7000

IMAGERY PHOTOGRAPHY 2315 W. 12th St. Sioux Falls, SD 57104 605-336-9378

IMPRESSIONS PHOTOGRAPHY 5929 S. Louis Ln. Sioux Falls, SD 57108 605-335-1302

LANDSTROM'S PHOTO LOFT 314 Dakota Ave. S. Huron, SD 57350 605-352-8360

PHOTOGRAPHIC IMAGES 27984 US Highway 281 Armour, SD 57313 605-724-2559

PHOTOGRAPHY BY SCOTT 118 N. Main Street Chamberlain, SD 57325 605-734-6312

PHOTOGRAPHY UNLIMITED 519 N. Main St. Mitchell, SD 57301 605-996-3273

RICHTER'S HOUSE OF PORTRAITS 12 N. Broadway Watertown, SD 57201 605-886-3435

SAMUELS STUDIOS 2820 W. Main St. Rapid City, SD 57702 605-343-6844

SCHNELLER PHOTOGRAPHY 116 S. Main St. Canton, SD 57013 605-987-4187

SMITH-JONES PHOTOGRAPHY 1802 Valentine St. Rapid City, SD 57702 605-342-7285

SPORT PHOTO 3714 S. Westport Ave Sioux Falls, SD 57106 605-362-8866

TENNESSEE

ARDINGER'S STUDIO 643 N. Riverside Dr. Clarksville, TN 37040 931-647-8305

ART-WORKS PHOTOGRAPHY 624 Jefferson ST. #A Nashville, TN 37208 615-242-3736

BARRY ASLINGER PHOTOGRAPHY 5402 Longview Dr. Hixson, TN 37343 423-842-9114

BING GEE STUDIO 3922 Gallatin Pike Nashville, TN 37216 615-226-1325

BLOOD WORTH PHOTOGRAPHY 814 Meadowlark Ln. Goodlettsville, TN 37072 615-859-1009

BOB GRAY PHOTOGRAPHY 6743 Stage Rd. Memphis, TN 38134 901-386-3900

BOYD'S PHOTOGRAPHY 630 Neely St. Bolivar, TN 38008 731-658-2107

CHRISTIAN LANGE PHOTOGRAPHY 1520 Highland Ave. Knoxville, TN 37916 865-522-6853

COLEMAN'S STUDIO 400 E. Elk Ave. Elizabethton, TN 37643 423-543-2405

CRICHTON PHOTOGRAPHY 940 4th Ave. S Nashville, TN 37210 615-244-4663

DON SPEARS PHOTOGRAPHY 121 E. Broadway Ave. Maryville, TN 37804 865-982-5872

EDDIE LE SUEUR PHOTOGRAPHY 212 ½ E. Main St. Johnson City, TN 37604 423-926-9851

EMMONS STUDIO 104 E. Church St. Union City, TN 38261 731-885-2367

FRANCES DOGGRELL PHOTOGRAPHY 688 New York St. Memphis, TN 38104 901-272-1222

FRANK BRADEN PHOTOGRAPHY 829 Mount Moriah Rd. Memphis, TN 38117 901-767-7897

FRED CANNON PHOTOGRAPHY 4930 N. Broadway St. Knoxville, TN 37918 865-687-5531

GIL MICHAEL PHOTOGRAPHY 2984 Oak Allee St. Memphis, TN 38115 901-362-2935

GLAMOUR SHOTS 5252 Hickory Hollow Pkwy #2401 Antioch, TN 37013 615-731-1470

HAMPTON HOUSE 6108 Quince Rd. Memphis TN 38119 901-365-1529

HOLLAND STUDIO OF PHOTO 3780 S. Mendenhall Rd. Memphis, TN 38115 901-362-1818

HOPE POWELL PHOTOGRAPHY 4700 Trousdale Dr. Nashville, TN 37220 615-833-4673

HOUSE OF PHOTOGRAPHY 4406 Shelborne Dr. Chattanooga, TN 37416 423-894-6448

HUE COUNTS PHOTOGRAPHY 119 Main Ave. N Fayetteville, TN 37334 931-433-2598

JERRY SEALS PHOTO STUDIO 186 W. Main St. Morristown, TN 37814 423-586-7383

JIMMY ALFORD STUDIOS 3061 Millbranch Rd. Memphis, TN 38116 901-332-1512

KEN ROSS PHOTOGRAPHY 5168 Wheelis Dr. Memphis, TN 38117 901-761-0334

LARRY MILLER PHOTOGRAPHY 115 Reese Rd. Sevierville, TN 37862 865-453-5547

LAUGHLIN PHOTOGRAPHY 2412 W. Andrew Johnson Hwy Morristown, TN 37814 423-581-3682

LEROY MONSEY STUDIOS 1300 MCCord Dr. Manchester, TN 37355 931-728-3907

LEROY MUNSEY STUDIOS 930 N. Jackson St. Tullahoma, TN 37388 931-455-0040

LOVELESS FINE PHOTOGRAPHY 305 E. Clark Blvd. Murfreesboro, TN 37130 615-890-1558

MC CLANAHAN STUDIO 126 S. College St. Trenton, TN 38382 731-855-1067

MC GUIRE STUDIO 1320 MC Carthur Rd. Maryville, TN 37804 865-983-2425

MIKE FESMIRE PHOTOGRAPHY 3 N. Broad St Lexington, TN 38351 731-968-8977

MILES HERITAGE STUDIO 508 Troy Ave Dyersburg, TN 38024 731-285-9385

NEWLON STUDIO 8805 Kingston Pike # G Knoxville, TN 37923 865-690-3316

OAK RIDGE PORTRAIT 303 Broadway Ave. Oak Ridge, TN 37830 865-483-8288

PERRIN TODD PHOTOGRAPHY 3171 Poplar Ave # 210 Memphis, TN 38111 901-278-3686

PHOTOGRAPHIC SERVICE 481 Georgetown Rd. Clarksville, TN 37043

PHOTOGRAPHY-DON WHITE WALKER 422 Blockhouse Rd. Maryville, TN 37803 865-984-0388

PICTURE PERFECT 105 Mathis Dr. Dickson, TN 37055 615-441-1300

QUICKPRO PHOTO IMAGING 162 Woodmere Mall Crossville, TN 38555 931-484-9555

RAMSEY PHOTOGRAPHY 5101 Sanderlin Ave. # 195 Memphis, TN 38117 901-685-8183

ROBERT PIERCE PHOTOGRAPHY 121 S. 11th St Nashville, TN 37206 615-227-0718

SANDRA STROH PHOTOGRAPHY 7503 Queens Ct. Germantown, TN 38138 901-755-1452

STANRICH STUDIO 3021 Broad St. Chattanooga, TN 37408 423-265-2357

TOGUE UCHIDA PHOTOGRAPHY 7620 Hwy 70 S #253 Nashville, TN 37221 615-297-5344

TOM MITCHELL JR PHOTOGRAPHY 555 S. Highland St. Memphis, TN 38111 901-324-8521

WAYNE HOLMES PHOTOGRAPHY 63 Gooden Ct Jackson, TN 38305 731-664-0909

WILSON STUDIO 6503 Hixson Pike #D Hixson, TN 37343 423-843-2444

TEXAS

A APIX-ROLLAND KRUEGER 200 Claremont Dr. San Marcos, TX 78666 512-392-2244

ACCENT PHOTOGRAPHY 1623 W. Park Row Dr. Arlington, TX 76013 817-461-0135

AL OESTER PHOTOGRAPHY 2202 Hialeah Dr Houston, TX 77018 713-686-2457

ANDERSON PHOTOGRAPHY 1832 Fir St. Pampa, TX 79065 806-665-2080

BEARDEN PHOTOGRAPHY 125 W. Nocharg Stamford, TX 79553 915-773-2397

BILL PHILLIPS PHOTOGRAPHY 2213 Scott Blvd. Temple, TX 76504 254-778-2121

BINEGAR PHOTOGRAPHY 1931 NW Military Hwy #203 San Antonio, TX 78213 210-344-0041

BLACKBURN PHOTOGRAPHY 8707 Katy # 106 Houston, TX 77024 713-464-0094

BRUCE BERMAN PHOTOGRAPHY 140 N. Stevens St. #301 El Paso, TX 79905 915-544-0352

BUD SHANNON PHOTOGRAPHY 10417 Gulfdale St. San Antonio TX 78216 210-530-0471

C & M PHOTOGRAPHERS 800 Staitti St Humble, TX 77338 281-446-0366

C & S PHOTOGRAPHY 2004 N Camp St. Seguin, TX 78155 830-379-6646

CASE PHOTOGRAPHY 426 S. Main St. Grapevine, TX 76051 817-481-4854

CREATIVE IMAGES BY ANNETTE 605 SW 16th St. Seminole, TX 79360 915-758-2008

DARST-IRELAND PHOTOGRAPHY 2321 Bassett Ave El Paso, TX 79901 915-542-0547

DON ROGERS PHOTOGRAPHY 3939 Bee Caves Dr. #B17 Austin, TX 78746 512-328-9300

F-16 PHOTOGRAPHY 8711 Burnet Rd. #B38 Austin, TX 78757 512-447-4711

GARCIA'S STUDIO 313 S 17th St. McAllen, TX 78501 956-686-9935

GERDES PHOTOGRAPHER 1905 E Red River St Victoria, TX 77901 361-573-6141

GLAMOURCRAFT STUDIOS 7375 S Hulen St Fort Worth, TX 76113 817-292-8989

HAVENCRAFT CREATIVE SVE P.O. Box 1363 Medina, TX 78055 830-589-7299

IMAGE SPECIALISTS 1954 Calder St Beaumont, TX 77701 409-833-8420

IMAGES BY TERRY LEWIS 1607 Cambridge Cir Nacogdoches, TX 75961 936-569-6959

JEFF CAVE PHOTOGRAPHY 3501 Xanadu St. Corpus Christi, TX 78415 361-853-3669

JIM ALLEN PHOTOGRAPHY 4020 N. Macarthur Blvd. #122-288 Irving, TX 75038 972-717-2951

JIM ASHFORD PHOTOGRAPHY 2808 Avonhill Dr. Arlington, TX 76015 817-468-0275

JOHN SENTER PHOTOGRAPHY 733 w. mill St New Braunfels, TX 78130 830-629-0628

LANGMORE PHOTOGRAPHY 5800 Broadway St. # 203 San Antonio, TX 78209 210-826-6300

LEGENDARY PORTRAITS 612 W. Bluff St Granbury, TX 76048 817-573-4747

LEO WEEKS PHOTOGRAPHERS 1117 Port Neches Ave Port Neches, TX 77651 409-722-1041

MADEARIS STUDIO 1304 W. Abram St. Arlington, TX 76013 817-277-0759

MADISON PHOTOGRAPHIC 2243 34th St. Lubbock, TX 79411 806-763-6693

MARK CANADA PRO PHOTOGRAPHY 400 Galveston St Conroe, TX 77301 936-539-2450

MEMORIES UNLIMITED PHOTOGRAPHY 2212 N. Frazier St. Conroe, TX 77303 936-756-1267

O'BRIEN STUDIO OF PHOTOGRAPHY 101 S. Main St. Irving, TX 75060 972-254-3835

PHOTOGRAPHICS UNLIMITED 2207 Marlandwood Rd. Temple, TX 76502 254-773-0988

PHOTOGRAPHIX 1008 s. Adams St. Amarillo, TX 79101 806-372-1706

QUIN STUDIO 315 W. Mulberry St Sherman, TX 75090 903-893-0219

RANDY PHILLIPS PHOTOGRAPHY 2011 Rickety Ln Tyler, TX 75703 903-561-4212

RITTER PHOTOGRAPHY 4381 Calder Ave. Beaumont, TX 77706 409-892-3053

RUBIN'S STUDIO OF PHOTOGRAPHY 301 W. Ohio Ave. Midland, TX 79701 915-684-7519

STUDIO 305 W Thompson Ave. Temple, TX 76501 254-778-2141

TERRY CREATIVE PHOTOGRAPHY 1021 Vine Ave. McAllen, TX 78501 956-682-1000

VISUAL SPORTS NETWORK 226 Springwood Ln. San Antonio, TX 78216 210-930-2876

WAGNER'S STUDIO 1921 s. Washington St. Amarillo, TX 79109 806-374-5942

WENDE WOOLLEY PHOTOGRAPHY 1137 Bayshore Dr. Rockwall, TX 75087 972-771-4392

WINSTON PHOTOART 1608 Chapman St. Orange, TX 77630 409-886-7377

UTAH

BOWERS PHOTOGRAPHY 712 E 50 S # 700 American Fork UT 84003 801-756-9846

BUSATH PHOTOGRAPHY 701 E South Temple Salt Lake City, UT 84102 801-364-6645

DON BLAIR PHOTOGRAPHY 4883 S State St. Murray, UT 84107 801-262-2685

ENGEL PHOTOGRAPHY 590 N Main St Orem, UT 84057 801-225-7012

G P STUDIO PHOTOGRAPHY 2690 Highland Dr. Salt Lake City, UT 84106 801-466-9510

GIBBY PHOTOGRAPHY 614 23rd St. Ogden, UT 84401 801-394-1644

GLEN THOMAS BROWN PHOTOGRAPHER 140 S 300 W. Kaysville, UT 84037 801-544-4918

GROVER PHOTOGRAPHY 4120 Highland Dr. Holladay, UT 84124 801-277-5322

HAZEN IMAGING INC 172 W. 36th St. Ogden, UT 84405 801-621-6400

LITTLE NORWAY STUDIO 920 28th St. Ogden, UT 84403 801-392-8684

LYNNE CLARK PHOTOGRAPHY 65 N. 400 E St. George, UT 84770 435-628-0879

MAR DEL PHOTOGRAPHY 9424 Union Sq. Sandy, UT 84070 801-572-4399

MARTINEZ PHOTOGRAPHY 2704 N 500 E Vernal, UT 84078 435-789-8422

PERPETUAL IMAGES Castleton Moab, UT 84532 435-259-6919

PHOTOGRAPHY BY LAURIE 4649 S 900 E Salt Lake City, UT 84117 801-261-4284

ROBERT MUNK PHOTOGRAPHY 1121 E 2100 S. Salt Lake City, UT 84106 801-484-4999

RUSS ROBINSON PHOTOGRAPHY 4016 Highland Dr Holladay, UT 84124 801-278-4444

SCOTT BREEN PHOTOGRAPHY 3955 Highland Dr. Holladay, UT 84124 801-272-4965

SCOTT HANCOCK 214 S. Main St. Pleasant Grove, UT 84062 801-785-8317

SCOTT SMITH PHOTOGRAPHY 280 S 1015 W Orem, UT 84058 801-226-6031

SHARPE PHOTOGRAPHY 234 S University Ave Provo, UT 84601 801-375-9005

STUDIO ONE 12 N State St Morgan, UT 84050 801-829-3673

THOMAS PHOTOGRAPHY 7 N Main St. Tooele, UT 84074 435-882-0525

VIRGINIA

ACCENT PHOTOGRAPHY 210 Rock Creek Ct. Yorktown, VA 23693 757-877-9716

ALLEN STUDIO 115 W Washington St. Middleburg, VA 20117 540-687-5281

ANDRE STUDIO INC. 221 S. Main St. Lexington, VA 24450 540-463-2139

ASPEN PHOTOGRAPHY 1600 Oxford Rd. Charlottesville, VA 22903 804-971-3568

ATLAS ONE HOUR PHOTO 8112 Arlington Blvd. #A Falls Church, VA 22042 703-641-8622

AUFENGER STUDIO 223 W York St. Norfolk, VA 23510 757-622-1144

BARRY BROOKS PHOTOGRAPHY 219 Walnut Ave Vinton, VA 24179 540-345-9355

BETH'S PHOTOGRAPHY 316 Hendren Ave Staunton, VA. 24401 540-885-7765

BRANT GAMMA PHOTOGRAPHY 1240 Old Garth Rd. Charlottesville, VA 22901 804-977-3545

BRUMFIELD STUDIOS 1050 Main St. Danville, VA.24541 804-792-7261

CASTON STUDIO 9000 Quioccasin Rd. Richmond, VA 23229 804-754-2800

CHRISTIANA STUDIOS 3966 Dumfries Rd. Catlett, VA 20119 540-788-4921

COMPSON STUDIOS 701—Patton St. Danville, VA 24541 804-792-2056

COOK'S PHOTO ART STUDIO 135 Park St. NE Vienna, VA 22180 703-938-5885

CREATIVE ARTS PHOTOGRAPHY 63 Riflemen Ln. Winchester, VA 22601 540-722-9000

DAVID REYNOLDS PHOTOGRAPHY 7909 Lomond Ct. Manassas, VA 20109 703-368-9659

DEYERLE STUDIOS 340 Boulevard Salem, VA 540-387-9139

DON GARDNER PHOTOGRAPHY 10 Omera Pl. Hampton, VA. 23666 757-826-2846

FISHER PHOTOGRAPHIC SVE RR 1 Box 339 Tazewell, VA 24651 540-988-5809

GILL COMMERCIAL PHOTOGRAPHY 802 Birdie Ln. Newport News, VA 23602 757-988-1100

GITCHELL'S STUDIO 107 E. Main St. Charlottesville, VA. 22902 804-296-7558

GREENE GALLERY 118 N. Main St. Woodstock, VA 22664 540-459-4883

JEAN LYNN PHOTOGRAPHY 401 Montour Dr. Richmond VA 23236 804-560-0160

LIFE TOUCH 121 Landmark Sq. Virginia Beach, VA 23452 757-463-3261

O'NEAL'S STUDIO OF PORTRAITURE 231 Pinner St. Suffolk, VA 23434 757-539-3711

PHOTO FLASH 1836 Rio Hill Ctr. Charlottesville, VA 22901 804-977-3959

PHOTO SOLUTIONS 2213 Mount Vernon Ave. Alexandria, VA 22301 703-549-3511

PHOTOGRAPHY BY DAVID 422 Crawford St. Portsmouth, VA. 23704 757-393-3777

RAPID PHOTO 2160 Barracks Rd. Charlottesville, VA 22903 804-979-0777

ROBERT THOMAS PHOTOGRAPHY 5809 Lakeside Ave #G1C Richmond, VA 23228 804-266-5458

ROGER RIDDLE'S PHOTOGRAPHY 391 Lynnwood Dr. Bristol VA 24201 540-669-3222

SOLOMON PHOTOGRAPHY 106 Plum Tree Ct. Sterling, VA. 20164 703-430-0121

STUDIO M INC. 1709 Wainwright Dr. Reston, VA 20190 703-471-4666

TRI-CITY PHOTOGRAPHY 3217 Tyre Neck Rd. VA 23703 757-484-5515

WHITMORE PHOTOGRAPHY 1640 Lafayette Blvd. Fredericksburg, VA 22401 540-371-0144

WHITT PHOTOGRAPHY 7222 Dogwood Ct. Radford VA 24141 540-639-5092

WILLIAM MC INTOSH PHOTOGRAPHY 1505 Baycliff Ln Virginia Beach VA 23454 757-496-8222

WOODY'S HOUSE OF PHOTOGRAPHY 202 Johnson St. Bristol, VA 24201 540-669-6189

VERMONT

AFTER IMAGE PHOTOGRAPHY 26 State St. Montpelier, VT 05602 802-229-4924

BELTRAMI STUDIOS 4516 Williston Rd. Williston, VT 05495 802-863-6223

CREATIVE IMAGE STUDIO Pageant Park Rd. Barton, VT 05822 802-525-3268

GLEN MOODY PHOTOGRAPHY 456 Shunpike Rd. Williston, VT 05495 802-862-1984

H-O PHOTOGRAPHERS 197 Main St. Hartford, VT. 05047 802-295-6321

LAYTON IMAGE PHOTOGRAPHY 1463 Union Village Rd. Norwich, VT 05055 802-649-1973

LIZZARI PHOTOGRAPHIC 32 Main St. Montpelier, VT 05602 802-223-7474

MARY CARROLL PHOTOGRAPHER 88 Browns Ct. Richmond, VT 05477 802-434-2312

MOUNTAIN IMAGES PHOTOGRAPHY HC 63 Box 15 Wilmington, VT 05363 802-464-5977

PERSPECTIVES 70 Landmark Hill Dr. # 1 Brattleboro, VT 05301 802-254-5711

PHOTIQUES 1 Scale Ave. # 106 Rutland, VT 05701 802-775-5367

ROSLUND PHOTOGRAPHY Town Highway 17 Lyndonville, VT 05851 802-626-9641

TAD MERRICK PHOTOGRAPHY 64 Main St. Middlebury, VT 05753 802-388-9598

WASHINGTON

BAUMGARDNER STUDIO 210 S 5th Ave. Yakima, WA 98902 509-575-1555

BAYSIDE PHOTOGRAPHY 2379 Garfield Ave SE Port Orchard, WA 98366 360-871-2162

BENHAM STUDIO GALLERY 1216 1st Ave. Seattle, WA 98101 206-622-2480

BRANT PHOTOGRAPHERS 8 100 Ave NE Bellevue, WA 98004 425-454-7676

BRUNO STUDIOS 1005 Main St. Vancouver, WA 98660 360-693-6751

CARROLL'S PHOTOGRAPHY 408 W. Main St. Centralia, WA 98531 360-736-3882

CASCADE PHOTOGRAPHICS 6906 Martin Way E Olympia, WA 98516 360-491-5473

CUNNINGHAM STUDIO 9013 E Frederick Ave Spokane, WA 99212 509-924-1700

DAREL ROA PHOTOGRAPHY 4110 110th Ave. E Puyallup WA 98372 253-848-6463

DORIAN STUDIO 14820 15TH Ave. NE #A Seattle, WA 98155 206-368-7770

EATON & TENNEFOSS PHOTOGRAPHY 413 Railroad Ave. Shelton, WA 98584 360-426-3272

GARY DELP & ASSOC 2005 Birchfield Rd. Yakima, WA 98901 509-452-5408

GAYLE RIEBER PHOTOGRAPHY 1121 A St. Tacoma, WA 98402 253-627-5455

HORIZON PHOTO 2034 Borst Ave. Centralia, WA 98531 360-736-0125

JUST IN TIME STUDIO 20015 Mountain Hwy E Spanaway, WA 98387 253-847-8281

MARTIN'S PHOTOGRAPHY 127 N. Bagley Creek Rd. Port Angeles, WA. 988362 360-452-7429

MC CUTHEON FOSHAUG STUDIO 120 W Main Puyallup, WA 98371 253-845-2101

MILLER PHOTOGRAPHY 213 W Division Ave Ephrata, WA 98823 509-754-4807

NORTH LIGHT STUDIO 1950 Keene Rd. Bldg # M Richland, WA 99352 509-735-8393

PHOTOGRAPHY PLUS 10217 144th St. E Puyallup, WA 98374 253-848-2275

PORTRAITS BY DESIGN 1500 Silver Beach Rd. Bellingham, WA 98226 360-671-4120

R V PHOTOGRAPHY 10618 SE 240th St. # 203 Kent, WA 98031 253-854-0413

RICH'S PORTRAIT STUDIO 7104 Central Park Dr. Aberdeen, WA 98520 360-532-9412

RICHERT PHOTO CTR 422 N. 3rd St. Shelton, WA 98584 360-426-6163

SAMUEL LEE PHOTOGRAPHY STUDIO 444 Front St. # 202 Lynden, WA 98264 360-354-1565

TERRY LOSS PHOTOGRAPHY 11893 Spromberg Cny Rd. Leavenworth, WA 98826 509-548-7286

VISUAL IMAGES PORTRAIT STUDIO 15020 Pacific Ave S Tacoma, WA 98444 253-535-0327

YEARWOOD STUDIO 1115 W Pioneer Ave Puyallup, WA 98371 253-841-2967

WISCONSIN

A POSITIVE IMAGE 6305 Catalpa St Greendale, WI 53129 414-423-1113

ADS PHOTOGRAPHY 1208 2nd Ave W Ashland, WI 54806 715-682-8885

BACH PHOTOGRAPHY 609 Silent Sunday Ct. Racine, WI 53402 262-639-3135

BERARD PORTRAIT DESIGN 711 Glenna Dr. Hudson, WI 54016 715-386-5880

BILL FRANTZ PHOTOGRAPHY 814 E Wisconsin St. Delavan, WI 53115 262-728-3733

BUCKLEY STUDIO OF PHOTOGRAPHY 2223 Fairfax St Eau Claire, WI 54701 715-834-3800

CANDID STUDIO 4915 S. 12th St. Sheboygan, WI 53081 920-457-4678

DAVID'S STUDIO & FRAMING N7667 910th St. River Falls, WI 54022 715-425-2435

DON KERKHOF STUDIO 2042 Pennsylvania Ave. Madison, WI 53704 608-244-1199

DREAMSCAPES PHOTOGRAPHY 1733 Rapids Dr. Racine, WI 53404 262-632-7060

EVENSON PHOTOGRAPHY 1212 Marine St. Green Bay, WI 54301 920-433-0313

FOEMMEL STUDIO 2133 Main St. Stevens Point, WI. 54481 715-341-3411

GILES PHOTOGRAPHY STUDIO 1412 S. Hastings Way # A Eau Claire, WI 54701 715-834-2993

GREG NOWAK PHOTOGRAPHY 10546 W. Cortez Cir. # 29 Franklin, WI 53132 414-529-2244

JEFF NOOYEN PHOTOGRAPHY 1347 W. Wisconsin Ave. Appleton, WI 54914 920-731-6341

LOMBARD STUDIOS 201 North Ave Hartland, WI 53029 262-367-8456

MC DERMOTT'S PHOTOGRAPHY 6015 60TH St. Kenosha, WI 53144 262-657-3686

MC NITT STUDIOS 38 N. Main St. Rice Lake, WI 54868 715-234-4949

NATE EDWARDS PHOTOGRAPHY 2821 N 4th St. Milwaukee, WI 53212 414-265-9077

OSWALD PHOTOGRAPHY 421 N. Main St. Oshkosh, WI 54901 920-235-4459

PEARCE PHOTOGRAPHY 1599 Western Ave. Green Bay, WI 54303 920-592-9494

PHOTO ARTS 210 W Chestnut St. Pardeeville, WI 53954 608-742-8786

RES PHOTOGRAPHY 301 S. 4th Ave Abbotsford, WI 54405 715-223-4562

RICHARD LONG PHOTOGRAPHY 2189 Eastridge Ctr Eau Claire, WI 54701 715-833-0536

STRUKEL PHOTOGRAPHY 3615 Erie Ave Sheboygan, WI 53081 920-457-1188

THOMPSON PHOTO IMAGERY 114 High Ave Oshkosh, WI 54901 920-235-5830
TRUMBLE PHOTOGRAPHY 514 Broadway Wisconsin Dells, WI 53965 608-254-4033
TURBA PHOTOGRAPHY 106 S. Broadway De Pere, WI 54115 920-336-6700
WALTERS PHOTOGRAPHY 1013 Suffolk Dr. Janesville, WI 53546 608-752-8808
WILLIAM NEIMAN PHOTO 130 E. Grand Ave Wisconsin Rapids, WI 54494 715-424-1870
WUTTKE STUDIO 817 Geneva St. Lake Geneva, WI 53147 262-248-3486
ZANDER STUDIO 320 E Green Bay St. Shawano, WI 54116 715-526-5040

WEST VIRGINIA

BELL STUDIO 328 New St. Bridgeport, WV 26330 304-842-3721
BUFFINGTON STUDIO OF PHOTOGRAPHY 127 W Main St. Clarksburg, WV 26301 304-622-1366
C & S PHOTOGRAPHY 61 Oak Circle Dr. Wheeling, WV 26003 304-233-4693
CARDINAL PHOTOGRAPHICS 318 W. Washington St. Lewisburg, WV 24901 304-645-3344
CHAPS PHOTOGRAPHY 108 Mount Lebanon Dr. Wheeling, WV 26003 304-232-0125
CRESS-GILSON PHOTOGRAPHY 97 Waddles Run Rd. Wheeling, WV 26003 304-232-3686
D-MAX PHOTOGRAPHY 400 Maple Ave Clarksburg, WV 26301 304-623-2222
ED'S PHOTOGENICS 221 Church St. S Ripley, WV 25271 304-372-3905
FRANK MAURITZ STUDIO 136 Lewis St. Oak Hill, WV 25901 304-469-9121
GERSON STUDIO 117 Ellen Ln Morgantown, WV 26505 304-599-2311
GLENN STUDIO 405 4th Ave Montgomery, WV 25136 304-442-8251
GRUBB PHOTO SVE 1316 Bland St Bluefield, WV 24701 304-327-7876
HEDGECOCK'S STUDIO 514 20th St. Huntington, WV 25703 304-525-4657
KEN BLAKE PHOTOGRAPHY 249 Jefferson Ave Moundsville, WV 26041 304-845-8970
LINDSAY'S STUDIO 1607 Washington St E Charleston, WV 25311 304-346-1091
MAJESTIC PHOTO STUDIO 43 25th St. Wheeling, WV 26003 304-233-7551
MANTINI'S STUDIO OF PRO PHOTO 318 High St. Morgantown, WV 26505 304-292-3232
NEWBROUGH PHOTOGRAPHY 1112 Kanawha St. Albans, WV 25117 304-722-2986

NICHOLAS PHOTOGRAPHY 321 Fairview Heights Rd Summersville, WV 26651 304-872-6786

PLUMLEY'S STUDIO 459 20th St. Dunbar, WV 25064 304-768-9656

SCHNEIDER STUDIO 1127 Main St. Wheeling, WV 26003 304-233-8678

STARR PHOTOGRAPHY 2500 Fairmont Ave Fairmont, WV 26554 304-363-4722

TIM RAY PHOTOGRAPHY 1813 Martha Ave Fairmont, WV 26554 304-363-8395

TURNER'S STUDIO Bar Run Rd. Ravenswood, WV 26164 304-273-4736

WARNER PHOTOGRAPHY 307 1st St. Fairmont, WV 26554 304-366-8819

WYOMING

DAVID HUBER PHOTOGRAPHY 1104 Wilson Dr. Worland, WY 82401 307-347-6304

6th DIMENSION PHOTOGRAPHY 2505 Meadow Ln. Gillette, WY 82718 307-686-1023

DOVE STUDIOS 1518 Converse Ave. Cheyenne, WY 82001 307-638-3397

FREMONT PHOTOGRAPHY 1396 Mortimore Ln Lander, WY 82520 307-332-4867

HEDE PHOTOGRAPHERS 705 Lillian Ln. Casper, WY 82609 307-234-7531

K-BAR STUDIO 19 N. Main St. Buffalo, WY 82834 307-684-5462

LEHMAN STUDIO 210 W. Main St. Riverton, WY 82501 307-856-3941

LUDWIG ONE HOUR PHOTO 17th St. Cheyenne, WY 82001 307-634-8818

NEW STUDIO 420 S. Main St. Rock Springs, WY 82901 307-362-3942

OLIE RINIKER PHOTOGRAPHY 530 Hall Ave Jackson, WY 83001 307-733-3505

PERFECT IMAGE PHOTOGRAPHY P.O. Box 6322 Laramie, WY 82073 307-742-3406

PHOTOGRAPHY BY GEORGE DUNLAP 425 S Gillette Ave Gillette, WY 82716 307-686-3094

PHOTOGRAPHY BY PAUL 3204 Fir Dr. Rock Springs, WY 82901 307-362-9448

RON MAIER PHOTOGRAPHY 2538 Cowgill Rd. Cody, WY 82414 307-587-6570

SINGER'S STUDIO 2218 E 19th St. Cheyenne, WY 82001 307-632-7794

SPECIAL EFFECTS PHOTOGRAPHY 241 Tyler St. Rock Springs, WY 82901 307-382-5508

STANLEY STUDIO 710 W. Main St. Riverton, WY 82501 307 856-7872

SUNLIGHT PHOTOGRAPHICS 101 N. Bent St. Powell, WY 82435 307-754-5731

WIT'S END PHOTOGRAPHY 851 S. McKinley St. Casper, WY 82601 307-237-4714

4

MODELING AGENCIES

Modeling agencies from around the country are listed alphabetically in this chapter, first by state, then by agency.

An asterisk (*) has been placed next to the agencies that are members of either SAG (Screen Actors Guild) or AFTRA (American Federation of Television and Radio Artist) unions.

Agencies that work with infants and children are listed separately in Chapter Five.

If you don't see an agency listing for your city, go to your local phone book and look in the yellow pages under "Modeling Agencies."

The licensing and regulating of this industry varies widely, state by state, and many states don't require any licensing at all.

Before you hire an agency you need to know a little bit about them. How long have they been in business? What kind of models do they represent? (Adult, runway, print, etc.)

By simply calling them, an established modeling agency will gladly answer all of your questions.

As the modeling industry grows and moves in different directions, so do the modeling agencies. They are constantly in search of new faces they can market to the industry.

Modeling agencies get paid on a commission basis. They find their models work, and they get paid a percentage of the model's pay. The percentage varies by agency but is usually between ten and twenty percent. It should never be more than that.

Legitimate modeling agencies do not charge you fees. When they sell your, "look" and find you work they make money, not before that.

A lot of agencies feed off of your vanity. If something sounds too good to be true, it probably is.

If an agency makes you promises or assures you that they have a lot of work waiting for you "after" you pay them for their representation or photo shoots, then they probably aren't reputable and they're making their money off of you, not the work that they are supposed to be finding you. (Read Chapter 9, Modeling Scams & Pitfalls.)

Don't let the glitz and glamour of this industry blind you or your common sense. Ask other models and friends questions about the agencies that they have representing them or that they have worked with.

MODELING AGENCIES

ALABAMA

ACT PRODUCTIONS MODELS—Hueytown, AL 35023 (205) 491-3205

BAREFOOT MODELS & TALENT—4317 Downtowner Loop North Mobile, AL 36609 (334) 344-5554

CATHI LARSEN AGENCY—1675 Montclair Road #136 Birmingham, AL 35210 (205) 951-2445

ELAN MODELS INC—1446 Montgomery Highway Vestavia Hills, AL 35216 (205) 823-9180, (11+)

GRAY-CHILD MODELS AND TALENT—P.O. Box 1857 Daphne, AL 36526-1857 (334) 626-8933, e-mail: Kgraychild@aol.com, Website: http://www.graychildmodels.com and http://www.casting-america.com

KIDDIN' AROUND MODELS & TALENT—714–32nd St. South Birmingham, AL 35233 (205) 323-5437

RARE QUALITY MODELS & TALENT—P.O. Box 1545 Dothan, AL 36302 (334) 671-2200, e-mail: Website: http://www.snowhill.com/-donnalyn/, (6+)

READY FOR THE WORLD MODELING—4429 Troy Hwy Montgomery, AL 36116 (334) 284-3006

STUDIO VOGUE—104–1st Ave. Southwest Fayette, AL 35555 (205) 932-6615

VOHN LEON'S MODELING AGENCY—P.O. Box 180723 Mobile, AL 36618 (334) 460-2770

ALASKA

ALASKA IMAGE DESIGN—600 West 41st Ave. #102 Anchorage, AK 99501 (907) 561-5739, e-mail: akimage@gci.net, Website: http://www.alaskaoutdoors.com/Image/index.htm

ALASKA MODELS & TALENT—600 W 41st Ave. #102 Anchorage, AK 99503 (907) 561-5739

APOGEE STUDIOS—5432 E Northern Lights Blvd. PMB 510 Anchorage, AK 99508 (907) 561-9766, e-mail: levi@apogee studios.com, Website: www.apogee-studios.com (8+)

ARIZONA

*ACTION TALENT—2720 E. Broadway Blvd. Tucson, AZ 85716 (520) 881-6535

*DANI'S AGENCY—1 E. Camelback Rd. #550 Phoenix, AZ 85012 (602) 263-1918

ELIZABETH SAVAGE TALENT AGENCY—4949 E. Lincoln Dr. Scottsdale, AZ 85253 (602) 840-3530

*FORD/BLACK AGENCY, ROBERT—4300 N. Miller Rd. #202 Scottsdale, AZ, 85251 (480) 966-2537

*FOSI'S TALENT AGENCY—2777 N. Campbell Ave. Tucson, AZ 85016 (520) 795-3534

*LEIGHTON AGENCY INC—2231 E. Camelback Rd. #319 Phoenix, AZ 85016 (602) 224-9255

LEIGHTON AGENCY INC—333 N. 44th St. Phoenix, AZ 85016 (602) 224-9255

MISS ARIZONA OLYMPIC—3921 E. Morrow Dr. Phoenix, AZ 85024 (602) 788-4463

MODEL & TALENT MANAGEMENT—7426 E. Stetson Dr. Scottsdale, AZ 85251 (602) 941-4941

*SIGNATURE MODELS & TALENT AGENCY—2600 N. 44th St. #209 Phoenix, AZ 85008 (602) 966-1102

TONDU STUDIOS—1850 N. Central Ave. #120 Phoenix, AZ 85004 (602) 252-5565

VOGUE STUDIO—1606 N. Miller Rd. Scottsdale, AZ 85257 (602) 675-0119

ARKANSAS

AGENCY INC—910 W. 6th St. Little Rock, AR 72201 (501) 374-6447

EXCEL MODELS & TALENT—8201 Cantrell Rd. Little Rock, AR 72227 (501) 227-4232

FERGUSON MODELING & TALENT—1100 W. 34th St. Little Rock, AR 72206 (501) 375-3519

JOHN CASABLANCAS MTM AGENCY—416 W. Meadows Fayetteville, AR 72701 (501) 444-7972

MODELS, INC./AARON-WINDSOR—660 Lollar Lane Fayetteville, AR 72701 (501) 973-9700

SOLUTIONS, 10801 Executive Ctr. #400 Little Rock, AR 72211 (501) 554-2850

TERRY LONG MODELS—P.O. Box 7353 Little Rock, AR 72217 (501) 221-2202

CALIFORNIA

A CLASS ACT MODELING—2950 Bechelli Lane Redding, CA 96002 (530) 222-3111

***A TOTAL ACTING EXPERIENCE**—20501 Ventura Blvd., #399 Woodland Hills, CA 91364 (818) 340-9249

***ABRAMS ARTISTS AGENCY**—9200 Sunset Blvd., #1130 Los Angeles, CA 90069 (310) 859-0625

***ACME TALENT & LITERARY**—6310 San Vicente Blvd., #520 Los Angeles, CA 90048 (323) 954-2263

***AGENCY 2 MODEL & TALENT (SD)**—1717 Kettner Blvd., #200 San Diego, CA 92101 (619) 645-7744

***AKA TALENT AGENCY**—6310 San Vicente Blvd. Los Angeles, CA 90048

ALESE MARSHALL MODEL—22730 Hawthorne Blvd. #201 Torrance, CA 90505 (310) 378-1223

***ALICE FRIES AGENCY**—1927 Vista Del Mar Ave. Los Angeles, CA 90068 (323) 464-1404

***ALLEN TALENT AGENCY**—P.O. Box 1498 Los Angeles, CA 90078 (213) 605-1110

AMERICAN MODELS—542 College Avenue Modesto, CA 95350

***ANGEL CITY TALENT**—1680 Vine St. #716 Hollywood, CA 90028

***ARTIST MANAGEMENT AGENCY**—835 5th Ave. #411 San Diego, CA 92101 (619) 235-6655

***ARTISTS GROUP, LTD.**—10100 Santa Monica Blvd., #2490 Los Angeles, CA 90067 (310) 552-1100

*A.S.A.—4430 Fountain Ave., #A Hollywood, CA 90029 (323) 662-9787

*BALDWIN TALENT, INC.—8055 W. Manchester Ave. Playa Del Rey, CA 90292 (310) 827-2422

*BALL TALENT AGENCY, BOBBY—4342 Lankershim Blvd. Universal City, CA 91602 (818) 506-8188

BASS INTERNATIONAL MODEL SCOUT—10877 Palms Blvd. Los Angeles, CA 90034 (310) 839-1097

*BENNETT AGENCY, SARA—6404 Hollywood Blvd. #316 Los Angeles, CA 90028 (323) 965-9666

*BERZON AGENCY, MARIAN—336 e 17TH St. Costa Mesa CA 92627

BEVERLY HILLS MODEL & TALENT—9107 Wilshire Blvd. #500 Beverly Hills, CA 90210 (310) 276-3505

BEVERLY AGENCY—371 Mobil Ave. Camarillo, CA 93010 (805) 445-9262

*BONNIE BLACK TALENT AGENCY—5318 Wilkinson #A Valley Village, CA 91607 (818) 753-5424

*BOOM MODELS & TALENT AGCY—2325 Third St. #223 San Francisco, CA 94107 (415) 626-6591

*BRAND MODEL & TALENT AGENCY—1520 Brookhollow Dr. #39, Santa Ana, CA 92705 (714) 850-1158

*BUCHWALD TALENT GROUP, INC., A Youth Agency—Commercial Department 6300 Wilshire Blvd. #910 Los Angeles, CA 90048 (323) 852-9555

BUILTMORE PRODUCTIONS—P.O. Box 571 Santa Monica, CA 90406 (310) 458-6360

*BURKETT TALENT AGENCY, INC.—27001 La Paz Rd. #418, Mission Viejo, CA 92691 (949) 830-6300

*BURTON AGENCY, INC., IRIS—1450 Belfast Dr. Los Angeles, CA 90069 (310) 288-0121

C R TALENT AGENCY—PO Box 1951 Palm Springs, CA 92263 (760) 327-7777

*CAMERON & ASSOC., INC., BARBARA—8369 Sausalito Ave. #A West Hills, CA 91304 (818) 888-6107

*CAREER ARTISTS INTERNATIONAL—11030 Ventura Blvd. #3 Studio City, CA 91604 (818) 980-1315

CAST IMAGES—1125 Firehouse Alley Sacramento, CA 95814 (916) 444-9720

*CASTLE HILL ENTERPRISES—1101 S. Orlando Ave. Los Angeles, CA 90035 (323) 653-3535

CATHY STEELE MODEL & TALENT—1610 Oak Park Blvd. Pleasant Hill, Ca 94523 (925) 932-4426

*CAVALERI & ASSOCIATES—178 S. Victory Blvd. #205 Burbank, CA 91506 (818) 955-9300

CHIC MODELING—236 Quincy Ave. Long Beach, CA 90803 (562) 438-5088

CINDY OSBRINK PRINT KIDS—4605 Lankershim Blvd. North Hollywood, CA 91602 (818) 760-2803

CINDY ROMANO MODELING & TALENT—PO Box 1951 Palm Springs, CA 92263 (760) 323-3333

*CLARK CO., W. RANDOLPH—13415 Ventura Blvd. #3 Sherman Oaks, CA 91423 (818) 385-0583

*CLER TALENT AGENCY, COLEEN—178 S. Victory Blvd. #108 Burbank, CA 91502 (818) 841-7943

*CNA & ASSOCIATES—1925 Century Park East, #750 Los Angeles, CA 90067 (310) 556-4343

*COAST TO COAST TALENT GROUP, INC.—3350 Barham Blvd. N. Hollywood, CA 90068 (323) 845-9200

COLLEEN CLER MODELING INSTITUTE—120 South Victory Blvd. Burbank, CA 91502 (818) 841-7943

*COLOURS MODEL & TALENT MGMT.—8344 ½ W. 3rd St. Los Angeles, CA 90048 (213) 658-7072

*COMMERCIALS UNLIMITED—8383 Wilshire Blvd., #850 Beverly Hills, CA 90211 (323) 655-0069

*CONTEMPORARY ARTISTS, LTD.—1317 5th St., #200 Santa Monica, CA 90401-2210 (310) 395-1800

*CORALIE THEATRICAL AGENCY, JR.—4789 Vineland Ave. #100 N. Hollywood, CA 91602 (818) 766-9501

*COSDEN ENT. LTD. ROBERT—3518 Cahuenga Blvd. # 200 Los Angeles, CA 90068 (213) 874-7200

COVER MODELS—1266 Quail Creek Circle San Jose, CA 95120 (408) 997-9200.

*CUNNINGHAM, ESCOTT, DIPENE & ASSOC., INC.—10635 Santa Monica Blvd. #130 Los Angeles, CA 90025 (310) 475-2111

*D.H. TALENT—1800 N. Highland #300 Los Angeles, CA 90028 (323) 962-6643

*DADE-SCHULTZ ASSOC.—23905 Plaza Gavilan, Valencia, CA 91355 (818) 760-3100

*DALE GARRICK INTERNATIONAL—8831 Sunset Blvd. #402 Los Angeles, CA 90069 (310) 657-2661

*DAVID & DAVID AGENCY, INC., 7461 Beverly Blvd., #402 Los Angeles, CA 90036 (323) 634-7777

*DIVERSE TALENT GROUP—1875 Century Park East #2250 Los Angeles, CA 90067 (310) 201-6565

*DON BUCHWALD & ASSOC., INC. PACIFIC—6500 Wilshire Blvd. 22nd Floor Los Angeles, CA 90048 (323) 655-7400

DOROTHY SHREVE MODELING—2665 N. Palm Canyon Dr. Palm Springs, CA 92262 (760) 327-5855

DZA & A PRINT DIVISION—8981 W. Sunset Blvd. #303 Los Angeles, CA 90069 (310) 274-5088

*EDWARDS & ASSOCIATES LLC—5455 Wilshire Blvd. #1614 Los Angeles, CA 90036 (323) 964-0000

ELEGANCE TALENT AGENCY—2975 Madison St. Carlsbad, CA 92008 (760) 434-3397

*ELEGANCE MODEL & TALENT—2763 State St. Carlsbad, CA 92008 (619) 434-3397

ELITE NEW FACES—345 North Maple Dr. #397 Beverly Hills, CA 90210 (310) 859-7767

*EPSTEIN—WYCKOFF—CORSA—ROSS & ASSOCIATES, 280 S. Beverly Dr. #400, Beverly Hills, CA 90212 (310) 278-7222

EXTRAORDINAIRE MODELS—200 New Stine Rd. Bakersfield, CA 93309 (805) 397-1157

*FILM ARTISTS ASSOC.—13563 Ventura Blvd. 2nd Fl. Sherman Oaks, CA 91423 (818) 386-9669

*FLICK EAST-WEST TALENT, INC.—9057 Nemo St. West Hollywood, CA 90069 (310) 271-9111

*FONTAINE AGENCY, JUDITH, 205 South Beverly Dr. #212 Beverly Hills, CA 90212 (310) 471-8631

FORD MODELS INC—8826 Burton Way Beverly Hills, CA 90211 (310) 276-8100

GENERATIONS MODEL & TALENT—350 Townsend St., San Francisco, CA 94107 (415) 777-9099

*GENERATIONS MODEL & TALENT—340 Brannan St. #302 San Francisco, CA 94107 (415) 777-9099

*GOLD, MARSHAK, LIEDTKE & ASSOC.—3500 W. Olive #1400 Burbank, CA 91505 (818) 972-4300

*GRADY AGENCY, MARY—348 East Olive Ave., #E Burbank, CA 91502 (818) 567-1400

*GRANT, SAVIC, KOPALOFF & ASSOCIATES—6399 Wilshire Blvd. # 414 Los Angeles, CA 90048 (323) 782-1854

*GWYN FOXX TALENT AGENCY—1342 E. Tujunga Ave. Burbank, CA 91501 (818) 848-0918

*HALPERN & ASSOC.—12304 Santa Monica Blvd. #104 Los Angeles, CA 90025 (310) 571-4488

HALVORSON MODEL MANAGEMENT—2858 Stevens Creek Blvd. San Jose, CA 95128 (408) 983-1038

*HERVEY-GRIMES TALENT AGENCY, INC.—10561 Missouri #1 Los Angeles, CA 90025

*HOLLANDER TALENT GROUP—3518 Cahuenga Blvd., #316 Los Angeles, CA 90068 (323) 845-4160

*HOWARD TALENT WEST—11374 Ventura Blvd. Studio City, CA 91604 (818) 766-5300

INDUSTRY MODELS & TALENT—942 Market St. San Francisco, CA 94102 (415) 986-6151

*INNOVATIVE ARTISTS YOUNG TALENT DIVISION—3000 Olympic Blvd. Bldg. 4 # 1200 Santa Monica, CA 90404 (310) 553-5200

*INNOVATIVE ARTISTS TALENT & LITERARY AGENCY—3000 Olympic Blvd., Bldg. 4 Ste. 1200 Santa Monica, CA 90404 (310) 553-5200

INTEGRITY CASTING—1825 Pruneridge Ave. #B Santa Clara, CA 95050 (408) 243-9466

*JANA LUKER AGENCY—1923½ Westwood Blvd. #3 Los Angeles, CA 90025 (310) 441-2822

JANICE PATTERSON AGENCY—2254 Moore St. #104 San Diego, CA 92110 (619) 295-9477

*KAZARIAN-SPENCER & ASSOC., INC.—11365 Ventura Blvd. #100 Studio City, CA 91604 (818) 769-9111

*KJAR AGENCY, TYLER—5116 Lankershim Blvd. N. Hollywood, CA 91601 (818) 760-0321

*LA TALENT, INC.—7700 W. Sunset Blvd. Los Angeles, CA 90046 (323) 656-3722

*LANE AGENCY, STACEY—13455 Ventura Blvd. #240 Sherman Oaks, CA 91423 (818) 501-2668

*LEVIN TALENT AGCY., SID—8484 Wilshire Blvd. #750 Beverly Hills, CA 90211 (323) 653-7073

*LOOK MODEL AGENCY—166 Geary St. #1400 San Francisco, CA 94108 (415) 781-2822

LOS LATINOS TALENT AGENCY—2801 Moorpark Ave. #11 San Jose, CA 95128 (408) 296-2213

*LYNNE & REILLY AGENCY—10725 Van Owen St. #113 North Hollywood, CA 91605-6402 (213) 755-6434

MAC MODELING—9454 Wilshire Blvd #720 Beverly Hills, CA 90212 (310) 273-2566 (3+)

MARI SMITH PRESENTS INC—101 State Place #D Escondido, CA 92029 (760) 745-1627

*MARIS AGENCY, 17620 Sherman Way #213 Van Nuys, CA 91406 (818) 708-2493

*MARLA DELL TALENT—2124 Union St. San Francisco, CA 94123 (415) 563-9213

*MARSHALL MODEL & TALENT., ALESE—22730 Hawthorne Blvd. #201 Torrance, CA 90505 (310) 378-1223

*MEDIA ARTISTS GROUP—8383 Wilshire Blvd. #954 Beverly Hills, CA 90211 (323) 658-5050

*MITCHELL K. STUBBS & ASSOCIATES—1450 S. Robertson Blvd. Los Angeles, CA 90035 (310) 888-1200

MODELS CENTER—151 Kalmus Dr. #J1 Costa Mesa, CA 92626 (714) 662-1000

*MODELS GUILD OF CALIFORNIA—8489 W. 3rd Street Los Angeles, CA 90048 (323) 782-0393 (323) 801-2132

MONTGOMERY TALENT & MODEL AGENCY—981 Hopkins Way Pleasanton, CA 94566 (925) 417-7480

*NATHE & ASSOC., SUSAN (CPC)—8281 Melrose, #200 Los Angeles, CA 90046 (323) 653-7573

*OSBRINK TALENT AGENCY, CINDY—4343 Lankershim Blvd., #100 Universal City, CA 91602 (818) 760-2488

PACIFIC TALENT & MODELS—1924 S Pacific Coast Hwy. #E Redondo Beach, CA 90277 (310) 543-1018

PANACHE MODELS INTERNATIONAL—520 W. Santa Ana Blvd. Santa Ana, CA 92701 (714) 541-6091

*****PANDA TALENT AGENCY**—3721 Hoen Ave. Santa Rosa, CA 95405 (707) 576-0711

*****PARADIGM, A TALENT & LITERARY AGENCY**—10100 Santa Monica Blvd. #2500 Los Angeles, CA 90067 (310) 277-4400

PARADISE PRODUCTIONS—PO Box 6249 Santa Barbara, CA 93160 (805) 963-8817

PASCUCCI PRODUCTION INC—26 farrell St. #600 San Francisco, CA 94108 (415) 248-3900

*****PLAYBOY MODEL AGENCY**—9242 Beverly Blvd. Beverly Hills, CA 90210 (310) 246-4000

*****PREMIERE ARTISTS AGENCY, INC.**—1875 Century Park E. #2250 Los Angeles, CA 90067 (310) 271-1414

PROMOTIONAL MODELING SERVICE—731 South Hwy. 101 Solana Beach, CA 92075 (619) 259-8808

*****SAN DIEGO MODEL MANAGEMENT**—438 Camino Del Rio S. #116 San Diego, CA 92108 (619) 296-1018

SAN DIEGO MODEL MANAGEMENT—824 N. Camino Del Rio #552 San Diego, CA 92108 (619) 296-1018

*****SANDERS AGENCY**—8831 Sunset Blvd. #304 Los Angeles, CA 90069 (310) 652-1119

*****SARNOFF COMPANY, INC.**—10 Universal City Plaza # 200 Universal City, CA 91608

*****SAVAGE AGENCY, INC.**—6212 Banner Ave. Los Angeles, CA 90038 (213) 461-8316

*****SCAGNETTI AGENCY, JACK**—5118 Vineland Ave. #102 N. Hollywood, CA 91601 (818) 762-3871

*****SCHIOWITZ/CLAY/ROSE, INC.**—1680 N. Vine #614 Los Angeles, CA 90028 (323) 463-7300

*****SHAPIRA & ASSOC., INC., DAVID**—15821 Ventura Blvd. #235 Encino, CA 91436 (818) 906-0322

*****SHUMAKER AGENCY**—6533 Hollywood Blvd. #401 Hollywood, CA 90028 (323) 464-0745

*****SPECIAL ARTISTS AGENCY**—345 N Maple Dr. #302 Beverly Hills, CA 90210 (310) 859-9688

STARS THE AGENCY—777 Davis St. San Francisco, CA 94111 (415) 421-6272

*STARS-THE AGENCY (SF)—23 Grant Ave. 4th Fl. San Francisco, CA 94108 (415) 421-6272

*STONE MANNERS—8436 W. 3rd St., #740 Los Angeles, CA 90048 (323) 655-1313

SUSAN LANE MODEL & TALENT AGENCY—14071 Windsor Pl. Santa Ana, CA 92705 (714) 731-7827

TALENT ENTERTAINMENT NETWORK—8833 W. Sunset Blvd #406 West Hollywood, CA 90069 (312) 659-4855

*TALENT PLUS AGENCY/LOS LATINOS (Hispanic Division)—Dyer Building, 2801 Moorpark Ave. #11 San Jose, CA 95128 (408) 296-2213

*TALENT GROUP, INC., 6300 Wilshire Blvd. #900 Los Angeles, CA 90048 (323) 852-9559

TANNEN & ASSOC., HERB—10801 National Blvd. #101 Los Angeles, CA 90064 (310) 466-5822

*THE AGENCY—1800 Avenue of the Stars #400 Los Angeles, CA 90067 (310) 551-3000

*THE SUN AGENCY—8961 Sunset Blvd. # D Los Angeles, CA 90069 (310) 888-8737

*THE ORANGE GROVE GROUP, INC.—12178 Ventura Blvd. #205, Studio City, CA 91604 (818) 762-7498

*TONRY TALENT—885 Bryant Street, # 201 San Francisco, CA 94103 (415) 543-3797

*TOP MODELS & TALENT AGENCY—The Flood Building, 870 Market St. #1076 San Francisco, CA 94102

TOP MODELS AND TALENT—870 Market Street #1076 San Francisco, CA 94102 (415) 391-1800

*UNITED TALENT AGENCY, 9560 Wilshire Blvd. Beverly Hills, CA 90212

VICKI BUSCH TALENT & MODEL—199 E. Linda Mesa Avenue Danville, CA 94526 (925) 552-0740

*WAUGH AGENCY, ANN—4741 Laurel Canyon Blvd. #200 North Hollywood, CA 91607

WILHELMINA MODELS INC—8383 Wilshire Blvd. #650 Beverly Hills, CA 90211 (323) 655-0909

WORLD MODELING AGENCY—4253 Van Nuys Blvd. Sherman Oaks, CA 91403 (818) 986-4316

YOKO INTERNATIONAL—1744 Carmel Dr. #204 Walnut Creek, CA 94596 (925) 960-0117

COLORADO

APPLAUSE MODEL MANAGEMENT—2171 S. Trenton Way #208 Denver, CO 80231 (303) 743-0616 13+

ASPIRE MODEL & TALENT, INC.—126 West 5th Ave. Denver, CO 80204 (303) 733-3888; e-mail: aspire@aspireagency.com Website: http://aspireagency.com (13+)

*BARBIZON TALENT AGENCY—7535 E. Hampton Ave. #108 Denver, CO 80231

BELLA MODELS & TALENT—2708 W. Colorado Colorado Springs, CO 80904 (303) 471-3030 e-mail: info@bellamodels.com

*DONNA BALDWIN TALENT INC.—Historic Wheeler Block Bldg. 2150 W. 29th Ave. #200 Denver, CO 80211 (303) 561-1199

JOHN CASABLANCAS MODELING CENTER—7600 E. Eastman Ave. Denver, CO 80231 (303) 337-5100 (10+)

JOHN ROBERT POWERS MODELING—14231 E. 4th Ave. #200 Aurora, CO 80011 (303) 340-2838

KIDSKITS INC.—136 Kalamuth St. Denver, CO 80223 (303) 446-8200 e-mail: info@kiddskitsinc.com, website: www.kidskitsinc.com

MARBLES KIDS MANAGEMENT INC.—240 Josephine St #205 Denver, CO 80206 (303) 322-5004

MAXIMUM TALENT INC.—1720 S. Bellaire St #907 Denver, CO 80222 (303) 691-2344

MIRAGE MODELS—2137 S. Birch St. Denver, CO 80222 (303) 758-4004 e-mail: modelesque@aol.com, website: http://www.mirage-models.com

MODEL & TALENT MANAGEMENT—7600 E. Eastman Ave. Denver, CO 80231 (303) 337-4541 (8+)

SILHOUETTES MODELING & ACTING—3980 Broadway St. Boulder, CO 80304 (303) 449-7765

UNIQUE MODELING AGENCY—P.O. Box 47164 Denver, CO 80201 (303) 821-2957

VECTRA SEARCH—2850 W. Serendipity Circle #201 Colorado Springs, CO 80917 (719) 597-3883

VIA ENTERTAINMENT—320 N. Academy Blvd. #302 Colorado Springs, CO 80909 (719) 597-3883 (5+)

CONNECTICUT

ALLISON DANIELS MODEL MANAGEMENT—1260 New Britain Ave. W. Hartford, CT 06110 (860) 561-4483

BLUSH MODELS MANAGEMENT—2 Pomperaug Office Park #2 Main Street S., Southbury, CT 06488 (203) 264-7782

COASTAL MODELS LTD.—2012 King's Hwy. E. Fairfield, CT 06430 (203) 254-7722 e-mail: coastalmod@aol.com, contact: Marty Kanawall

JOHN CASABLANCAS MODELING CTR.—461 Farmington Ave. Hartford, CT 06105 (860) 232-4421 (5+)

JOHNSTON MODELING AGENCY—50 Washington St. Norwalk, CT 06854 (203) 838-6188

NEWSTAR INC.—55 Griswold Rd. Wethersfield, CT 06109 (860) 529-7761

DELAWARE

ROBERT TAYLOR TALENT—901 N. Washington St. Wilmington, DE 19801 (302) 427-3675

FLORIDA

40 PLUS MODEL & TALENT—P.O. Box 611298 Miami, FL 33261 (305) 538-6773

ALEXA MODEL & TALENT MANAGEMENT AGENCY—4100 W. Kennedy Blvd. #228 Tampa, FL 33609 (813) 289-8020

ANDERSON GREENE ENTERTAINMENT—1210 Washington Ave. Miami Beach, FL 33139 (305) 675-9881

ANNE O'BRIANT AGENCY INC—1260 Fran Mar Ct. Clermont, FL 34711 (352) 242-9983

ARIZA TALENT & MODELING AGENCY—909 State Rd. 436 Casselberry, FL 32707 (407) 332-0011

AUSTIN TALENT INTL.—1323 63rd Ave. E. Bradenton, FL 34203 e-mail: promodel10@aol.com

AVENUE PRODUCTIONS INC—2810 E. Oakland Park Blvd. #308 Ft. Lauderdale, FL 33306 (954) 561-1226

*AZUREE TALENT AGENCY—140 N. Orlando Ave. #120 Winter Park, FL 32789 (407) 629-5025

BARONS MODEL TEAM—7365 Southwest 8th St. Miami, FL 33144 (305) 264-1550

BELLA MODEL & TALENT MANAGEMENT—1553 San Marco Blvd. Jacksonville, FL 32207 (904) 298-9811

*BERG TALENT AGENCY—3825 Henderson Blvd. Tampa, FL 33629 (813) 877-5533 (3+)

*BOCA TALENT & MODEL AGENCY—829 Southeast 9th St. Palm Plaza #4 Deerfield Beach, FL 33441 (305) 428-4677

BOOM MODEL & TALENT AGENCY—13012 N. Dale Mabry Hwy. Tampa, FL 33618 (813) 264-1373

BOOM MODELS—126 3rd Ave. North Safety Harbor, FL 34695 (727) 265-2204

BOSS MODELS INC—539 Euclid Ave. Miami Beach, FL 33139 (305) 531-4244

BREVARD TALENT GROUP—405 Palm Springs Blvd. Indian Harbor Beach, FL 32937 (407) 773-1355

CENTRAL FLORIDA CASTING, INC—2601 Wells Ave. #181 Fern Park, FL 32730 (407) 830-9226

COCONUT GROVE TALENT AGENCY—3525 Vista Court Miami, FL 33133 (305) 858-3002

DENISE CAROL MODELING STUDIO—2223 Atlantic Blvd. Jacksonville, FL 32207 (904) 399-0824

*DIMENSIONS III MODELING & TLNT—5205 S. Orange Ave. Orlando, FL 32809 (407) 851-2575

ELITE MODEL MANAGEMENT MIAMI—1200 Collins Ave. Miami Beach, FL 33139 (305) 674-9500

FAMOUS FACES ENTERTAINMENT CO—2013 Harding St. Hollywood, FL 33020 (954) 922-0700

FLORIDA STARS MODEL & TALENT—225 W. University Ave. #A Gainesville, FL 32601 (322) 338-1086 website: http/www.afloridastar.com

FORD MODELS INC—826 Ocean Dr. Miami Beach, FL 33139 (305) 534-7200

*GREEN & GREEN MODEL & TALENT AGENCY.—1688 Meridian Ave. #1000 Miami Beach, FL 33139 (305) 532-9880

*HALEY TALENT, SUSAN—618 Wymore Rd. #2 Winter Park, FL 32789-2862 (407) 644-0600

*HURT-GARVER TALENT & MODELS—400 N. New York Ave. Winter Park, FL 32789 (407) 740-5700

IMAGE PRODUCTIONS—300 Biscayne Way Blvd. #1120 Miami, FL 33131-2210 (305) 531-9096

IMAGE LIFESTYLE TALENT AGENCY—420 Lincoln Rd. Miami Beach, FL 33139

INTERNATIONAL MODELS INC—8415 Coral Way #205 Miami, FL 33155 (305) 266-6331

JOBS & MODELS UNLIMITED—337 8TH Street Daytona Beach, FL 32117 (386) 253-6730

LAS OLAS MODELS & TALENT—1119 E. Las Olas Blvd. Ft. Lauderdale, FL 33301 (954) 763-3869

MARIAN POLAN TALENT AGENCY—10 Northeast 11th Ave. Ft. Lauderdale, FL 33301 (954) 525-8351

*MARIE INC., IRENE—728 Ocean Dr. Miami Beach, FL 33139-6203 (305) 672-2344 (954) 771-1400

*MARTIN-DONALDS INC. DBA—1915A Hollywood Blvd. Hollywood, FL 33020 (954) 921-2321

MARY LOU'S MODELS—P.O. Box 5127 Navarre, FL 32566-0127 (850) 939-3204

MICHELE & GROUP MODELING AGENCY—305 W. Granada Blvd. Ormond Beach, FL 32174 (386) 676-1702

MODELSCOUT INC—651 Rugby St. Orlando, FL 32804 (407) 420-5888

MODEL'S EXCHANGE—2425 E. Commercial Blvd. #206 Ft. Lauderdale, FL 33308 (954) 491-4266

NOUVEAU PRODUCTIONS—2600 Broadway #A, West Palm Beach, FL 33407 (561) 659-3656

PAGE PARKES MODEL'S REP—763 Collins Ave. Miami Beach, FL 33139 (305) 672-4869

PARKER AGENCY—47 S. Palm Ave. #106 Sarasota, FL 34236 (941) 316-0505

*POLAN TALENT AGENCY, MARION—10 N.E. 11th Ave. Ft. Lauderdale, FL 33301 (954) 525-8351

*POMMIER MODELS, MICHELE—81 Washington Ave, Miami Beach, FL 33139 (305) 672-9344

PROTOCOL MODES OF THE GULF—4949 Tamiami Trail North Naples, FL 34103 (941) 417-1200

REEVE AGENCY—1917 Boothe Circle #151 Longwood, FL 32750-6708 (407) 331-1784 (4+)

*ROXANNE MCMILLAN TALENT AGCY, 12100 N.E. 16th Ave. #106 N. Miami, FL 33161 (305) 899-9150

RUNWAYS—1688 Meridan Ave. #700 Miami Beach, FL 33139 (305) 673-8245

SANTA MARIA ENTERTAINMENT PRODUCTIONS—6025 45TH Ave. N. St. Petersburg, FL 33709 (727) 545-8686

SARAH PARKER MODEL & TALENT—410 Datura St. West Palm Beach, FL 33401 (561) 655-4400

SELECT MODELS—817 Washington Ave. Miami Beach, FL 33139 (305) 672-5566

SELECT MODELS—3699 Morton Street Jacksonville, FL 32217 (904) 730-2045

SESSIONS MODELING STUDIO—10991 San Jose Blvd. #16B Jacksonville, FL 32223 (904) 292-4366

*SHEFFIELD AGENCY, THE—P.O. Box 101418 Ft. Lauderdale, FL 33310 (954) 523-5887

STELLA JAY BROWN ENTERPRISES—605 Yorktown Dr. Leesburg, FL 34748 (352) 787-7004

*STELLAR TALENT AGENCY—407 Lincoln Rd. #2K, Miami Beach, FL 33139 (305) 672-2217

WILHELMINA MODELS—927 Lincoln Rd #200 Miami Beach, FL 33139 (305) 672-9344

*WORLD OF KIDS INC—1460 Ocean Dr. Miami Beach, FL 33139 (305) 672-5437

GEORGIA

ARLENE WILSON MODEL MGMT—887 West Marietta St. N.W. Atlanta, GA 30318 (404) 876-8555

*ATLANTA MODELS & TALENT INC—2970 Peachtree Road N.W. Atlanta, GA 30305 (404) 261-9627

ATLANTA'S YOUNG FACES—6075 Roswell Rd. N.E. Atlanta, GA 30328 (404) 255-3080

AUSTON'S PROFESSIONAL MODELING—3391 Peachtree Rd. N.E. #410 Atlanta, GA 30326 (404) 237-9800

BENNIE'S MODELING SERVICE—Highway 99 Darien, GA 31305 (912) 437-6415

BOHANNON MODELING AGENCY—4820 Old National Hwy Atlanta, GA 30337 (404) 209-0909

ELITE MANAGEMENT CORP—181 14ᵗʰ St. N.E. Atlanta, GA 30309 (404) 872-7444

ELLIS-CROSS ASSOCIATES INC—1422 W Peachtree St. N.W. Atlanta, GA 30309 (404) 874-1709

*GENESIS MODELS & TALENT INC—1465 Northside Dr. N.W. Atlanta, GA 30318 (404) 350-9212

*GLYN KENNEDY, INC.—975 Hunterhill Dr. Roswell, GA 30075 (678) 461-4444

IMAGE—530 Huntwick Place Roswell, GA 30075 (770) 993-2493

KATY'S PROFESSIONAL MODELING—4283 Memorial Dr. Decatur, GA 30032 (404) 292-0073

LORREN & MACY'S MODELING—405 Broad St. #A Rome, GA 30161 (706) 235-1175

L'AGENCE MODELS—5901 Peachtree Dun Rd. N.E. #60 Atlanta, GA 30328 (770) 396-9015

MADEMOISELLE MODELING AGENCY—2901 University Ave. Columbus, GA 31907 (706) 561-9449

MICHELLE JAMES HAIR PRODUCTION—467 Highland Ave. Augusta, GA 30909 (706) 738-7707

MILLIE LEWIS OF SAVANNAH—7011 Hodgson Memorial Dr Savannah, GA 31406 (912) 354-9525

PEOPLE STORE INC—2004 Rockledge Rd. N.E. Atlanta, GA 30324 (404) 874-6448

POPE MODELING CONSULTANT—3060 N. Pharr Court N.E. Atlanta, GA 30305 (404) 261-0736

*TALENT GROUP/HOT SHOT KIDS—561 W. Pike St. Lawrenceville, GA 30045 (678) 215-1500

TALENT SOURCE—107 E. Hall St. Savannah, GA 31401 (912) 232-9390

TARA MODELING ACADEMY & AGENCY—650 Morrow Industrial Blvd. Jonesboro, GA 30236 (770) 968-7700

*THE BURNS AGENCY—3800 Bretton Woods Rd. Decatur, GA 30032 (866) 744-5037

*THE PEOPLE STORE—2004 Rockledge Rd. N.E. Atlanta, GA 30324 (404) 874-6448

WILLIAM REYNOLDS AGENCY—1932 N. Druid Hills Rd. N.E. #100 Atlanta, GA 30319 (404) 636-1974

*WILSON INC., ARLENE—887 W. Marietta St. #N-10, Atlanta, GA 30318 (404) 876-8555

HAWAII

ACE OF HEARTS MODELS & TALENT—801 Ala Nioi Pl #1102 Honolulu, HI 96818 (808) 839-6934

ADR PRODUCTIONS, INC.—419 Waiakamilo Rd. #204 Honolulu, HI 96817 (808) 842-1313, e-mail: ryan@adragency.com, website: http://www.adragency.com

CHAMELEON TALENT AGENCY—590 Lipoa Pky. Kihei, HI 96753 (808) 875-2511

CIA CENTRAL ISLAND AGENCY—41-846 Laumilo St. Waimanalo, HI 96795 (808) 259-7914

ENCORE TALENT—74-4989 Mamalahoa Hwy. Holualoa, HI 96725 (808) 326-1636

KANIU KINIMAKA MODEL & TALENT—69 Railroad Ave. Hilo, HI 96720 (808) 961-0031

KATHY MULLER TALENT & MODELING—619 Kapahulu Ave. #205 Honolulu, HI 96815 (808) 737-7917

KOTOMORI AGENCY—1441 Kapiolani Blvd. #1206 Honolulu, HI 96814 (808) 955-6511

TALENT'ED INTERNATIONAL AGENCY—Kealakekua, HI 96750 (808) 323-3333

VOGUE INTERNATIONAL MODELING & TALENT AGENCY 2153 N. King St. #323-A Honolulu, HI 96819 (808) 842-0881

IDAHO

METCALF'S MODELING & TALENT—1851 Century Wy. #3 Boise, ID 83709 (208) 378-8777

TALENT POOL INC—P.O. Box 8322 Boise, ID 83707 (208) 384-1707

ILLINOIS

*AMBASSADOR TALENT AGENTS, INC—333 N. Michigan Ave. #910 Chicago, IL 60601 (312) 641-3491

ANNE O'BRIANT AGENCY—11819 Chisholm Trail Orland Park, IL 60467 (708) 460-3677

*ARIA MODEL & TALENT MGMT LTD—1017 W. Washington Blvd. Chicago, IL 60607 (312) 243-9400

ARLENE WILSON MODEL & TALENT—430 W. Erie St. #210 Chicago, IL 60610 (312) 573-0200

AUDITION DIVISION LIMITED—1084 Industrial Dr. Bensenville, IL 60106 (630) 766-6100

*BAKER & ROWLEY TALENT AGY INC—1347 W. Washington #1B Chicago, IL 60607 (773) 252-7900

BEST FACES OF CHICAGO—1152 N. La Salle Dr. Chicago, IL 60610 (312) 944-3009

*BIG MOUTH TALENT AGENCY—935 W. Chestnut #415 Chicago, IL 60622 (312) 421-4400

CLAIRE MODEL & TALENT—Wheeling, IL 60090 (847) 459-4242

DAVID & LEE MODEL MANAGEMENT—70 w. Hubbard St. Chicago, IL 60610 (312) 661-0500

ELITE MODEL MANAGEMENT CORP—58 W. Huron Chicago, IL 60610 (312) 943-3226

EMILIA LAURENCE LIMITED—325 W. Huron St. #404 Chicago, IL 60610 (312) 717-2033 (4+)

EYE FOR I AMERICA—314 W. Institute Chicago, IL 60610 (312) 664-1609

FORD TALENT GROUP—641 W. Lake St. #402 Chicago, IL 60661 (312) 707-9000

INFINITE IMAGES INC—2426 N. Austin Ave, Chicago, IL 60639 (773) 804-1630

*JENNIFER'S TALENT UNLIMITED—740 N. Plankinton, #300 Milwaukee, WI 53203-2403 (414) 277-9440

JOHN ROBERT POWERS MODELING—27 E. Monroe St. #200 Chicago, IL 60603 (312) 726-1404

*LINDA JACK TALENT—230 E. Ohio #200 Chicago, IL 60611 (312) 587-1155

*LORENCE LTD, EMILIA—325 W. Huron #404 Chicago, IL 60610 (312) 787-2033

*LORI LINS LTD—7611 W. Holmes Ave. Greenfield, WI 53220 (414) 282-3500

M L INTERNATIONAL MODELING INC—162 N. Franklin St. Chicago, IL 60606 (312) 849-9190

MARKETING UNLIMITED MODELING—1921 5th Ave. Moline, IL 61265 (309) 762-1978 (5+)

NATIONAL TALENT ASSOCIATES—6326 N. Lincoln Ave. Chicago, IL 60659 (773) 539-8575

ROYAL MODEL MANAGEMENT—1051 Perimeter Dr. Schaumburg, IL 60173 (847) 240-4215

SALAZAR TALENT AGENCY—760 N. Ogden Ave. Chicago, IL 60622 (312) 666-1677

SHAWNEE STUDIOS—102 W. Main St. Mount Olive, Il 62069 (217) 999-2522

SHIRLEY HAMILTON INC.—333 E. Ontario St. Chicago, IL 60611 (312) 787-4700

STEWART TALENT AGENCY—58 W. Huron Chicago, IL 60610 (312) 943-3131

STEWART'S NORTHWEST TALENT—4227 Connecticut Trail Crystal Lake, IL 60012 (815) 455-6311

TALENT GROUP—4637 N. Magnolia Ave. Chicago, IL 60640 (773) 561-8814

INDIANA

*ACT I MODEL & TALENT AGENCY—6100 N. Keystone Ave. #105 Indianapolis, IN 46220 (317) 255-3100

AMERICAN MODELS INTERNATIONAL MODELING—2500 Harmony Way Evansville, IN 47720 (812) 422-5064

COVER SHOTS—14370 State Road 23 Granger, IN 46530 (219) 271-1992 (5+)

*HELEN WELLS INC—11711 N Meriden St. Carmel, IN 46032 (317) 843-5363

MODEL MAKERS INC—10 W Market St. Indianapolis, IN 46204 (317) 464-5215

SUPER MODELS INTERNATIONAL—14420 Cherry Tree Rd. Carmel, IN 46033 (317) 846-4321

IOWA

AMERICAN ETHNIC MODEL AGENCY—326 N. Walnut St. Monticello, IA 52310 (319) 395-7772

CORRINE SHOVER AGENCY—326 N. Walnut St. Monticello, IA 52310 (319) 465-5507

MODEL CONSULTANTS—2625 S.E. 18th St. Des Moines, IA 50320 (515) 244-5500

KANSAS

CAREER IMAGES MODEL & TALENT—8519 Lathrop Ave. Kansas City, KS 66109 (913) 334-2200

GAIL BOWEN MODELS & PROPS—2300 E. Douglas Ave. Wichita, KS 67214 (316) 262-8338

GREGORY AGENCY—3873 E. Harry St. Wichita, KS 67218 (316) 687-5666

HOFFMAN INTERNATIONAL—6705 W. 91st St. Shawnee Mission, KS 66212 (913) 642-1060

KSKID PRODUCTIONS—1201-1/2 W. Douglas Ave. Wichita, KS 6721 (316) 680-4243 e-mail: kskidproductions@hotmail.com, website: http://www.kskid.com

MODEL'S & IMAGES—1619 N. Rock Rd. Wichita, KS 67206 (316) 634-2777

KENTUCKY

ALIX ADAMS MODEL SCHOOL-AGENCY—9813 Merioneth Dr. Jeffersontown, KY 40299 (502) 266-6990

BARBARANS SCHOOL OF MODELING—105 Princess Dr. Ashland, KY 411101 (606) 324-6683

COSMO MODEL & TALENT—7410 La Grange Rd. #204 Louisville, KY 40222 (502) 425-8000

MJK MODELS—414 Baxter Ave. Louisville, KY 40204 (502) 585-4152

LOUISIANA

ABOUT FACES MODELING & TALENT—201 St. Charles Ave. Fl. 25 New Orleans, LA 70170 (504) 522-3030

FAME MODELING & TALENT—4518 Magazine St. New Orleans, LA 70115 (504) 891-2001 email info@fameagency.com, website: http://www.fameagency.com

GLAMOUR MODELING AGENCY—P.O. Box 1526 Meraux, LA 70075 (504) 279-7313

IMAGES MODEL & TALENT AGENCY—511 Jefferson St. Lafayette, LA 70501 (318) 269-5610

METRO MODEL & TALENT MGMT—201 St. Charles Ave. #2587 New Orleans, LA 70170 (504) 897-6686

MICHAEL TURNEY AGENCY—733 Olive St. Shreveport, LA 71104 (318) 221-2628

MODEL MASTERS INC—Van Ave. New Orleans, LA 70122 (504) 288-3315

MTP—1 Galleria Blvd. #825 Metairie, LA 70001 (504) 831-8118

NEW ORLEANS MODEL & TALENT—1347 Magazine St. New Orleans, LA 70130 (504) 525-0100

STANWYCKS STUDIOS—4139 Tchoupitoulas St. New Orleans, LA 70115 (504) 899-9394

MAINE

MAINE TALENT—Winthrop Rd. Belgrade, ME 0491, (207) 495-2143

PORT CITY MODELS INC—217 Commercial St. #202 P.O. Box 6820 Portland, ME 04103 (207) 415-4015 e-mail: info@portcitymodels.com, website: http://www.portcity-models.com

MARYLAND

ANNAPOLIS MODELING AGENCY—130 Manns Rd Severna Park, MD 21146 (410) 647-1200

BELLA NOVA MODEL MANAGEMENT—206 N. Liberty St #3 Baltimore, MD 21201

CENTRAL CASTING—2229 N. Charles St. Baltimore, MD 21218 (410) 889-3200

ELEGANZA—P.O. Box 416 Aberdeen, MD 21001 (410) 272-7409

NOVA MODELS INC—2120 N. Charles St. Baltimore, MD 21218 (410) 752-6682

RAMP MODEL MANAGEMENT—932 N. Charles St. Baltimore, MD 21201 (410) 727-0000

*****THE BULLOCK AGENCY**—5200 Bullock Ave. #102 Hyattsville, MD 20781 (301) 905-9598

MASSACHUSETTS

*****ACTUAL TALENT**—1260 New Britain Rd. #65 W. Hartford, CT 06110 (860) 920-5322

AGENCY ROYALE MODELING—65 Clinton St. Malden, MA 02148 (781) 397-0993

COPLEY 7 MODELS & TALENT—P.O. Box 535 Boston MA 02117 (617) 267-4444

FORD AGENCY—297 Newbury St. Boston, MA 02115 (617) 262-9300

FORD MODEL MANAGEMENT—297 Newbury St. Boston, MA 02115 (617) 266-6939

HEART & SOUL PROMOTIONS INC—30 Main St. Ashland, MA 01721 (508) 881-4881

JOHN ROBERT POWERS MODELING—390 Main St. #740 Worcester, MA 01608 (508) 753-6343

*MAGGIE INC—35 Newbury St. Boston, MA 02116 (617) 536-2639

MODEL CLUB—229 Berkeley St. Boston, MA 02116 (617) 247-9020

MODEL & TALENT MANAGEMENT—1 Gateway Center #180 Newton, MA 02158 (617) 969-3555

*MODELS GROUP—374 Congress St. Boston, MA 02210 (617) 426-4711

*MODELS INC—218 Newbury St. 2nd Fl. Boston, MA 02116 (617) 437-6212

PROFESSIONAL TEAM MODELS & PROMOTION—244 Newburyport Turnpike Rowley, MA 01969 (978) 948-2495

MICHIGAN

AAA AGENCY-POWERS MODEL—16250 Northland Dr #239 Southfield, MI 48075 (810) 569-2247

ABBEY'S PEOPLE—2309 Columbia Ave. W. Battle Creek, MI 49015 (616) 965-8285

*AFFILIATED MODELS INC—1680 Crooks Rd #200 Troy, MI 48084 (248) 244-8770

*CLASS MODELING TALENT AGENCY—2722 E. Michigan Ave. Lansing, MI 48912 (517) 482-1833

FACES FOR PLACES—22255 River Ridge Trail Farmington Hills, MI 48335 (248) 471-6611

FEMINIQUE-LESHOMME MODELING—P.O. Box 530606 Livonia, MI 48153 (810) 471-1218

MADELINE'S MODELING AGENCY—157 S. Kalamazoo Mall Kalamazoo, MI 49007 (616) 344-0755

MODEL & TALENT MANAGEMENT—44450 Pinetree Drive Plymouth, MI 48170 (734) 455-0801

MODELS UNLIMITED 18437 Roselawn St. Detroit, MI 48221 (313) 345-1331

PRO TALENT—1345 Monroe N.W, Grand Rapids, MI 49505 (616) 458-2513

*****PRODUCTIONS PLUS**—30600 Telegraph Rd. #2156 Bingham Farms, MI 48025 (248) 644-5566

PROFESSIONAL TALENT—1345 Monroe Ave. N.W. Grand Rapids, MI 49505 (616) 458-2513

SUCCESS MODELING & TALENT AGENCY—101 Brookside Lane Brighton, MI 48116 (810) 220-5902

TA-DAH PRODUCTIONS—2737 W. 12 Mile Rd. Berkley, MI 48072 (248) 548-2324

*****THE I GROUP, LLC**—29540 Southfield Rd. #200 Southfield, MI 48076 (810) 552-8842

*****THE TALENT SHOP**—30100 Telegraph Rd. #116 Birmingham, MI 48025 (810) 644-4877

MINNESOTA

AGENCY MODELS AND TALENT—210 N. Second St. #002 Minneapolis, MN 55410 (612) 664-1174

*****CARYN MODEL & TALENT AGENCY**—100 N. 6th St. #270B Minneapolis, MN 55403 (612) 349-3600

IMAGE 1 PROFESSIONAL MODELING & ACTING—601 9th Ave. N. St. Cloud, MN 56303 (320) 251-0101

KARYN'S MODELING AGENCY—6651 Hwy 7 St. Louis Park, MN 55426 (612) 915-1912

*****MEREDITH MODEL & TALENT**—800 Washington Ave. N. #511 Minneapolis, MN 55401 (612) 340-9555

*****MOORE CREATIVE TALENT INC**—1610 W. Lake St. Minneapolis, MN 55408 (612) 827-3823

*****NEW FACES MODELS & TALENT INC**—6301 Wayzata Blvd. Minneapolis, MN 55416 (612) 544-8668

SUSAN WEHMANN MODELS & TALENT—1128 Harmon Pl. #205 Minneapolis, MN 55403 (612) 333-6393

MISSISSIPPI

COLOR CAMPUS MODELING & ACTING—240 Eisenhower Dr. Biloxi, MS 39531 (228) 388-2465

MISSOURI

AJH ENTERPRISES—P.O. Box 63262 St. Louis, MO 63163 (314) 352-7248

ALLURE MODELS—144 W. Madison Ave. St. Louis, MO 63122 (314) 909-0666

AMERICAN ARTISTS AGENCY—1808 Broadway St. Kansas City, MO 64108 (816) 474-9988

*CITY TALENT—2101 Locust St. #2, W. St. Louis, MO 63103 (314) 621-7200

*ENTERTAINMENT PLUS—114 A W. 3rd St. Kansas City, MO 64105 (816) 474-4778

*EXPOSURE MODEL & TALENT—215 W. 18th St. Kansas City, MO 64108 (816) 842-4494

*HOFFMAN INTERNATIONAL—6705 W. 91st St. Overland Park, KS 66212 (913) 642-1030

I & I MODEL GROUP—1509 Westport Rd. #200 Kansas City, MO 64111 (816) 410-9950

IMAGES OF ST. LOUIS—715 Frontenac Square St. Louis, MO 63131 (314) 993-0605

IMPRESSIONS & IMAGES MODELS—207 Westport Rd. Kansas City, Mo 64111 (816) 931-9950

KAY MODELING SCHOOL & AGENCY—1201 w. 7TH St. Joplin, MO 64801 (417) 781-4540 (8+)

MODEL RESOURCE GROUP—13 Maryland Plaza St. Louis, MO 63108 (314) 361-1312

NORMA'S MODELING SCHOOL & AGCY—3638 S. Campbell Ave. Springfield, MO 65807 (417) 882-2436

PATRICIA STEVENS MODEL AGENCY—2000 Baltimore Ave. Kansas City, MO 64108 (816) 221-1188

POWERS PROMOTIONS—713 Old Frontenac Sq. St. Louis, MO 63131 (314) 993-9339

*PRIMA MODELS—522 S. Hanley Rd. St. Louis, MO 63105 (314) 721-1235

*TALENT PLUS INC—1222 Lucas #300 St. Louis, MO 63103 (314) 421-9400

*TALENT UNLIMITED—4049 Pennsylvania Ave. Kansas City, MO 64111 (816) 561-9040

TALENTPLUS-CENTRO MODELS—55 Maryland Plaza St. Louis, MO 63108 (314) 421-9400

*THE AGENCY/MODELS & TALENT—10 E. Cambridge Circle Dr. Kansas City, KS 66103 (913) 342-8382

MONTANA

CREATIVE WORLD MODELING—27 N. 27th St. Billings, Mt 59101 (406) 259-9540

NASS TALENT MGMT—P.O. Box 3244 Bozeman, MT 59772 (406) 586-7045

WINSLOW STUDIO & GALLERY—16 S. Tracy Ave. Bozeman, MT 59715 (406) 587-8826

NEBRASKA

INTERNATIONAL SCHOOL-MODELING—8602 Cass St. Omaha, NE 68114 (402) 399-8787

NEVADA

A BASKOW TALENT AGENCY & ASSOC—2948 E. Russell Rd. Las Vegas, NV 89120 (702) 733-7818 (4+)

ALEXIA MODELING AGENCY—6370 W. Flamingo Rd. Las Vegas, NV 89103 (702) 248-0896

ALWAYS ENTERTAINING—3690 S. Eastern Ave. #103 Las Vegas, NV 89109 (702) 737-3232

ANNE O'BRIANT AGENCY—4528 W. Charleston Blvd. Las Vegas, NV 89102

BEST MODEL & TALENT—4270 Cameron St. #6 Las Vegas, NV 89103 (702) 889-2900

CLASSIC MODELS LIMITED—3305 Spring Mountain Rd. #12 Las Vegas, NV 89102 (702) 367-1444

CONVENTION EASE—3720 W. Desert Inn Rd. #A Las Vegas, NV 89102 (702) 365-1057

FARRINGTON PRODUCTIONS INC—4350 Arville St. #27 Las Vegas, NV 89103 (702) 735-7353

HOLIDAY MODELS INC—900 E. Desert Inn Rd. #101 Las Vegas, NV 89109 (702) 735-7353

JUDY VENN & ASSOCIATES—3401 W. Charleston Blvd. Las Vegas, NV 89102 (702) 259-4494

LENZ AGENCY—1591 E. Desert Inn Rd. Las Vegas, NV 89109 (702) 733-6888

NEVADA CASTING GROUP INC—100 Washington St. Reno, NV 89503, (702) 322-8187

PARKS PEOPLE—50 S. Jones Blvd. Las Vegas, NV 89107 (702) 870-0555

PREMIERE MODELS—2700 State St. #18 Las Vegas, NV 89103 (702) 362-3000

SKY MODELING INC—4350 Arville St. #27 Las Vegas, NV 89103 (702) 362-3000

VICTORIA'S DESTINATION SERVICE—2929 E. Desert Inn Rd. Las Vegas, NV 89121 (702) 794-2492

WILD STREAK TALENT INTERNATIONAL—3355 Spring Mountain Rd #247 Las Vegas, NV 89102 (702) 252-8382

NEW HAMPSHIRE

CINDERELLA MODELING STUDIO—9 Brook St. Manchester, NH 03104 (603) 627-4125

EAST COAST FOCUS—3 Pleasant St. Concord, NH 03301 (603) 228-6377

NEW ENGLAND MODELS GROUP—250 Commercial Lane #2022 Manchester, NH 03101 (603) 624-0555

PROFILE MODEL AGENCY—50 Northwestern Dr. Salem, NH 03079 (603) 893-2414

WEBB MODEL MANAGEMENT—452 Packers Falls Rd. Lee, NH 03824 (603) 659-0110

NEW JERSEY

AMERICAN BEAUTY POSE INC—Sewaren, NJ 07077 (732) 634-1111

AXIS MODELS & TALENT INC—24-26 Church St. Montclair, NJ 07042 (973) 783-4900

CAMELOT MODELING CONSULTANTS—20 Church St. Montclair, NJ 07042 (201) 509-8522

CHRISTINE MODELS & CASTING—43 Rock Rd. Wayne, NJ 07470 (973) 904-0300

CLERI MODEL MANAGEMENT CORP—145 Talmadge Rd. #11 Edison, NJ 08837 (732) 650-9730

DELL MODELING & MANAGEMENT CTR—370 Ganttown Rd. Sewell, NJ 08080 (609) 589-4099

L & M MODELING INC—232 Boulevard Hasbrouck Heights, NJ 07604 (201) 288-2253

MC CULLOUGH MODELS INC—8 S. Hanover Ave. Margate City, NJ 08402 (609) 822-2222

MEREDITH MODEL EAST—767 Fredrick Wycoss, NJ 07481 (201) 560-9992

MODEL TEAM—55 Central Ave. Ocean Grove, NJ 07756 (732) 988-3648 (5+)

MODELS ON THE MOVE—1200 Route 70 E. #6 Cherry Hill, NJ 08034 (856) 667-1060

NEW TALENT MANAGEMENT—590 Route 70 Brick, NJ 08723 (732) 477-3355

NEW MEXICO

APPLAUSE TALENT AGENCY—225 San Pedro Dr. N.E. Albuquerque, NM 87108 (505) 262-9733

DESIREE MODELING ACTING & TLNT—2645 Missouri Ave. #6 Las Cruces, NM 88011 (505) 521-8000

EATON AGENCY INC—3636 High St. N.E. Albuquerque, NM 87107 (505) 344-3149

MANNEQUIN AGENCY—2021 San Mateo Blvd. N.E. Albuquerque, NM 87110 (505) 266-6823

SOUTH OF SANTA FE—6921 Montgomery Blvd. N.E. Albuquerque, NM 87109 (505) 880-8550

NEW YORK

*****ABRAMS ARTISTS & ASSOC**—725 Seventh Av. 26th Fl. New York, NY 10001 (646) 486-4600

ACME TALENT & LITERARY—875 Avenue of the Americas #2108 New York, NY 10001 (212) 328-0388

*__ACTUAL TALENT__—1260 New Britain Rd. #65 W. Hartford, CT 06110 (860) 920-5322

ADELE'S KIDS—33 Rupert Ave. Staten Island, NY 10314 (718) 494-5000

AGENCE CHRISTIE—2124 Broadway #134 New York, NY 10023 (888) 579-5392 e-mail Director@Agence Christie.com, Website: www.AgenceChristie.com

*__AMATO AGENCY, MICHAEL__—1650 Broadway #307 New York, NY 10019 (212) 247-4456

*__AMERICAN INT'L TALENT AGENCY__—303 W. 42nd St. #608 New York, NY 10036 (212) 245-8888

AMERICAN MODEL MANAGEMENT CORP—155 Spring St. New York, NY 10012 (212) 941-5858

*__ANDREADIS TALENT AGENCY__—119 W. 57th St. #711 New York, NY 10019 (212) 315) 0303

*__ANN STEELE AGENCY__—240 W. 44th St. #1 Helen Hayes Theatre, New York, NY 10036 (212) 278-0896

BARBIZON MODELING AGENCY—Montauk Hwy & Route 109 West Babylon, NY 11704 (516) 587-6100

BARBIZON MODELING AGENCY—15 Penn Plaza New York, NY 10001 (212) 239-1110

*__BAUMAN REDANTY & SHAUL__—250 W. 57th St. #473 New York, NY 10019 (212) 757-0098

*__BEILIN AGENCY INC., PETER__—230 Park Ave. #923 New York, NY 10169 (212) 949-9111

*__BERNARD LIEBHABER AGENCY__—352 Seventh Ave. 7th Fl. New York, NY 10001 (212) 631-7561

BEYOND ONE GENERATION MODELS INC—David Picow & Jo-Jo 1133 Broadway #904 New York, NY 10010 (212) 367-7280 e-mail Bigmodel@aol.com.

*__BIENSTOCK INC., N.S.__—1740 Broadway 24th Fl. New York, NY 10019 (212) 765-3040

BLACKWOOD-STEELE INC—694 Macedon Ctr. Rd. Fairport, New York, NY 14450 (716) 425-7099

BLACKWOOD-STEELE INC—P.O. Box 690 Fairport, NY 14450 (716) 425-1306

BLUE MODEL MANAGEMENT—625 Broadway #6M New York, NY 10012 (212) 253-9416

BOSS MODELS INC—1 Gansevoort St. New York, NY 10014 (212) 242-2444

*BUCHWALD & ASSOC., DON—10 E. 44th St. New York, NY 10017 (212) 867-1200

CAMERA TWO MODELING & ACTING—7206 Austin St. Flushing, NY 11375 (718) 793-3661

CANVAS 42—P.O. Box 14, Hewlett, New York (516) 791-4191

*CARSON ORGANIZATION LTD., THE—240 W. 44th St. PH New York, NY 10036 (212) 221-1517

*CARSON-ADLER AGENCY INC—250 W. 57th St. New York, NY 10107 (212) 307-1882

CLICK RUNWAY MODELS—129 W. 27th St. New York, NY 10001 (212) 206-1414

*CUNNINGHAM, ESCOTT, DIPENE & ASSOC—257 Park Ave. S. #900 New York, NY 10010 (212) 477-1666

*DICCE TALENT AGENCY, GINGER—1650 Broadway #714 New York, NY 10019 (212) 974-7455

DNA MODEL MANAGEMENT—145 Hudson St. New York, NY 10013 (212) 226-0080

ELITE MODEL MANAGEMENT CORP—111 E. 22nd St. New York, NY 10010 (212) 529-9700

*EWCR & ASSOCIATES—311 W. 43rd St. #204 New York, NY 10036 (212) 586-9110

FACES—6814 Main St. #110 Williamsville, NY 14221 (716) 634-5634

*FLAUNT MODEL MANAGEMENT—114 E 32nd St. New York, NY 10016 (212) 679-9011

FORD—142 Greene St. 4th Floor New York, NY, (212) 219-6500

*FRESH FACES AGENCY, INC.—108 S. Franklin Ave., #11 Valley Stream, NY 11580 (516) 223-0034

*FRONTIER BOOKING INT'L, INC.—1560 Broadway #1110 New York, NY 10036 (212) 221-0220

FUNNY FACE TODAY INC—151 E. 31st St. #24J New York, NY 10016 (212) 686-4343

GILLA ROOS LTD, 16 W. 22ND St. #3 New York, NY 10010 (212) 727-7820

*GOLDNADEL INC—234 Fifth Ave. #406 New York, NY 10001 (212) 532-2202

GONZALEZ MODEL & TALENT—112 E. 23rd St. Ph New York, NY 10010 (212) 982-5626

GRACE DE MARCO—350 5th Ave. New York, NY 10118 (212) 629-6404

*HENDERSON/HOGAN AGENCY INC—850 Seventh Ave. #1003 New York, NY 10019 (212) 765-5190

*HWA TALENT REPRESENTATIVES—220 E. 23RD St. #400 New York, NY 10010 (212) 889-0800

IKON NEW YORK—140 W. 22nd Street New York, NY 10011 (212) 691-2363

IMAGES MANAGEMENT—30 E. 20th St. New York, NY 10003 (212) 228-0300

IMG MODELS—304 Park Ave. S. New York, NY 10010 (212) 253-8882

*JORDAN, GILL & DORNBAUM AGCY INC—156 Fifth Ave. #711 New York, NY 10010 (212) 463-8455

JUNE 2 MODEL & TALENT AGENCY—143 Allen St. Buffalo, NY 14201 (716) 883-0700

*KERIN-GOLDBERG ASSOCIATES—155 E 55th St. #5D New York, NY 10022 (212) 838-7373

*KOLSTEIN TALENT AGENCY dba NAOMI'S WORLD OF ENTERTAINMENT INC—85 C Lafayette Ave. Suffern, NY 10901 (845) 357-8301

*LEVY AGENCY, BRUCE—311 W. 43rd St. #602 New York, NY 10036 (212) 262-6845

LYONS GROUP—505 8th Ave. New York, NY 10018 (212) 239-3539

MARY THERESE FRIEL INC—1251 Pittsford Mendon Rd. Mendon, NY 14506 (716) 624-5510

MC DONALD RICHARDS INC—156 5th Ave. #222 New York, NY 10010 (212) 627-3100 (7+)

*MCCULLOUGH ASSOCIATES—8 S. Hanover Ave. Margate, NJ 08402 (609) 822-2222

MEGA MODEL MANAGEMENT—26 W. 17th St. New York, NY 10011 (212) 366-4049

*MEREDITH MODEL MGMT—10 Furler St. Totawa, NJ 07512 (651) 812-0122

MODELS SERVICE AGENCY INC—570 7th Ave. #702 New York, NY 10018 (212) 944-8896

MODELS & TALENT—45 W. 21st St. New York, NY 10010 (212) 219-1616

*MORRIS AGENCY, WILLIAM—1325 Avenue Of the Americas New York, NY 10019 (212) 586-5100

*NEEDHAM METZ & KOWALL INC—19 W 21st St. #401 New York, NY 10010 (212) 741-7000

NEW FACES—6814 Main St., Williamsville, NY 14221 (716) 634-5634

NEXT MANAGEMENT CO—23 Watts St. #5 New York, NY 10013 (212) 925-5100

NEXUS PERSONAL MANAGEMENT INC—694 Macedon Ctr. Rd. Fairport, NY 14450 (716) 425-1306

*****NOUVELLE TALENT INC**—453 W. 17th St. #3 New York, NY 10011 (212) 645-0940

ORB AGENCY—130 W. 56th St. New York, NY 10019 (212) 957-2862

*****OSCARD AGENCY INC., FIFI**—24 W. 40th St. 17th Fl. New York, NY 10018 (212) 764-1100

*****PARADIGM**—200 W. 57th St. #900 New York, NY 10019 (212) 246-1030

PARTS MODELS—500 E. 77th St. #917 New York, NY 10162 (212) 744-6123

PASARELA MODELING & TALENT LTD—231 W. 29th St. New York, NY 10001 (212) 594-1043

PAULINES MODEL MANAGEMENT—379 W. Broadway New York, NY 10012 (212) 941-6000

R&L MODEL MANAGEMENT—203 W. 23rd St. #400 New York, NY 10011 (212) 935-2300

*****ROOS LTD., GILLA**—16 W. 22nd St. 7th Fl. New York, NY 10010 (212) 727-7820

*****SCHIFFMAN, EKMAN, MORRISON & MARX INC (S.E.M & M)**—22 W. 19th St. 8th Fl. New York, NY 10011 (212) 627-5500

*****SCHILL AGENCY INC., WILLIAM**—302A W. 12th St. #183 New York, NY 10014 (877) 813-3923

*****SCHULLER TALENT/NEW YORK KIDS**—276 Fifth Ave. New York, NY 10001 (212) 532-6005

STARS MODEL MANAGEMENT INC—303 E. 60th St. New York, NY 10022 (212) 758-3545

*****THE LEUDTKE AGENCY**—1674 Broadway #7A New York, NY 10019 (212) 220-3532

THOMPSON MODEL AGENCY INC—50 W. 34th St. #6C6 New York, NY 10001 (212) 947-6711

*****TRANUM, ROBERTSON & HUGHES**—600 Madison Ave. New York, NY 10017 (212) 371-7500

U S MODEL-TALENT MANAGEMENT—250 Goodman St. N. Rochester, NY 14607 (716) 244-0592

*****WATERS & NICOLOSI**—1501 Broadway #1305 New York, NY 10036 (212) 302-8787

WILHELMINA MODELS INC—300 S. Park Ave. #2 New York, NY 1001, (212) 473-0700

*WRIGHT REPRESENTATIVES, ANN—165 W 46th St. #1105 New York, NY 10036 (212) 764-6770

*WRITERS & ARTISTS AGENCY—19 W. 44th St. #1000 New York, NY 10036 (212) 391-1112

NORTH CAROLINA

BROCK AGENCY—329 13th Ave. N.W. Hickory, NC 28601 (704) 322-8553

CAROLINA TALENT INC—312 Rensselaer Ave. Charlotte, NC 28203 (704) 332-3218

DIRECTIONS USA—3717 W. Market St. #D Greensboro, NC 27403 (336) 292-2800

DIRECTIONS USA—206 E. Tremont Ave. Charlotte, NC 28203 (704) 377-3151

ICE MODEL TALENT MGMT INT'L—8318 Pineville Matthews Rd. Charlotte, NC, (704) 544-1550 (5+)

IMAGE & FASHION ACADEMY—580 12th Ave. N.E. Hickory, NC 28601 (704) 327-3349

KICK 277 MODELING AGENCY—210 W. Main St. Dallas, NC 28034 (704) 922-5425 (12+)

MARILYN'S INC—601 Norwalk St. Greensboro, NC 27407 (336) 292-5950

MAULTSBY MODEL & TALENT AGENCY—1213 Culbreth Dr. Wilmington, NC 28405 (910) 313-0922

MODEL SELECT INC—4500 Central Ave. #A Charlotte, NC 28205 (704) 536-7760

ON TRACK MODELING INC—5500 Executive Ctr. Dr. Charlotte, NC 28212 (704) 532-6577 (13+)

PROFESSIONAL MODEL'S GUILD—1819 Charlotte Dr. Charlotte, NC 28203, (704) 377-9299

RICK'S TALENT & MODELING AGENCY—806 Summit Ave. Greensboro, NC 27405 (336) 379-0033

STAR TALENT NETWORK—616 Guy Walker Way Durham, NC 27703 (919) 596-5876

TALENT CONNECTION—338 N. Elm St. Greensboro, NC 27401 (336) 274-2499

TALENT TREK AGENCY—825-C Merrimon Ave. Box 356, Asheville, NC 28804

THE AGENCY, DIV. OF CARL MIZE INC—116 E Kivett Dr. P.O. Box 464 High Point, NC 27261 (336) 887-7025 e-mail CM0511@aol.com

NORTH DAKOTA

FARGO—220-1/4 Broadway Fargo, ND 58102 (701) 235-8132

OHIO

A GOLDEN TOUCH TALENT AGENCY—8527 Refugee Rd. Pickerington, OH 43147 (614) 837-0629

A GREAT AMERICAN MODEL SEMINAR—3622 Belmont Ave. Youngstown, OH 44505 (330) 759-4848

ACTIVE IMAGE MANAGEMENT COMPANY—Worthington, OH 43085 (614) 885-7770

ASHLEY TALENT AGENCY—10948 Reading Rd. #310 Cincinnati, OH 45241 (513) 554-4836

*CAM TALENT AGENCY, COLUMBUS—1350 W. 5th Ave. #25 Columbus, OH 43212 (614) 488-1122

*CAM TALENT, CINCINNATI—1150 W. Eight St. #262 Cincinnati, OH 45203 (513) 421-1795

*CREATIVE TALENT—1102 Neil Ave Columbus, OH 43201 (614) 294-7827

DIMENSIONS PLUS SIZE MODEL—551 36th St. N.W. Canton, Oh 44709 (330) 649-9809

FORD TALENT GROUP INC—1300 E. 9th St. #1640 Cleveland, OH 44114 (216) 522-1300

GLORIA SUSTAR AGENCY—35 E. 7th St. #401 Cincinnati, OH 45202 (513) 721-3737

*GOENNER TALENT, JO—10019 Paragon Rd. Dayton, OH 45458 (937) 885-2595

*HEYMAN TALENT AGENCY—3308 Brotherton Rd. Cincinnati, OH 45209 (513) 533-3113

IMPACT MGMT TALENT (IMI)—9700 Rockside Rd. #410 Cleveland, OH 44125 (216) 901-9710

JACK MORAN ALL STAR TALENT—5714 Scarborough Dr. Cincinnati, OH 45238 (513) 922-0621

JO GOENNER-TALENT—4700 Reed Rd. E. Columbus, OH 43220 (614) 459-3582

MARSHA MODEL & TALENT AGENCY—Box 7141–118 W. High St. Bryan, OH 43506 (419) 636-5334

MICHAEL STEPHEN STUDIOS—650 Youngstown Warren Rd. Niles, OH 44446 (330) 544-5355

NEW VIEW MANAGEMENT GROUP INC—10680 McSwain Dr. Cincinnati, OH 45241 (513) 733-4444

PRO-MODEL MANAGEMENT—3926 W. Market St. Akron, OH 44333 (330) 867-4125

RIGHT DIRECTION—5701 N. High St. Worthington, OH 43085 (614) 848-3367

RIGHT KIDS—5701 N. High St. Worthington, OH 43085 (614) 848-4301

SHARKEY AGENCY INC—1299 Lyons Rd #H Dayton, OH 45488 (937) 434-4461

Z MODELS—985 Mediterranean Ave. Columbus, OH 43229 (614) 436-9006

Z MODELS INC—3067 W. Market St. #5 Fairlawn, OH 44333 (330) 869-5050

OKLAHOMA

ALLEN INTERNATIONAL MODELING,LLC.—P.O. Box 701416 Tulsa, OK 74170 (918) 481-4477 website: www.allenmodels.com

HARRISON-GERS MODEL & TALENT—2624 W. Britton Rd. Oklahoma City, OK 73120 (405) 840-4515

J BALLARD MODEL & TALENT INSTITUTE—300 N. Meridian Ave. #201 N. Oklahoma City, OK 73107 (405) 942-8383

JOHN CASABLANCAS MODEL MANAGEMENT—5009 N. Pennsylvania Avenue Oklahoma City, Ok 73112 (405) 842-000

KIRBY KASTING & MODELING—8136 S. Harvard Ave. #A Tulsa, OK 74137 (918) 491-3410

LINDA LAYMAN AGENCY LIMITED—3546 e. 51ST St. Tulsa, OK 74135 (918) 744-0888

MODEL & TALENT MGMT—5009 N. Pennsylvania Ave. Oklahoma City, OK 73112 (405) 842-0090

OREGON

ABC KIDS-N-TEENS ARTS CTR—1144 Willagillespie Rd. Eugene, OR 97401 (541) 485-6960

ABC KIDS-N-TEENS PERFORMING—3829 N.E. Tillamook St. Portland, OR 97212 (503) 249-2945

CINDERELLA'S SCHOOL-MODEL AGCY—317 N.E. Ct. St. Upper Lvl, Salem, OR 97301 (503) 581-1073

*CUSICK'S TALENT AGENCY—1009 N.W. Hoyt St. #100 Portland, OR 97209 (503) 274-8555

*ERHART TALENT—037 S.W. Hamilton St. Portland, OR 97201 (503) 243-6362

JOHN CASABLANCAS MODELING—5440 S.W. Westgate Dr. #350 Portland, OR 97221 (503) 297-7730

*ROSE CITY TALENT—239 N.W. 13TH Ave. #215 Portland, OR 97209 (503) 274-1005

RYAN ARTISTS—239 N.W. 13th Ave. #215 Portland, OR 97209 (503) 228-5648

SPORTS UNLIMITED INC—1991 N.W. Upshur St. Portland, OR 97209 (503) 227-3449

PENNSYLVANIA

*ASKINS MODELS, DENISE—55 N. Third St. Philadelphia, PA 19106 (215) 925-7795

BOWMAN AGENCY—1040 Woodridge Blvd. Lancaster, PA 17601 (717) 898-7716

*CLARO AGENCY INC., THE—1513 W. Passyunk Ave. Philadelphia, PA 19145 (215) 465-7788

*DOCHERTY INC—109 Market St. Pittsburgh, PA 15222 (412) 765-1400

*EXPRESSIONS MODELING & TALENT AGENCY INC—110 Church St. Philadelphia, PA 19106 (215) 923-4420

*GREER LANGE ASSOC—40 Lloyd Ave., #104 Malvern, PA 99355 (610) 647-5515

*MCCULLOUGH ASSOC—8 S. Hanover Ave Atlantic City, NJ 08402-2615 (609) 822-2222

*MODELS ON THE MOVE—1200 Route 70 #6 Barclay Towers, P.O. Box 4037, Cherry Hills, NJ 08034 (609) 667-1060

*PLAZA 7—160 N. Gulph Rd. King of Prussia, PA 19406 (610) 337-2693

*PRO MODEL—1107 Union Blvd, Allentown, PA 18103 (610) 820-5359

*REINHARD AGENCY—2021 Arch St. #404 Philadelphia, PA 19103 (215) 567-2008
*THE TALENT GROUP—2820 Smallman St. Pittsburgh, PA 15222 (412) 471-8011

RHODE ISLAND

DONAHUE MODELS—14 Rome Ave. Providence, RI 02904 (401) 353-4950
EXPOSURE AGENCY & STUDIO—43 Arnold Ave. Providence, RI 02905 (401) 941-6611
JOHN CASABLANCAS MODEL MGMT—1 Lambert Lind Hwy. Warwick, RI 02886 (401) 463-5866
MODEL CLUB—355 S. Water St. Providence, RI 02903 (401) 273-7120

SOUTH CAROLINA

COLLINS MODELS-STUDIO & AGENCY—1441 Greenhill Rd. Columbia, SC 29206 (803) 216-0550
MILLIE LEWIS—1228 S. Pleasantburg Dr. Greenville, SC 29605 (864) 299-1101
MILLIE LEWIS OF COLUMBIA INC—3612 Landmark Dr. Columbia, SC 29204 (803) 782-7338
MODEL'S IN MOTION—Oak Grove Rd. Spartanburg, SC 29301 (864) 574-1783

SOUTH DAKOTA

J K'S CONNECTION—24050 Highway #385 Custer, SD 57730 (605) 574-9555
PROFESSIONAL IMAGE BY ROSEMARY—2815 E. 26TH Street Sioux Falls, SD 57103 (605) 334-0619

TENNESSEE

18 KARAT TALENT & MODELING—6409 Deane Hill Dr. Knoxville, TN 37919 (865) 558-0004
ADVANTAGE MODELS & TALENT—4825 Trousdale Dr #230 Nashville, TN 37220 (615) 833-3005
AMAX—4121 Hillsboro Rd. Nashville, TN 37215 (615) 292-0246
COLORS TALENT AGENCY—269 S. Front St. Memphis, TN 38103 (901) 523-9900

DONNA GROFF AGENCY INC—P.O. Box 382517 Germantown, TN 38183 (901) 854-5561

FLAIR MODELS—672 Lake Terrace Dr. Nashville, TN 37217 (615) 361-3737

HARPER AGENCY—4004 Hillsboro Rd. Nashville, TN 37215 (615) 383-1455

JO-SUSAN—2817 W. End Ave. Nashville, TN 37203 (615) 327-8726

MITCH KARAM MODEL & TALENT—1807-1/2 21st Ave. S. Nashville, TN 37212 (615) 383-4016

RASNIC MODELING INC—2400 Merchants Dr. Knoxville, TN 37912 (865) 525-7011

ROBBINS MODELS & TALENT—176 S. Walnut Bend Rd. Cordova, TN 38018 (901) 753-8360

*TALENT & MODEL LAND INC—P.O. Box 40763 Nashville, TN 37204 (615) 321-5596

TALENT TREK AGENCY—406 Eleventh St. Knoxville, TN 37916 (865) 977-8735

*TALENT TREK AGENCY—1701 W. End Ave. Nashville, TN 37203 (615) 244-6411

*TALENT TREK*NASHVILLE—2021 21st Ave. S. #102 Nashville, TN 37212 (615) 279-0010

TEXAS

*ACCLAIM PARTNERS—4107 Medical Pkwy #210 Austin, TX 78756 (512) 323-5566

*ACTORS ETC. INC—2620 Fountainview #210 Houston, TX 77057, (713) 785-4495

ALINA MODEL AND TALENT MGMT—2600 S. Loop W. #300D Houston, TX 77054 (713) 218-7255 e-mail alinatalentAusa.com, website: http://www.alinatalent.entrepreneur.com

ALL AMERICAN BLONDES—Dallas, TX 75243 (214) 521-5852

AVANT MODELS & CASTING—85 N.E. Loop 410 #218A San Antonio, TX 78216 (210) 308-8411

BOMBSHELL BLONDES—1200 E. Davis St. Mesquite, TX 75150 (214) 720-1333

CHERIE EATON LTD—704 University Village Dr. Richardson, TX 75081 (972) 644-5744

CHERIE EATON LIMITED—P.O. Box 18160, Dallas TX 75081 (972) 644-5744

CONDRA/ARISTA MODELING AGENCY—1330 Old Blanco Rd., #201 San Antonio, TX 78216 (210) 492-9947

DALLAS MODEL GROUP—12700 Hillcrest Rd. #147, Dallas, TX 75230 (972) 980-7647

***DAWSON AGENCY INC., KIM**—2710 N. Stemmons Fwy. #700, Tower North, Dallas, TX 75207-2208 (214) 630-5161

EBONY'S QUEEN'S—9625 Webb Chapel Rd. Dallas, TX 75220 (214) 686-5483

ENTOURAGE MODEL & TALENT—6800 Park Ten Blvd. San Antonio, TX 78213 (210) 733-5007

EVERETT ASBURY AGENCY—P.O. Box 21865, Waco TX 76702, (817) 751-9570

FIRST MODELS & TALENT AGENCY—5433 Westheimer Rd. #305 Houston, TX 77056 (713) 850-9611

HOLLYWOOD STUDIOS—4130 La Luz Ave. El Paso, TX 79903 (915) 566-6060

***INTERMEDIA AGENCY**—5353 W. Alabama #222 Houston, TX 77056 (713) 622-8282

JOHN ROBERT POWERS MODELING—6320 Camp Bowie Blvd., Ft. Worth, TX 76116 (817) 738-2021

K HALL MODELS & TALENT—700 Rio Grande St. Austin, TX 78701 (512) 476-7523

K D STUDIO—2600 N. Stemmons Fwy #117 Dallas, TX 75207 (214) 638-0484

LA MADEMOISELLE'S MODELING—10651 Harry Hines Blvd. Dallas, TX 75220 (214) 351-9542

MAD HATTER MODEL & TALENT AGENCY 2620 Fountain View Dr. #212 Houston, TX 77057 (713) 266-5800

MARGO MANNING CASTING & ACTING—6360 Lyndon B Johnson Fwy Dallas, TX 75240 (972) 239-2882

MODELS WEST 3405 S. Western St. #201 Amarillo, TX 79109 (806) 352-1943

***NEAL HAMIL AGENCY**—7887 San Felipe St. #227 Houston, TX 77063 (713) 789-1335

P S IMAGES—1105 Pueblo Midland, TX 79705 (915) 683-0844

PAGE PARKES MODELS REP—3303 Lee Pkwy Dallas, TX 75219 (214) 526-4434

***PASTORINI-BOSBY TALENT AGENCY**—3013 Fountain View Dr. #240 Houston, TX 77057 (713) 266-4488

PREMIERE PROMOTIONS—5902 Irvington Blvd. Houston, TX 77009, (713) 699-9858, website: www/premierepromotions.cc

REFLECTIONS INC TALENT—3817 S. Alameda St. Corpus Christi, TX 78411 (512) 857-5414

SELECT MODELING & TALENT—3405 S. Western St. Amarillo, TX 79109 (806) 352-1173

TALENT HOUSE—812 N. Virginia St. #204 El Paso, TX 79902 (915) 533-1945

*TAYLOR TALENT INC., PEGGY—1825 Market Ctr. Blvd. #320 LB37 Dallas, TX 75207 (214) 651-7884

*THE THOMAS AGENCY—14275 Midway Rd. #220 Dallas, TX 75244 (972) 687-9181

*YOUNG AGENCY, SHERRY—2620 Fountainview #212 Houston, TX 77057 (713) 266-5800

UTAH

COLLETTE'S DISTINCTIVE MDLNG—1033 Revere Circle Holladay, UT 84117 (801) 262-2462 (5+)

KLC NEW FACES—56 E. Broadway Salt Lake City, UT 84111 (801) 322-3648

VERMONT

DEBRA LEWIN PRODUCTIONS & TLNT—269 Pearl St. Burlington, VT 05401 (802) 865-2234

VIRGINIA

ASHGROVE PLANTATION—1960 Horse Shoe Dr. Vienna, VA 22182 (703) 556-9233

BARONE & COMPANY—5599 Seminary Rd. Falls Church, CA 22041 (703) 768-2231

ENCORE MODEL & TALENT AGENCY—826 Rivergate Pl. Alexandria, VA 22314 (703) 548-0900

EVIE MANSFIELD MODELING AGENCY—505 S. Independence Blvd. #205 Virginia Beach, VA 23452 (757) 490-5990

GLAMOUR MODELING & TALENT LIMITED—1115 Independence Blvd. #110 Virginia Beach, VA 23455 (757) 363-8844

KING'S ENTERTAINMENT—3424 Brambleton Ave. Roanoke, VA 24018 (540) 989-5464

MODEL CONNECTION—11140 Pennway Dr. Richmond, VA 23236 (804) 794-8598

MODEL MANAGEMENT—249 S. Van Dorn St. Alexandria, VA 22304 (703) 823-5203

MODELOGIC—2501 E. Broad St. Richmond, VA 23223 (804) 644-1000
NEW FACES MODELS—8230 Leesburg Pike #520 Vienna, VA 22182 (703) 821-0786
ON-CALL MODELS—946 Ferryman Quay Chesapeake, VA 23323 (757) 485-1201
SATCHI AGENCY—8201 Greensboro Dr. #214 Mc Lean, VA 22102 (703) 356-3580
STEINHART-NORTON TALENT MANAGEMENT—312 Arctic Crescent Virginia Beach, VA 23451 (757) 422-9535
STUDIOS LIMITED MODEL-TALENT NET—118 Campbell Ave. S.E. Roanoke, VA 24011 (540) 345-6300
WRIGHT MODELING AGENCY—12638 Jefferson Ave. #16 Newport News, VA 23602 (757) 886-5884 (5+)

WASHINGTON

BOOL MODELS—1700 Westlake Ave. N. Seattle WA (206) 286-8888
CLASSIC PROMOTIONS INC/AFTRA—1500 Eastlake Ave. E. #2000 Seattle, WA 98102 (206) 720-1110
*COLLEEN BELL MODELING & TALENT AGENCY—14205 S.E. 36th St. #100 Bellevue, WA 98006 (425) 649-1111
*DRAMATIC ARTISTS AGENCY—1000 Lenora St. #511 Seattle, WA 98121 (206) 442-9190
EMERALD CITY MODEL & TALENT—1980 Harvard Ave. E. Seattle, WA 98102 (206) 329-7768
*HEFFNER MANAGEMENT—1601 5th Ave. #2301 Seattle, WA 98101 (206) 622-2211
JEWEL IMAGES MODEL & TALENT—6145 Maureen Dr, Ferndale, WA 98248 (360) 380-6728 e-mail jewelcorp@aol.com
KID BIZ TALENT AGENCY—One Bellevue Center 411 108th Ave. N.E. #2050 Bellevue, WA 98004 (425) 455-8800
KIM BROOKE GROUP—2044 Eastlake Ave. E. Seattle, WA 98102 (206) 329-1111
NORTHWEST FASHION INSTITUTE—19009 33rd Ave. W. #100 Lynwood, WA (425) 775-8385
PERSISTENT IMAGE—P.O. Box 1284 Renton, WA 98057 (425) 271-9123
*SEATTLE MODELS GUILD—1809 7th Ave. #303 Seattle, WA 98101 (206) 622-1406
TCM INC—2200 6th Ave. #100 Seattle, WA 98121 (206) 728-4826
TCM MODELS—3311 W. Clearwater Ave. Kennewick, WA 99336 (509) 783-5868

TEAM MODELS—3431 96th Ave. N.E. Clyde Hill, WA 9800 (425) 455-2969
THE WARD AGENCY—Edmonds, WA (425) 787-1982

WEST VIRGINIA

REFER to your local phone book, yellow pages

WISCONSIN

AGENCE CHRISTIE—5524 N. 12th St. Milwaukee, WI 53209 (888) 579-5392 e-mail Director@AgenceChristie.com, website: www.AgenceChristie.com
GERED MODELS INTERNATIONAL LIMITED—2702 Monroe St. Madison, WI 53711 (608) 238-6372
JENNIFER'S TALENT UNLIMITED—740 N. Plankinton Ave. Milwaukee, WI 53203 (414) 277-9440
*LINS LTD LORI—7611 W. Holmes Greenfield, WI 53220 (414) 282-3500

WYOMING

REFER to your local phone book, yellow pages

WASHINGTON D.C.

ANNE SCHWAB'S MODEL STORE—906 D St. N.E. Washington, DC 20002 (202) 333-3560
ARTIST AGENCY—3333 K Street N.W. #50 Washington, DC 20007 (202) 342-0933
CENTRAL CASTING INC—623 Pennsylvania Avenue S.E. Washington, DC 20003 (202) 547-6300

5

BABY & CHILD MODELING AGENCIES

"Everybody says my baby is beautiful and that she should be in magazines." "My two year old mimics characters on the television; everyone says he should be on TV." "My daughter has won numerous beauty pageants and loves being on stage. Everybody says I should get her into modeling."

If you've thought about the modeling industry then you've probably asked yourself some of the following questions:

How and where do I get started?

How much money can my baby or toddler make?

Do I have to spend a lot of money on their cloths?

Do I pay an agency or school for training?

The first step is evaluating your child. They don't need to be blond or beautiful. They do need to be photogenic, outgoing and a good listener. For babies, good temperaments, along with a great smile are a must.

You don't need to buy expensive clothes or spend a lot of money on photographs, although some photographers and bogus talent scouts make a great living convincing you that you do. (Read Chapter Nine, Modeling Scams & Pitfalls.)

Modeling agencies for children of all ages are listed in this chapter, first by state, then by agency. Some of the agencies only accept older children. These are separately marked to the right of the agency's phone number.

For example: If you see: 6+ then that means that the agency does not take children under the age of six.

The most important question you need to ask yourself before jumping into modeling is: Do I have a lot of free time and am I willing to travel on a moment's notice?

The thrill and excitement of seeing your baby or child on the cover of a magazine tends to block the reality of the commitment and responsibility that comes with the profession.

You will have to travel to numerous interviews on a moment's notice and, if your child is not selected for the job, he or she does not get paid.

You must also be able to keep a positive outlook at all times. You don't want your toddler to feel he or she has failed you just because they didn't get picked for a job.

If you have the time and you can make this kind of a commitment then you're ready for the next step, finding an agent.

Children modeling agencies receive hundreds of phone calls every week from excited, eager parents.

Agencies in Los Angeles, New York, and Miami are the biggest and the busiest.

To find a modeling agency for your toddler, first look up your state in this chapter, and then look for the agencies that are close to your hometown. If there aren't any agencies listed for your general area, then go to your local phone book and look under "Modeling Agencies."

Call each and every agency in your general vicinity and ask them if they are interested in your baby or toddler. Most if not all of the modeling agencies will be interested but will need to see pictures of your child before they will make a commitment.

Immediately send them current color pictures of your little one as follows:

A head shot, which is a close-up of your child's face (without make-up.)

A body shot, which is a picture of your toddler from head to toes.

A posed shot, which is a picture of your little one with that special grin,

or with that perfect smile that only your baby or toddler has.

Don't cover your child's head with hats or clutter their bodies with a cute costume or stuffed animal. The agencies want to see what your little one "really" looks like.

Don't run to a photographer or portrait studio. The pictures should be current (no older than 30 days) because at these ages kids are constantly changing. Small 3"x 5" pictures are fine.

Put your name, phone number and your toddler's name and age on the back of each picture.

If your child is under the age of three, list your toddler's or baby's age by how many months old he or she is. For example: 18 months not 1-1/2 years old.

Send the pictures out to each and every agency that requested them.

Sending large 8"x10" pictures gets expensive and doesn't guarantee your toddler will get work. Keep the pictures small; this will save you money on both the cost of the pictures and on postage.

It's not wise to send out pictures to agencies that are over a hundred miles away from your hometown, because you will have to drive back and forth a lot to the agency, sometimes more than once a week. The jobs that your baby or toddler gets are usually in your agent's city, not yours. Keeping a toddler confined in a car two to six hours a day can be very stressful for both of you, so be realistic about what agencies you send your child's pictures to.

When an agency calls you they will want to meet and talk to your child. A lot of agencies see new clients at a specific day or time of the month. Make your appointment as soon as possible. Don't put it off for two to three weeks. If you don't show up for the appointment (or call and change it) you've already lost that agency.

You may have the most talented, good-looking child in North America, but if you're not reliable, the modeling industry wants nothing to do with you.

When you go to the interview, relax. Remember, this is supposed to be a fun experience. If you're calm your toddler will be calm. Usually the agency will ask you to sign a nonexclusive contract for one year.

Congratulations! You now have your foot in the door. To keep the door open you need to follow your agency's request, which is usually sending them new current snapshots of your child, every thirty to sixty days.

Each and every interview you share with your child should be approached as an enjoyable, new experience.

The more interviews you go on, the more confident your toddler will become.

A special lunch or a stop at the park together after each interview is a wonderful way to reward your child, whether they got the job or not.

BABY & CHILDREN AGENCIES

ALABAMA

ACT PRODUCTIONS MODELS—Hueytown, AL 35023 (205) 491-3205

BAREFOOT MODELS & TALENT—4317 Downtowner Loop North Mobile, AL 36609 (334) 344-5554

CATHI LARSEN AGENCY—1675 Montclair Road #136 Birmingham, AL 35210 (205) 951-2445

ELAN MODELS INC—1446 Montgomery Highway Vestavia Hills, AL 35216 (205) 823-9180 (11+)

GRAY-CHILD MODELS AND TALENT—P.O. Box 1857 Daphne, AL 36526-1857 (334) 626-8933 e-mail: Kgraychild@aol.com, Website: http://www.graychildmodels.com and http://www.casting-america.com

KIDDIN' AROUND MODELS & TALENT—714–32nd St. South Birmingham, AL 35233 (205) 323-5437

RARE QUALITY MODELS & TALENT—P.O. Box 1545 Dothan, AL 36302, (334) 671-2200 e-mail: Website: http://www.snowhill.com/-donnalyn/ (6+)

ALASKA

ALASKA IMAGE DESIGN—600 West 41st Ave. #102 Anchorage, AK 99501 (907) 561-5739 e-mail: akimage@gci.net, Website: http://www.alaskaoutdoors.com/Image/index.htm

ALASKA MODELS & TALENT—600 W 41st Ave. #102 Anchorage, AK 99503 (907) 561-5739

ARIZONA

*ACTION TALENT**—2720 E. Broadway Blvd. Tucson, AZ 85716 (520) 881-6535

*DANI'S AGENCY**—1 E. Camelback Rd. #550 Phoenix, AZ 85012 (602) 263-1918

ELIZABETH SAVAGE TALENT AGENCY—4949 E. Lincoln Dr. Scottsdale, AZ 85253 (602) 840-3530

*FORD/BLACK AGENCY, ROBERT**—4300 N. Miller Rd. #202 Scottsdale, AZ, 85251 (480) 966-2537

*FOSI'S TALENT AGENCY—2777 N. Campbell Ave. Tucson, AZ 85016 (520) 795-3534

*LEIGHTON AGENCY INC—2231 E. Camelback Rd. #319 Phoenix, AZ 85016 (602) 224-9255

*SIGNATURE MODELS & TALENT AGENCY—2600 N. 44th St. #209 Phoenix, AZ 85008 (602) 966-1102

ARKANSAS

AGENCY INC—910 W. 6th St. Little Rock, AR 72201 (501) 374-6447

JOHN CASABLANCAS MTM AGENCY—416 W. Meadows Fayetteville, AR 72701 (501) 444-7972

MODELS, INC./AARON-WINDSOR—660 Lollar Lane Fayetteville, AR 72701 (501) 973-9700

TERRY LONG MODELS—P.O. Box 7353 Little Rock, AR 72217 (501) 221-2202

CALIFORNIA

*A TOTAL ACTING EXPERIENCE—20501 Ventura Blvd. #399 Woodland Hills, CA 91364

*ABRAMS ARTISTS AGENCY—9200 Sunset Blvd., #1130 Los Angeles, CA 90069 (310) 859-0625

*ACME TALENT & LITERARY—6310 San Vicente Blvd., #520 Los Angeles, CA 90048 (323) 954-2263

*AKA TALENT AGENCY—6310 San Vicente Blvd. Los Angeles, CA 90048

ALESE MARSHALL MODEL—22730 Hawthorne Blvd. #201 Torrance, CA 90505 (310) 378-1223

*ALICE FRIES AGENCY—1927 Vista Del Mar Ave. Los Angeles, CA 90068 (323) 464-1404

*ANGEL CITY TALENT—1680 Vine St. #716 Hollywood, CA 90028

*ARTIST MANAGEMENT AGENCY INC—835 5th Ave. #411 San Diego, CA 92101 (619) 235-6655

*ARTISTS GROUP, LTD.—10100 Santa Monica Blvd., #2490 Los Angeles, CA 90067 (310) 552-1100

*BALDWIN TALENT, INC.—8055 W. Manchester Ave. Playa del Rey, CA 90292 (310) 827-2422

*BALL TALENT AGENCY, BOBBY—4342 Lankershim Blvd. Universal City, CA 91602 (818) 506-8188

*BENNETT AGENCY, SARA—6404 Hollywood Blvd. #316 Los Angeles, CA 90028 (323) 965-9666

*BERZON AGENCY, MARIAN—336 e 17TH St. Costa Mesa, CA 92627

BEVERLY HILLS MODEL & TALENT—9107 Wilshire Blvd. #500 Beverly Hills, CA 90210 (310) 276-3505

*BONNIE BLACK TALENT AGENCY—5318 Wilkinson #A Valley Village, CA 91607 (818) 753-5424

*BOOM MODELS & TALENT AGCY—2325 Third St. #223 San Francisco, CA 94107 (415) 626-6591

*BRAND MODEL & TALENT AGENCY—1520 Brookhollow Dr., #39 Santa Ana, CA 92705 (714) 850-1158

*BUCHWALD TALENT GROUP, INC., A Youth Agency—Commercial Department, 6300 Wilshire Blvd. #910, Los Angeles, CA 90048 (323) 852-9555

*BURTON AGENCY, INC., IRIS—1450 Belfast Dr. Los Angeles, CA 90069 (310) 288-0121

C R TALENT AGENCY—PO Box 1951 Palm Springs, CA 92263 (760) 327-7777

*CAMERON & ASSOC., INC., BARBARA—8369 Sausalito Ave. #A West Hills, CA 91304 (818) 888-6107

*CASTLE HILL ENTERPRISES—1101 S. Orlando Ave. Los Angeles, CA 90035 (323) 653-3535

CHIC MODELING—236 Quincy Ave. Long Beach, CA 90803 (562) 438-5088

CINDY OSBRINK PRINT KIDS—4605 Lankershim Blvd. North Hollywood, CA 91602 (818) 760-2803

*CLARK CO., W. RANDOLPH—13415 Ventura Blvd. #3 Sherman Oaks, CA 91423 (818) 385-0583

*CLER TALENT AGENCY, COLEEN—178 S. Victory Blvd. #108 Burbank, CA 91502 (818) 841-7943

*CNA & ASSOCIATES—1925 Century Park East, #750 Los Angeles, CA 90067 (310) 556-4343

*COAST TO COAST TALENT GROUP, INC.—3350 Barham Blvd. N. Hollywood, CA 90068 (323) 845-9200

COLLEEN CLER MODELING INSTITUTE—120 South Victory Blvd. Burbank, CA 91502 (818) 841-7943

*COLOURS MODEL & TALENT MGMT.—8344 ½ W. 3rd St. Los Angeles, CA 90048 (213) 658-7072

*COMMERCIALS UNLIMITED—8383 Wilshire Blvd., #850 Beverly Hills, CA 90211 (323) 655-0069

*CONTEMPORARY ARTISTS, LTD.—1317 5th St., #200 Santa Monica, CA 90401-2210 (310) 395-1800

*COSDEN ENT., LTD., ROBERT—3518 Cahuenga Blvd. #200 Los Angeles, CA 90068 (213) 874-7200

*CUNNINGHAM, ESCOTT, DIPENE & ASSOC., INC.—10635 Santa Monica Blvd. #130 Los Angeles, CA 90025 (310) 475-2111

*D.H. TALENT—1800 N. Highland #300 Los Angeles, CA 90028 (323) 962-6643

*DADE-SCHULTZ ASSOC.—23905 Plaza Gavilan, Valencia, CA 91355 (818) 760-3100

*DALE GARRICK INTERNATIONAL—8831 Sunset Blvd. #402 Los Angeles, CA 90069 (310) 657-2661

*DAVID & DAVID AGENCY, INC., 7461 Beverly Blvd., #402 Los Angeles, CA 90036 (323) 634-7777

*DIVERSE TALENT GROUP—1875 Century Park East #2250 Los Angeles, CA 90067 (310) 201-6565

*DON BUCHWALD & ASSOC., INC. PACIFIC—6500 Wilshire Blvd. 22nd Floor Los Angeles, CA 90048 (323) 655-7400

EQUINOX—8961 W. Sunset Blvd. Penthouse, Los Angeles, CA 90069 (310) 274-5088

*EDWARDS & ASSOCIATES LLC—5455 Wilshire Blvd. #1614 Los Angeles, CA 90036 (323) 964-0000

*EPSTEIN—WYCKOFF—CORSA—ROSS & ASSOCIATES 280 S. Beverly Dr. #400 Beverly Hills, CA 90212 (310) 278-7222

*FILM ARTISTS ASSOC.—13563 Ventura Blvd., 2nd Fl. Sherman Oaks, CA 91423 (818) 386-9669

*FONTAINE AGENCY, JUDITH, 205 South Beverly Dr. #212 Beverly Hills, CA 90212 (310) 471-8631

FORD MODELS INC—8826 Burton Way Beverly Hills, CA 90211 (310) 276-8100

*GENERATIONS MODEL & TALENT**—340 Brannan St. #302 San Francisco, CA 94107 (415) 777-9099

*GOLD, MARSHAK, LIEDTKE & ASSOC.**—3500 W. Olive #1400 Burbank, CA 91505 (818) 972-4300

*GRADY AGENCY, MARY**—348 East Olive Ave., #E Burbank, CA 91502 (818) 567-1400

*GRANT, SAVIC, KOPALOFF & ASSOCIATES**—6399 Wilshire Blvd. # 414 Los Angeles, CA 90048 (323) 782-1854

*GWYN FOXX TALENT AGENCY**—1342 E. Tujunga Ave. Burbank, CA 91501 (818) 848-0918

HALVORSON MODEL MANAGEMENT—2858 Stevens Creek Blvd. San Jose, CA 95128 (408) 983-1038

*HERVEY-GRIMES TALENT AGENCY, INC.**—10561 Missouri #1 Los Angeles, CA 90025

*HOLLANDER TALENT GROUP**—3518 Cahuenga Blvd., #316 Los Angeles, CA 9006, (323) 845-4160

*HOWARD TALENT WEST**—11374 Ventura Blvd., Studio City CA 91604 (818) 766-5300

*INNOVATIVE ARTISTS YOUNG TALENT DIVISION**—3000 Olympic Blvd. Bldg. 4 # 1200 Santa Monica, CA 90404 (310) 553-5200

*JANA LUKER AGENCY**—1933-1/2 Westwood Blvd. #3 Los Angeles, CA 90025 (310) 441-2822

*KAZARIAN-SPENCER & ASSOC., INC.**—11365 Ventura Blvd. #100 Studio City, CA 91604 (818) 769-9111

*KJAR AGENCY, TYLER**—5116 Lankershim Blvd, N. Hollywood, CA 91601 (818) 760-0321

*LA TALENT, INC.**—7700 W. Sunset Blvd. Los Angeles, CA 90046 (323) 656-3722

*LANE AGENCY, STACEY**—13455 Ventura Blvd. #240 Sherman Oaks, CA 91423 (818) 501-2668

*LEVIN TALENT AGCY., SID**—8484 Wilshire Blvd. #750 Beverly Hills, CA 90211 (323) 653-7073

*LOOK MODEL AGENCY**—166 Geary St. #1400 San Francisco, CA 94108 (415) 781-2822

LOS LATINOS TALENT AGENCY—2801 Moorpark Ave. #11 San Jose, CA 95128 (408) 296-2213

*LYNNE & REILLY AGENCY—10725 Vanowen St. #113 N. Hollywood, CA 91605-6402 (213) 755-6434

MAC MODELING—9454 Wilshire Blvd #720 Beverly Hills, CA 90212, (310) 273-2566 (3+)

*MARLA DELL TALENT—2124 Union St. San Francisco, CA 94123 (415) 563-9213

*MARSHALL MODEL & TALENT., ALESE—22730 Hawthorne Blvd. #201 Torrance, CA 90505 (310) 378-1223

*MEDIA ARTISTS GROUP—8383 Wilshire Blvd., #954 Beverly Hills, CA 90211 (323) 658-5050

*MODELS GUILD OF CALIFORNIA—8489 W. 3rd Street Los Angeles, CA 90048 (323) 782-0393

MODELS GUILD OF CALIFORNIA TALENT AGENCY—8489 W. 3rd St. #1107, Los Angeles, CA 90048 (323) 801-2132

*NATHE & ASSOC., SUSAN (CPC)—8281 Melrose, #200 Los Angeles, CA 90046 (323) 653-7573

*OSBRINK TALENT AGENCY, CINDY—4343 Lankershim Blvd. #100 Universal City, CA 91602 (818) 760—2488

PANACHE MODELS INTERNATIONAL—520 W. Santa Ana Blvd. Santa Ana, CA 92701 (714) 541-6091

*PANDA TALENT AGENCY—3721 Hoen Ave. Santa Rosa, CA 95405 (707) 576-0711

*PARADIGM, A TALENT & LITERARY AGENCY—10100 Santa Monica Blvd. #2500 Los Angeles, CA 90067 (310) 277-4400

PASCUCCI PRODUCTION INC—26 Ofarrell St. #600 San Francisco, CA 94108 (415) 248-3900

*PREMIERE ARTISTS AGENCY, INC.—1875 Century Park E. #2250 Los Angeles, CA 90067 (310) 271-1414

*SAN DIEGO MODEL MANAGEMENT—438 Camino Del Rio S. #116 San Diego, CA 92108 (619) 296-1018

*SANDERS AGENCY—8831 Sunset Blvd. #304 Los Angeles, CA 90069 (310) 652-1119

*SAVAGE AGENCY, INC.—6212 Banner Ave. Los Angeles, CA 90038 (213) 461-8316

*SCHIOWITZ/CLAY/ROSE, INC.—1680 N. Vine #614 Los Angeles, CA 90028 (323) 463-7300

*SHAPIRA & ASSOC., INC., DAVID—15821 Ventura Blvd. #235 Encino, CA 91436 (818) 906-0322

*SHUMAKER AGENCY—6533 Hollywood Blvd. #401 Hollywood, CA 90028 (323) 464-0745

STARS THE AGENCY—777 Davis St. San Francisco, CA 94111 (415) 421-6272

*STARS-THE AGENCY (SF)—23 Grant Ave. 4th Fl. San Francisco, CA 94108 (415) 421-6272

*STONE MANNERS—8436 W. 3rd St., #740, Los Angeles, CA 90048 (323) 655-1313

SUSAN LANE MODEL & TALENT AGENCY—14071 Windsor Pl. Santa Ana, CA 92705 (714) 731-7827

TALENT ENTERTAINTMENT NETWORK—8833 W. Sunset Blvd #406 West Hollywood, CA 90069 (312) 659-4855

*TALENT GROUP, INC., 6300 Wilshire Blvd. #900 Los Angeles, CA 90048 (323) 852-9559

*TALENT PLUS AGENCY/LOS LATINOS (Hispanic Division)—Dyer Building, 2801 Moorpark Ave. #11 San Jose, CA 95128 (408) 296-2213

TANNEN & ASSOC., HERB—10801 National Blvd. #101 Los Angeles, CA 90064 (310) 466-5822

*THE AGENCY—1800 Avenue of the Stars #40, Los Angeles, CA 90067 (310) 551-3000

*THE SUN AGENCY—8961 Sunset Blvd. # D Los Angeles, CA 90069 (310) 888-8737

*THE ORANGE GROVE GROUP, INC.—12178 Ventura Blvd. #205 Studio City, CA 91604 (818) 762-7498

*TONRY TALENT—885 Bryant Street, # 201 San Francisco, CA 94103 (415) 543-3797

*TOP MODELS & TALENT AGENCY—The Flood Building 870 Market St. #1076 San Francisco, CA 94102

*WAUGH AGENCY, ANN—4741 Laurel Canyon Blvd. #200 North Hollywood, CA 91607

WILHELMINA MODELS INC—8383 Wilshire Blvd. #650 Beverly Hills, CA 90211 (323) 655-0909

*WILSON & ASSOC., SHIRLEY—5410 Wilshire Blvd. #806 Los Angeles, CA 90036 (323) 857-6977

*WRITERS & ARTISTS AGENCY—8383 Wilshire Blvd. #550 Los Angeles, CA 90211 (323) 866-0900

COLORADO

APPLAUSE MODEL MANAGEMENT—2171 S. Trenton Way #208 Denver, CO 80231 (303) 743-0616 (13+)

ASPIRE MODEL & TALENT, INC.—126 West 5th Ave. Denver, CO 80204 (303) 733-3888; e-mail: aspire@aspireagency.com Website: http://aspireagency.com (13+)

*BARBIZON TALENT AGENCY—7535 E. Hampton Ave. #108 Denver, CO 80231

*DONNA BALDWIN TALENT INC.—Historic Wheeler Block Bldg., 2150 W. 29th Ave., #200 Denver, CO 80211 (303) 561-1199

JOHN CASABLANCAS MODELING CENTER—7600 e. Eastman Ave. Denver, CO 80231, (303) 337-5100 (10+)

JOHN ROBERT POWERS MODELING—14231 E. 4th Ave. #200 Aurora, CO 80011, (303) 340-2838

KIDSKITS INC.—136 Kalamuth St. Denver, CO 80223, (303) 446-8200 e-mail: info@kiddskitsinc.com, website: www.kidskitsinc.com

MARBLES KIDS MANAGEMENT INC.—240 Josephine St #205 Denver, CO 80206 (303) 322-5004

MAXIMUM TALENT INC.—1720 S. Bellaire St #907 Denver, CO 80222 (303) 691-2344

MODEL & TALENT MANAGEMENT—7600 E. Eastman Ave. Denver, CO 80231 (303) 337-4541 (8+)

SILHOUETTES MODELING & ACTING—3980 Broadway St. Boulder, CO 80304 (303) 449-7765

UNIQUE MODELING AGENCY—P.O. Box 47164 Denver, CO 80201 (303) 821-2957

VECTRA SEARCH—2850 W. Serendipity Circle #201 Colorado Springs, CO 80917 (719) 597-3883

VIA ENTERTAINMENT—320 N. Academy Blvd. #302 Colorado Springs, CO 80909 (719) 597-3883 (5+)

CONNECTICUT

JOHN CASABLANCAS MODELING CTR.—461 Farmington Ave. Hartford, CT 06105 (860) 232-4421 (5+)

JOHNSTON MODELING AGENCY—50 Washington St. Norwalk, CT 06854 (203) 838-6188

DELAWARE

REFER to your local phone book, yellow pages

FLORIDA

ALEXA MODEL & TALENT MANAGEMENT AGENCY—4100 W. Kennedy Blvd. #228 Tampa, FL 33609 (813) 289-8020

ANDERSON GREENE ENTERTAINMENT—1210 Washington Ave. Miami Beach, FL 33139 (305) 675-9881

AVENUE PRODUCTIONS INC—2810 E. Oakland Park Blvd. #308 Ft. Lauderdale, FL 33306 (954) 561-1226

*AZUREE TALENT AGENCY—140 N. Orlando Ave. #120 Winter Park, FL 32789 (407) 629-5025

BARONS MODEL TEAM—7365 Southwest 8th St. Miami, FL 33144 (305) 264-1550

BELLA MODEL & TALENT MANAGEMENT—1553 San Marco Blvd. Jacksonville, FL 32207 (904) 298-9811

*BERG TALENT AGENCY—3825 Henderson Blvd, Tampa, FL 33629 (813) 877-5533 (3+)

*BOCA TALENT & MODEL AGENCY—829 Southeast 9th St. Palm Plaza #4 Deerfield Beach, FL 33441 (305) 428-4677

BOOM MODEL & TALENT AGENCY—13012 N. Dale Mabry Hwy. Tampa, FL 33618 (813) 264-1373

BOOM MODELS—126 3rd Ave. N. Safety Harbor, FL 34695 (727) 265-2204

BOSS MODELS INC—539 Euclid Ave. Miami Beach, FL 33139 (305) 531-4244

BREVARD TALENT GROUP—405 Palm Springs Blvd. Indian Harbor Beach, FL 32937 (407) 773-1355

CENTRAL FLORIDA CASTING, INC—2601 Wells Ave. #181 Fern Park, FL 32730 (407) 830-9226

CLICK MODELS MIAMI—1688 Meridian Ave. Miami Beach, FL 33139 (305) 674-9900

DENISE CAROL MODELING STUDIO—2223 Atlantic Blvd. Jacksonville, FL 32207 (904) 399-0824

*DIMENSIONS III MODELING & TLNT—5205 S. Orange Ave. Orlando, FL 32809 (407) 851-2575

FLORIDA STARS MODEL & TALENT—225 W. University Ave. #A Gainesville, FL 32601 (322) 338-1086 website: http/www.afloridastar.com

*GREEN & GREEN MODEL & TALENT AGCY.—1688 Meridian Ave. #1000 Miami Beach, FL 33139 (305) 532-9880

*HALEY TALENT, SUSAN—618 Wymore Rd. #2 Winter Park, FL 32789-2862 (407) 644-0600

*HURT-GARVER TALENT & MODELS—400 N. New York Ave. Winter Park, FL 32789 (407) 740-5700

JOBS & MODELS UNLIMITED—337 8TH Street Daytona Beach, FL 32117 (386) 253-6730

LAS OLAS MODELS & TALENT—1119 E. Las Olas Blvd. Ft. Lauderdale, FL 33301 (954) 763-3869

*MARIE INC., IRENE—728 Ocean Dr. Miami Beach, FL 33139-6203 Dade (305) 672-2344, Broward (954) 771-1400

*MARTIN-DONALDS INC. DBA—1915A Hollywood Blvd. Hollywood, FL 33020 (954) 921-2321

MARY LOU'S MODELS—P.O. Box 5127 Navarre, FL 32566-0127 (850) 939-3204

MODELSCOUT INC—651 Rugby St., Orlando, FL 32804 (407) 420-5888

MODEL'S EXCHANGE—2425 E. Commercial Blvd. #206 Ft. Lauderdale, FL 33308 (954) 491-4266

*POLAN TALENT AGENCY, MARION—10 N.E. 11th Ave. Ft. Lauderdale, FL 33301 (954) 525-8351

*POMMIER MODELS, MICHELE—81 Washington Ave. Miami Beach, FL 33139 (305) 672-9344

REEVE AGENCY—1917 Boothe Circle #151 Longwood, FL 32750-6708 (407) 331-1784 (4+)

*ROXANNE MCMILLAN TALENT AGCY, 12100 N.E. 16th Ave. #106 N. Miami, FL 33161 (305) 899-9150

SARAH PARKER MODEL & TALENT—410 Datura St. West Palm Beach, FL 33401 (561) 655-4400

SELECT MODELS—817 Washington Ave. Miami Beach, FL 33139 (305) 672-5566

SELECT MODELS—3699 Morton Street Jacksonville, FL 32217 (904) 730-2045

SESSIONS MODELING STUDIO—10991 San Jose Blvd. #16B Jacksonville, FL 32223 (904) 292-4366

*SHEFFIELD AGENCY, THE—P.O. Box 101418 Ft. Lauderdale, FL 33310 (954) 523-5887

STELLA JAY BROWN ENTERPRISES—605 Yorktown Dr. Leesburg, FL 34748 (352) 787-7004

*STELLAR TALENT AGENCY—407 Lincoln Rd., #2K Miami Beach, FL 33139 (305) 672-2217

WILHELMINA MODELS—927 Lincoln Rd #200 Miami Beach, FL 33139 (305) 672-9344

*WORLD OF KIDS INC—1460 Ocean Dr. Miami Beach, FL 33139 (305) 672-5437

GEORGIA

ARLENE WILSON MODEL MGMT—887 West Marietta St. N.W. Atlanta, GA 3031, (404) 876-8555

*ATLANTA MODELS & TALENT INC—2970 Peachtree Road N.W. Atlanta, GA 30305 (404) 261-9627

ATLANTA'S YOUNG FACES—6075 Roswell Rd. N.E. Atlanta, GA 30328 (404) 255-3080

AUSTON'S PROFESSIONAL MODELING—3391 Peachtree Rd. N.E. #410 Atlanta, GA 30326 (404) 237-9800

BOHANNON MODELING AGENCY—4820 Old National Hwy Atlanta, GA 30337 (404) 209-0909

*GENESIS MODELS & TALENT INC—1465 Northside Dr. N.W. Atlanta, GA 30318 (404) 350-9212

*GLYN KENNEDY, INC.—975 Hunterhill Dr. Rosewell, GA 30075 (678) 461-4444

L'AGENCE MODELS—5901 Peachtree Dun Rd. N.E. #60 Atlanta, GA 30328 (770) 396-9015

MADEMOISELLE MODELING AGENCY—2901 University Ave. Columbus, GA 31907 (706) 561-9449

MICHELLE JAMES HAIR PRODUCTION—467 Highland Ave. Augusta, GA 30909 (706) 738-7707

MILLIE LEWIS OF SAVANNAH—7011 Hodgson Memorial Dr. Savannah, GA 31406 (912) 354-9525

PEOPLE STORE INC—2004 Rockledge Rd. N.E. Atlanta, GA 30324 (404) 874-6448

POPE MODELING CONSULTANT—3060 N. Pharr Court N.E. Atlanta, GA 30305 (404) 261-0736

*TALENT GROUP/HOT SHOT KIDS—561 W. Pike St. Lawrenceville, GA 30045 (678) 215-1500

TARA MODELING ACADEMY & AGENCY—650 Morrow Industrial Blvd. Jonesboro, GA 30236 (770) 968-7700

*THE BURNS AGENCY—3800 Bretton Woods Rd. Decatur, GA 30032 (866) 744-5037

*THE PEOPLE STORE—2004 Rockledge Rd. N.E. Atlanta, GA 30324 (404) 874-6448

*WILSON INC., ARLENE—887 W. Marietta St. #N-101 Atlanta, GA 30318 (404) 876-8555

HAWAII

ADR PRODUCTIONS, INC.—419 Waiakamilo Rd. #204 Honolulu, HI 96817 (808) 842-1313 e-mail: ryan@adragency.com, website: http://www.adragency.com

ENCORE TALENT—74-4989 Mamalahoa Hwy. Honolulu, HI 96725 (808) 326-1636

PREMIER AGENCY—1441 Kapiolani Blvd. #1206, Honolulu, HI 96814 (808) 955-6511

IDAHO

METCALF'S MODELING & TALENT—1851 Century Wy. #3 Boise, ID 83709 (208) 378-8777

ILLINOIS

*AMBASSADOR TALENT AGENTS, INC—333 N. Michigan Ave., #910 Chicago, IL 60601 (312) 641-3491

ARLENE WILSON MODEL & TALENT—430 W. Erie St. #210 Chicago, IL 60610 (312) 573-0200

AUDITION DIVISION LIMITED—1084 Industrial Dr. Bensenville, IL 60106, (630) 766-6100

*BAKER & ROWLEY TALENT AGY INC—1347 W. Washington #1B Chicago, IL 60607 (773) 252-7900

*BIG MOUTH TALENT AGENCY—935 W. Chestnut #415 Chicago, IL 60622 (312) 421-4400

ELITE MODEL MANAGEMENT CORP—58 W. Huron Chicago, IL 60610 (312)943-3226

EMILIA LORENCE LIMITED—325 W. Huron St. #404 Chicago, IL 60610 (312) 717-2033 (4+)

FORD TALENT GROUP—641 W. Lake St. #402 Chicago, IL 60661 (312) 707-9000

*JENNIFER'S TALENT UNLIMITED INC—740 N. Plankinton, #300 Milwaukee, WI 53203-2403 (414) 277-9440

JOHN ROBERT POWERS MODELING—27 E. Monroe St. #200 Chicago, IL 60603 (312) 726-1404

*LINDA JACK TALENT—230 E. Ohio #200 Chicago, IL 60611 (312) 587-1155

*LORENCE LTD, EMILIA—325 W. Huron #404 Chicago, IL 60610 (312) 787-2033

*LORI LINS LTD—7611 W. Holmes Ave. Greenfield, WI 53220 (414) 282-3500

M L INTERNATIONAL MODELING INC—162 N. Franklin St., Chicago, IL 60606 (312) 849-9190

MARKETING UNLIMITED MODELING—1921 5th Ave. Moline, IL 61265 (309) 762-1978, (5+)

NATIONAL TALENT ASSOCIATES—6326 N. Lincoln Ave. Chicago, IL 60659 (773) 539-8575

ROYAL MODEL MANAGEMENT—1051 Perimeter Dr. Schaumburg, IL 60173 (847) 240-4215

SHIRLEY HAMILTON INC.—333 E. Ontario St. Chicago, IL 60611 (312) 787-4700

STEWART TALENT AGENCY—58 W. Huron Chicago, IL 60610 (312) 943-3131

INDIANA

*ACT I MODEL & TALENT AGENCY—6100 N. Keystone Ave. #105 Indianapolis, IN 46220 (317) 255-3100

AMERICAN MODELS INTERNATIONAL MODELING—2500 Harmony Wy. Evansville, IN 47720 (812) 422-5064
COVER SHOTS—14370 State Road 23 Granger, IN 46530 (219) 271-1992 (5+)
*HELEN WELLS INC—11711 N Meridan St. Carmel, IN 46032 (317) 843-5363

IOWA

MODEL CONSULTANTS—2625 S.E. 18th St. Des Moines, IA 50320 (515) 244-5500
TALENT/IOWA—6545 S.E. Bloomfield Rd. Des Moines, IA 50320 (515) 285-8907

KANSAS

CAREER IMAGES MODEL & TALENT—8519 Lathrop Ave. Kansas City, KS 66109 (913) 334-2200
GREGORY AGENCY—3873 E. Harry St. Wichita, KS 67218 (316) 687-5666
HOFFMAN INTERNATIONAL—6705 W. 91st St. Shawnee Mission, KS 66212 (913) 642-1060
KSKID PRODUCTIONS—1201-1/2 W. Douglas Ave. Wichita, KS 67213, (316) 680-4243 e-mail: kskidproductions@hotmail.com website: http://www.kskid.com
MODEL'S & IMAGES—1619 N. Rock Rd. Wichita, KS 67206 (316) 634-2777

KENTUCKY

ALIX ADAMS MODEL SCHOOL-AGENCY—9813 Merioneth Dr. Jeffersontown, KY 40299 (502) 266-6990
COSMO MODEL & TALENT—7410 La Grange Rd. #204 Louisville, KY 40222 (502) 425-8000
MJK MODELS—414 Baxter Ave. Louisville, KY 40204 (502) 585-4152

LOUISIANA

ABOUT FACES MODELING & TALENT—201 St. Charles Ave. Fl. 25 New Orleans, LA 70170 (504) 522-3030
FAME MODELING & TALENT—4518 Magazine St. New Orleans, LA 70115 (504) 891-2001 email: info@fameagency.com website: http://www.fameagency.com

NEW ORLEANS MODEL & TALENT—1347 Magazine St. New Orleans, LA 70130 (504) 525-0100

MAINE

REFER to your local phone book, yellow pages

MARYLAND

ANNAPOLIS MODELING AGENCY—130 Manns Rd, Severna Park MD 21146 (410) 647-1200

BELA NOVA MODEL MANAGEMENT—206 N. Liberty St #3 Baltimore, MD 21201

KIDS INTERNATIONAL—938 E. Swan Creek Rd., #152 Ft. Washington, MD 20744 (301) 292-6094

NOVA MODELS INC—2120 N. Charles St., Baltimore MD 21218 (410) 752-6682

*THE BULLOCK AGENCY—5200 Bullock Ave. #102 Hyattsville, MD 20781 (301) 905-9598

MASSACHUSETTS

*ACTUAL TALENT—1260 New Britain Rd. #65 W. Hartford, CT 06110 (860) 920-5322

BOSTON AGENCY FOR CHILDREN—380 Broadway Somerville, MA 02145 (617) 666-0900

CAMEO MODEL & TALENT AGENCY—49 River St. #1 Waltham, MA 02453 (781) 647-8300, e-mail: thecameoagency@yahoo.com

FORD AGENCY—297 Newbury St. Boston, MA 02115 (617) 262-9300

FORD MODEL MANAGEMENT—297 Newbury St. Boston, MA 02115 (617) 266-6939

KIDS N THE BIZ—122 Veeley Rd. Southfield, MA 01259 (413) 734-2000

MODEL CLUB—229 Berkeley St. Boston, MA 02116 (617) 247-9020

MICHIGAN

ABBEY'S PEOPLE—2309 Columbia Ave. W. Battle Creek, MI 49015 (616) 965-8285

*AFFILIATED MODELS INC—1680 Crooks Rd #200 Troy, MI 48084 (248) 244-8770

*CLASS MODELING TALENT AGENCY—2722 E. Michigan Ave. Lansing, MI 48912 (517) 482-1833

FACES FOR PLACES—22255 River Ridge Trail Farmington Hills, MI 48335 (248) 471-6611

MODEL & TALENT MANAGEMENT—44450 Pinetree Drive Plymouth, MI 48170 (734) 455-0801

*PRODUCTIONS PLUS—30600 Telegraph Rd. #2156 Bingham Farms, MI 48025 (248) 644-5566

PROFESSIONAL TALENT—1345 Monroe Ave. N.W. Grand Rapids, MI 49505 (616) 458-2513

*THE I GROUP, LLC—29540 Southfield Rd. #200 Southfield, MI 48076 (810) 552-8842

*THE TALENT SHOP—30100 Telegraph Rd. #116 Birmingham, MI 48025 (810) 644-4877

MINNESOTA

AGENCY MODELS AND TALENT—210 N. Second St. #002 Minneapolis, MN 55410 (612) 664-1174

*CARYN MODEL & TALENT AGENCY—100 N. 6th St. #270B Minneapolis, MN 55403 (612) 349-3600

IMAGE 1 PROFESSIONAL MODELING & ACTING—601 9th Ave. N. St. Cloud, MN 56303 (320) 251-0101

*MEREDITH MODEL & TALENT—800 Washington Ave. N. #511, Minneapolis, MN 55401 (612) 340-9555

*MOORE CREATIVE TALENT INC—1610 W. Lake St. Minneapolis, MN 55408 (612) 827-3823

*NEW FACES MODELS & TALENT INC—6301 Wayzata Blvd. Minneapolis, MN 55416 (612) 544-8668

SUSAN WEHMANN MODELS & TALENT—1128 Harmon Pl. #205 Minneapolis, MN 55403 (612) 333-6393

MISSISSIPPI

REFER to your local phone book, yellow pages

MISSOURI

AJH ENTERPRISES—P.O. Box 63262 St. Louis, MO 63163 (314) 352-7248

ALLURE MODELS—144 W. Madison Ave. St. Louis, MO 63122 (314) 909-0666

AMERICAN ARTISTS AGENCY—1808 Broadway St. Kansas City, MO 64108 (816) 474-9988

*CITY TALENT—2101 Locust St. #2, W. St. Louis, MO 63103 (314) 621-7200

*ENTERTAINMENT PLUS—114 A W. 3rd St. Kansas City, MO 64105 (816) 474-4778

*EXPOSURE MODEL & TALENT—215 W. 18th St. Kansas City, MO 64108 (816) 842-4494

*HOFFMAN INTERNATIONAL—6705 W. 91st St. Overland Park, KS 66212 (913) 642-1030

IMAGES OF ST. LOUIS—715 Frontenac Square St. Louis, MO 63131 (314) 993-0605

KAY MODELING SCHOOL & AGENCY—1201 w. 7th St. Joplin, MO 64801 (417) 781-4540 (8+)

NORMA'S MODELING SCHOOL & AGCY—3638 S. Campbell Ave. Springfield, MO 65807 (417) 882-2436

PATRICIA STEVENS MODEL AGENCY—2000 Baltimore Ave. Kansas City, MO 64108 (816) 221-1188

*PRIMA MODELS—522 S. Hanley Rd. St. Louis, MO 63105 (314) 721-1235

*TALENT UNLIMITED—4049 Pennsylvania Ave. Kansas City, MO 64111 (816) 561-9040

TALENTPLUS-CENTRO MODELS—55 Maryland Plaza St. Louis, MO 63108 (314) 421-9400

*THE QUINN AGENCY—1062 Madison St. St. Charles, MO 63301 (636) 947-0120

MONTANA

CREATIVE WORLD MODELING—27 N. 27th St. Billings, Mt 59101 (406) 259-9540
NASS TALENT MGMT—P.O. Box 3244 Bozeman, MT 59772 (406) 586-7045

NEBRASKA

REFER to your local phone book, yellow pages

NEVADA

A BASKOW TALENT AGENCY & ASSOC—2948 E. Russell Rd. Las Vegas, NV 89120 (702) 733-7818 (4+)
CONVENTION EASE—3720 W. Desert Inn Rd. #A Las Vegas, NV 89102 (702) 365-1057
HOLIDAY MODELS INC—900 E. Desert Inn Rd. #101 Las Vegas, NV 89109 (702) 735-7353
WILD STREAK TALENT INTERNATIONAL—3355 Spring Mountain Rd #247 Las Vegas, NV 8910,(702) 252-8382

NEW HAMPSHIRE

CINDERALLA MODELING STUDIO—9 Brook St. Manchester, NH 03104 (603) 627-4125
EAST COAST FOCUS—3 Pleasant St. Concord, NH 03301 (603) 228-6377
NEW ENGLAND MODELS GROUP—250 Commercial Lane #2022 Manchester, NH 03101 (603) 624-0555

NEW JERSEY

AXIS MODELS & TALENT INC—24-26 Church St. Montclair, NJ 07042 (973) 783-4900
CHRISTINE MODELS & CASTING—43 Rock Rd. Wayne, NJ 07470 (973) 904-0300
CLASSIC MODEL & TALENT MGMT—213 W. 35th St. 10th Fl. Edison, NJ 08837 (732) 650-9730

MEREDITH MODEL EAST—767 Fredrick, Wycoss, NJ 07481 (201) 560-9992

MODEL TEAM—55 Central Ave. Ocean Grove, NJ 07756 (732) 988-3648 (5+)

MODELS ON THE MOVE—1200 Route 70 E. #6 Cherry Hill, NJ 08034 (856) 667-1060

NEW TALENT MANAGEMENT—590 Route 70 Brick, NJ 08723 (732) 477-3355

NEW MEXICO

MANNEQUIN AGENCY—2021 San Mateo Blvd. N.E. Albuquerque, NM 87110, (505) 266-6823

NEW YORK

*ABRAMS ARTISTS & ASSOC—725 Seventh Av. 26th Fl. New York, NY 1001 (646) 486-4600

ACME TALENT & LITERARY—875 Avenue of the Americas #2108 New York, NY 10001 (212) 328-0388

*ACTUAL TALENT—1260 New Britain Rd. #65 W. Hartford, CT 06110 (860) 920-5322

*AMATO AGENCY, MICHAEL—1650 Broadway #307 New York, NY 10019 (212) 247-4456

*AMERICAN INT'L TALENT AGENCY—303 W. 42nd St. #608 New York, NY 10036 (212) 245-8888

*ANDREADIS TALENT AGENCY—119 W. 57th St. #711 New York, NY 10019 (212) 315) 0303

*ANN STEELE AGENCY—240 W. 44th St. #1 Helen Hayes Theatre, New York, NY 10036 (212) 278-0896

*BERNARD LIEBHABER AGENCY—352 Seventh Ave. 7th Fl. New York, NY 10001 (212) 220-3532

*BIENSTOCK INC., N.S.—1740 Broadway 24th Fl. New York, NY 10019 (212) 765-3040

BLACKWOOD-STEELE INC—P.O. Box 690 Fairport, NY 14450 (716) 425-1306

*BUCHWALD & ASSOC., DON—10 E. 44th St. New York, NY 10017 (212) 867-1200

*CARSON ORGANIZATION LTD., THE—240 W. 44th St. PH New York, NY 10036 (212) 221-1517

*CARSON-ADLER AGENCY INC—250 W. 57th St. New York, NY 10107 (212) 307-1882

*CUNNINGHAM, ESCOTT, DIPENE & ASSOC—257 Park Ave. S. #900 New York, NY 10010 (212) 477-1666

*DICCE TALENT AGENCY, GINGER—1650 Broadway #714 New York, NY 10019 (212) 974-7455

*EWCR & ASSOCIATES—311 W. 43rd St. #204 New York, NY 10036 (212) 586-9110

FACES—6814 Main St. #110 Williamsville, NY 14221 (716) 634-5634

FORD—142 Greene St. 4th Floor New York, NY (212) 219-6500

FUNNY FACE TODAY INC—151 E. 31st St. #24J New York, NY 10016 (212) 686-4343

*GENERATION MODELING MGMT—20 W. 20th St. #1008, New York, NY 10011 (212) 727-7219

*GILLA ROOS LTD, 16 W. 22ND St. #3 New York, NY 10010 (212) 727-7820

*GOLDNADEL INC—234 Fifth Ave. #406 New York, NY 10001 (212) 532-2202

GONZALEZ MODEL & TALENT—112 E. 23rd St. Ph New York, NY 10010 (212) 982-5626 (5+)

*HENDERSON/HOGAN AGENCY INC—850 Seventh Ave. #1003 New York, NY 10019 (212) 765-5190

IKON NEW YORK—140 W. 22nd Street New York, NY 10011 (212) 691-2363

JUNE 2 MODEL & TALENT AGENCY—143 Allen St. Buffalo, NY 14201 (716) 883-0700

*KERIN-GOLDBERG ASSOCIATES—155 E 55th St. #5D New York, NY 10022 (212) 838-7373

MC DONALD RICHARDS INC—156 5th Ave. #222 New York, NY 10010 (212) 627-3100 (7+)

MODELS SERVICE AGENCY INC—570 7th Ave. #702 New York, NY 10018 (212) 944-8896

NEXUS PERSONAL MANAGEMENT INC—694 Macedon Ctr. Rd. Fairport, NY 14450 (716) 425-1306

*OSCARD AGENCY INC., FIFI—24 W. 40th St. 17th Fl. New York, NY 10018 (212) 764-1100

*PARADIGM—200 W. 57th St. #900 New York, NY 10019 (212) 246-1030

R&L MODEL MANAGEMENT—203 W. 23rd St. #400 New York, NY 10011 (212) 935-2300

*SCHIFFMAN, EKMAN, MORRISON & MARX INC (S.E.M & M)—22 W. 19th St. 8th Fl. New York, NY 10011 (212) 627-5500

*SCHILL AGENCY INC., WILLIAM—302A W. 12th St. #183 New York, NY 10014 (877) 813-3923

*SCHULLER TALENT/NEW YORK KIDS—276 Fifth Ave. New York, NY 10001 (212) 532-6005

*THE LEUDTKE AGENCY—1674 Broadway #7A New York, NY 10019 (212) 220-3532

THOMPSON MODEL AGENCY INC—50 W. 34th St. #6C6 New York, NY 10001 (212) 947-6711

*TRANUM, ROBERTSON & HUGHES—600 Madison Ave. New York, NY 10017 (212) 371-7500

U S MODEL-TALENT MANAGEMENT—250 Goodman St. N. Rochester, NY 14607 (716) 244-0592

*WATERS & NICOLOSI—1501 Broadway #1305 New York, NY 10036 (212) 302-8787

WILHELMINA MODELS INC—300 S. Park Ave. #2 New York, NY 10010 (212) 473-0700

*WRITERS & ARTISTS AGENCY—19 W. 44th St. #1000 New York, NY 10036 (212) 391-1112

NORTH CAROLINA

CAROLINA TALENT INC—312 Rensselaer Ave. Charlotte, NC 28203 (704) 332-3218

DIRECTIONS USA—3717 W. Market St. #D Greensboro, NC 27403 (336) 292-2800

DIRECTIONS USA—206 E. Tremont Ave. Charlotte, NC 28203 (704) 377-3151

ICE MODEL TALENT MGMT INT'L—8318 Pineville Matthews Rd. Charlotte, NC, (704) 544-1550 (5+)

KICK 277 MODELING AGENCY—210 W. Main St. Dallas, NC 28034 (704) 922-5425 (12+)

MARILYN'S INC—601 Norwalk St. Greensboro, NC 27407 (336) 292-5950

ON TRACK MODELING INC—5500 Executive Ctr. Dr. Charlotte, NC 28212 (202) 704) 532-6577 (13+)

PROFESSIONAL MODEL'S GUILD—1819 Charlotte Dr. Charlotte, NC 28203 (704) 377-9299

RICK'S TALENT & MODELING AGENCY—806 Summit Ave. Greensboro, NC 27405 (336) 379-0033

TALENT CONNECTION—338 N. Elm St. Greensboro, NC 27401 (336) 274-2499

NORTH DAKOTA

REFER to your local phone book, yellow pages

OHIO

A GOLDEN TOUCH TALENT AGENCY—8527 Refugee Rd. Pickerington, OH 43147 (614) 837-0629

ACTIVE IMAGE MANAGEMENT COMPANY—Worthington, OH 43085 (614) 885-7770

ASHLEY TALENT AGENCY—10948 Reading Rd. #310, Cincinnati, OH 45241 (513) 554-4836

CHILDREN'S MODEL AGENCY INTERNATIONAL—6407 Montgomery Rd. Cincinnati, OH 45213 (513) 351-2700

FORD TALENT GROUP INC—1300 E. 9th St. #1640 Cleveland, OH 44114 (216) 522-1300

GLORIA SUSTAR AGENCY—35 E. 7th St. #401 Cincinnati, OH 45202 (513) 721-3737

*HEYMAN TALENT AGENCY—3308 Brotherton Rd. Cincinnati, OH 45209 (513) 533-3113

IMPACT MGMT TALENT (IMI)—9700 Rockside Rd. #410 Cleveland, OH 44125 (216) 901-9710

JO GOENNER-TALENT—4700 Reed Rd. E. Columbus, OH 43220, (614) 459-3582

MARSHA MODEL & TALENT AGENCY—Box 7141 118 W. High St., Bryan, OH 43506 (419) 636-5334

MICHAEL STEPHEN STUDIOS—650 Youngstown Warren Rd. Niles, OH 44446 (330) 544-5355

NEW VIEW MANAGEMENT GROUP INC—10680 McSwain Dr. Cincinnati, OH 45241 (513) 733-4444

PRO-MODEL MANAGEMENT—3926 W. Market St. Akron, OH 44333 (330) 867-4125

RIGHT DIRECTION—5701 N. High St. Worthington, OH 43085, (614) 848-3367

RIGHT KIDS—5701 N. High St. Worthington, OH 43085 (614) 848-4301

SHARKEY AGENCY INC—1299 Lyons Rd #H Dayton, OH 45488 (937) 434-4461

Z MODELS—985 Mediterranean Ave. Columbus, OH 43229 (614) 436-9006

Z MODELS INC—3067 W. Market St. #5 Fairlawn, OH 44333 (330) 869-5050

OKLAHOMA

LINDA LAYMAN AGENCY LIMITED—3546 e. 51ST St. Tulsa, OK 74135 (918) 744-0888

MODEL & TALENT MGMT—5009 N. Pennsylvania Ave. Oklahoma City, OK 73112 (405) 842-0090

OREGON

ABC KIDS-N-TEENS ARTS CTR—1144 Willagillespie Rd. Eugene, OR 97401 (541) 485-6960

ABC KIDS-N-TEENS PERFORMING—3829 N.E. Tillamook St. Portland, OR 97212 (503) 249-2945

*CUSICK'S TALENT AGENCY—1009 N.W. Hoyt St. #100, Portland OR 97209 (503) 274-8555

*ERHART TALENT—037 S.W. Hamilton St. Portland, OR 97201 (503) 243-6362

JOHN CASABLANCAS MODELING—5440 S.W. Westgate Dr. #350 Portland, OR 97221 (503) 297-7730

*ROSE CITY TALENT—239 N.W. 13TH Ave. #215 Portland, OR 97209 (503) 274-1005

RYAN ARTISTS—239 N.W. 13th Ave. #215 Portland, OR 97209 (503) 228-5648

SPORTS UNLIMITED INC—1991 N.W. Upshur St. Portland, OR 97209 (503) 227-3449

PENNSYLVANIA

BOWMAN AGENCY—1040 Woodridge Blvd. Lancaster, PA 17601 (717) 898-7716

*CLARO AGENCY INC., THE—1513 W. Passyunk Ave., Philadelphia, PA 19145 (215) 465-7788

*MODELS ON THE MOVE—1200 Route 70 #6 Barclay Towers, P.O. Box 4037 Cherry Hills, NJ 08034 (609) 667-1060

*PLAZA 7—160 N. Gulph Rd. King of Prussia, PA 19406 (610) 337-2693

PROFESSIONAL IMAGE BY ROSEMARY—2820 Smallman St. Pittsburgh, PA 15222 (412) 471-8011

*THE TALENT GROUP—2820 Smallmann St. Pittsburgh, PA 15222 (412) 471-8011

RHODE ISLAND

DONAHUE MODELS—14 Rome Ave. Providence, RI 02904 (401) 353-4950

EXPOSURE AGENCY & STUDIO—43 Arnold Ave. Providence, RI 02905 (401) 941-6611

MODEL CLUB—355 S. Water St. Providence, RI 02903 (401) 273-7120

SOUTH CAROLINA

MILLIE LEWIS—1228 S. Pleasantburg Dr. Greenville, SC 29605 (864) 299-1101

MILLIE LEWIS OF COLUMBIA INC—3612 Landmark Dr. Columbia, SC 29204 (803) 782-7338

SOUTH DAKOTA

REFER to your local phone book, yellow pages

TENNESSEE

ADVANTAGE MODELS & TALENT—4825 Trousdale Dr #230 Nashville, TN 37220 (615) 833-3005

AMAX—4121 Hillsboro Rd. Nashville, TN 37215 (615) 292-0246

JO-SUSAN—2817 W. End Ave. Nashville, TN 37203 (615) 327-8726

*TALENT & MODEL LAND INC—P.O. Box 40763 Nashville, TN 37204 (615) 321-5596

TALENT TREK AGENCY—406 Eleventh St. Knoxville, TN 37916 (865) 977-8735
*****TALENT TREK AGENCY**—1701 W. End Ave., Nashville, TN 37203 (615) 244-6411
*****TALENT TREK**—2021 21ˢᵗ Ave. S. #102 Nashville, TN 37212 (615) 279-0010

TEXAS

*****ACCLAIM PARTNERS**—4107 Medical Pkwy #210 Austin, TX 78756 (512) 323-5566
*****ACTORS ETC. INC**—2620 Fountainview #210 Houston, TX 77057 (713) 785-4495
AVANT MODELS & CASTING—85 N.E. Loop 410 #218A San Antonio, TX 78216 (210) 308-8411
*****CAMPBELL AGENCY, THE**—3906 Lemmon Ave., #200 Dallas, TX 75219 (214) 522-8991
CONDRA/ARISTA MODELING AGENCY—1330 Old Blanco Rd., #201 San Antonio, TX 78216 (210) 492-9947
*****DAWSON AGENCY INC., KIM**—2710 N. Stemmons Fwy. #700 Tower North, Dallas, TX 75207-2208 (214) 630-5161
FIRST MODELS & TALENT AGENCY—5433 Westheimer Rd. #305 Houston, TX 77056 (713) 850-9611
*****INTERMEDIA AGENCY**—5353 W. Alabama #222 Houston, TX 77056 (713) 622-8282
K HALL MODELS & TALENT—700 Rio Grande St. Austin, TX 78701, (512) 476-7523
MODELS WEST 3405 S. Western St. #201 Amarillo, TX 79109 (806) 352-1943
*****NEAL HAMIL AGENCY**—7887 San Felipe St. #227 Houston, TX 77063 (713) 789-1335
*****PASTORINI-BOSBY TALENT AGENCY**—3013 Fountain View Dr. #240 Houston, TX 77057 (713) 266-4488
TALENT HOUSE—812 N. Virginia St. #204 El Paso, TX 79902 (915) 533-1945
*****TAYLOR TALENT INC., PEGGY**—1825 Market Ctr. Blvd. #320—LB37 Dallas, TX 75207 (214) 651-7884
*****THE THOMAS AGENCY**—14275 Midway Rd. #220 Dallas, TX 75244 (972) 687-9181
*****YOUNG AGENCY, SHERRY**—2620 Fountainview #212 Houston, TX 77057 (713) 266-5800

UTAH

COLLETTE'S DISTINCTIVE MDLNG—1033 Revere Circle, Holladay, UT 84117 (801) 262-2462 (5+)

VERMONT

<u>REFER to your local phone book, yellow pages</u>

VIRGINIA

MODELOGIC—2501 E. Broad St., Richmond, VA 23223 (804) 644-1000
WRIGHT MODELING AGENCY—12638 Jefferson Ave. #16 Newport News, VA 23602 (757) 886-5884 (5+)

WASHINGTON

*COLLEEN BELL MODELING & TALENT AGENCY—14205 S.E. 36th St. #100 Bellevue, WA 98006 (425) 649-1111
*DRAMATIC ARTISTS AGENCY—1000 Lenora St. #511 Seattle, WA 98121 (206) 442-9190
EMERALD CITY MODEL & TALENT—1980 Harvard Ave. E. Seattle, WA 98102 (206) 329-7768
FUTURE STARS TOTS N TEENS MDL—17900 Southcenter Pkwy #200 Seattle, WA 98102, (206) 329-7768
KID BIZ TALENT AGENCY—One Bellevue Center, 411 108th Ave. N.E. #2050 Bellevue, WA 98004 (425) 455-8800
KIM BROOKE GROUP—2044 Eastlake Ave. E. Seattle, WA 98102 (206) 329-1111
NORTHWEST FASHION INSTITUTE—19009 33rd Ave. W. #100 Lynwood, WA (425) 775-8385
PERSISTENT IMAGE—P.O. Box 1284 Renton, WA 98057 (425) 271-9123
*SEATTLE MODELS GUILD—1809 7th Ave. #303 Seattle, WA 98101 (206) 622-1406

WEST VIRGINIA

REFER to your local phone book, yellow pages

WISCONSIN

JENNIFER'S TALENT UNLIMITED—740 N. Plankinton Ave. Milwaukee, WI 53203 (414) 277-9440
*LINS LTD LORI—7611 W. Holmes Greenfield, WI 53220 (414) 282-3500

WYOMING

REFER to your local phone book, yellow pages

WASHINGTON D.C.

ANNE SCHWAB'S MODEL STORE—906 D St. N.E. Washington, DC 20002 (202) 333-3560

6

WORKING WITHOUT AN AGENT

◆

MODELING DOCUMENTS, FORMS, & INCOME TAXES

Standing in front of a camera is only a small portion of what a model does. Modeling is a business.

All businesses have to keep accurate bookkeeping records and are required to file income tax returns.

A model's income is considered independent contractor work. Therefore, he or she receives a check without any income taxes or social security taxes withheld. As an independent contractor the burden of paying these taxes falls on the model.

Two taxes are paid on this income: Social security taxes and income taxes. Both of these taxes are paid on yearly modeling net income. The (yearly) net modeling income is derived by totaling modeling income for the year, then subtracting modeling expenses for the year. If the total modeling expenses are more than the total modeling income, it's called a net loss, and no income taxes or social security are owed. (An income tax return needs to be filed for each and every year that you are self-employed, and/or working as a model, even if you have a net loss.)

The income tax system is very complex. Presently we have a 10, 15, 20, and 28 percent federal tax rate. Social security taxes are currently 15.3 percent. Employees pay half of the social security, employers pay the other half. An independent contractor pays both halves, or 15.3 percent.

Example: If you earned $5,000. and had $4,000. in modeling expenses for the year, then you'd have a net profit of $1,000.

On a net profit of $1,000. you pay $150. in social security taxes. Your income taxes on a net profit of $1,000. would depend on which tax bracket you're in. If you're in the (minimum) 10 percent tax bracket you pay $100. in federal income taxes.

It's wise to save 20 percent of your modeling income each year, to pay income taxes.

Do not let family or friends prepare your income tax returns. You're a model, in business, and you need a professional to help you. Do ask family and friends which accountants they use, and make an appointment. If you have questions about income and/or business expenses, ask a professional. Accountants are well versed in this area and the more you know, the better bookkeeper and business owner you will become.

Business expenses vary from model to model, and from job to job. Simply put, any expense you incur directly related to getting modeling jobs are tax deductible. Hotels, out-of-town meals (while away from home overnight), long distance phone calls to your agency, professional makeup, zed card fees, and photographer expenses are the most common modeling expenses.

Your vehicle, is also a business expense. A portion of actual vehicle expenses can be written off, including gasoline, repairs, maintenance, insurance, and lease payments. Or you can take a standard mileage allowance for each mile you drive for modeling. You cannot take both.

The standard mileage allowance changes yearly. It is currently 48.5 cents per mile.

Example: If you drove 3,500 miles a year as a model, you would be allowed an income tax deduction of $1,697.50.

For models who travel extensively, their cars are their largest tax deduction. It's important to keep accurate records of all of traveling related to modeling.

Every time you drive to interviews or to your agency's office, you accrue tax-deductible travel mileage. Driving to buy professional makeup or special clothes required for a photo shoot is all tax-deductible travel.

Keep accurate track of your tax-deductible mileage by writing it down in a business mileage logbook. You can obtain a mileage logbook at any stationary store, or ask your accountant for one.

Each and every time you get into your car for modeling, you need to make an entry in your mileage logbook. Keep your entries simple and concise.

For your reference, below is a page of entries from a mileage logbook.

Date	Business Destination	Business Mileage		No. Miles
		Odometer Reading		
		Start	Finish	
		✕	✕	
Jan 4th	Visit agency in Los Angeles	39,310	39,595	285
Feb 10th	Pick up pictures	41,003	41,063	60
Feb 25th	Photo shoot at Marriott hotel	41,610	41,745	135
March 9th	Zack Smith, photo job	42,045	42,080	35

Modeling expenses should be paid for by checks or by credit cards. Do not pay any tax-deductible modeling expenses by cash. Cash receipts easily get misplaced or fade, and if not carefully documented you can easily forget which business expense they were for.

If you pay by check, make a small notation in the memo section at the bottom left-hand corner of the check. Then save the check and receipt as shown below:

JOHN AND JANE DOE
PH. 760-777-7777
77777 Anywhere Rd.
Cathedral City, CA 92234

55-5555/7777   **5555**

DATE 3/1/07

Pay to the Order of **Staples** $ 7.54

Seven Dollars and 54/100 cents   Dollars

For Photo Labels   〜〜〜〜〜   MP

Write on the matching receipt whatever items you purchased for your business. See the example on the next page.

STAPLES

that was easy.

```
Low prices. Every item. Every day.
  110% Price-Match. Guaranteed.
   69-044 E. Palm Canyon Drive
    CATHEDRAL CITY, CA 92234
        (760) 328-7682
SALE                546028 15 001 12627
                    1384 03/01/07 07:57
QTY SKU                     OUR PRICE


   REWARDS NUMBER 4087467900
   *****Buy More / Save More*****
1   AVY INK/LSR LBL 7U
    072782052027            1.75
1   AVY INK/LSR LBL 7U
    072782052027            1.75
1   AVY INK/LSR LBL 7U
    072782052027            1.75
1   AVY INK/LSR LBL 7U
    072782052027            1.75
  Discount Amount <-2.00>
*****************************************
SUBTOTAL                    7.00
  Standard Tax 7.75%        0.54
TOTAL                      $7.54
```

File your receipts in a manila file folder, labeled "Modeling Expenses." As you become more experienced, you can separate your expenses into numerous categories, from: travel expenses to meal expenses. Ask your accountant how he or she would like you to keep track of your modeling income and expenses.

There also are numerous inexpensive, user-friendly computer software programs available that total and categorize business income and expenses.

Paying modeling expenses by credit cards may seem easier, but that process requires more bookkeeping time. If you pay by credit cards, you need to highlight or circle each business expense on each and every monthly credit card statement. If you use multiple credit cards this will prove to be very time consuming. Each modeling expense receipt must be matched with and kept with each monthly credit card statement. Further a note needs to be written next to each expense on the credit card statement which identifies the business nature.

A credit card statement with memo entries appears below. Refer to it when you receive your monthly credit card statements.

BANK OF OMAHA

TRANS DATE	POST DATE	TRANSACTION DESCRIPTION	REFERENCE NUMBER	AMOUNT CHARGES	CREDITS
06/05	06/05	PAYMENT - THANK YOU	1111222233334AAA444555B		-$40.00
05/25	05/28	CIC*Credit Monitoring	AB112222333344445555666	$9.95	
06/05	06/07	LA COSTA RESORT & SPA CARLSBAD CA	AB112222333344445555666	$83.56	←Hotel Exp.
06/07	06/09	LAS CASUELAS NUEVAS RANCHO MIRAGE CA	AB112222333344445555666	$16.49	
06/08	06/12	ALDO SHERMAN OAKS CA	AB112222333344445555666	$21.65	←Make Up
06/12	06/14	LAS CASUELAS NUEVAS RANCHO MIRAGE CA	AB112222333344445555666	$14.79	
06/14	06/16	TARGET 00007777 PALM DESERT CA	AB112222333344445555666	$50.20	←Modeling Clothes
06/14	06/16	LAS CASUELAS NUEVAS RANCHO MIRAGE CA	AB112222333344445555666	$15.83	

Some credit card companies track and categorize charged expenses. If possible, acquire and use a separate credit card for your modeling expenses.

Pay credit card bills off on a monthly basis. Credit card companies often charge a high rate of interest, which will quickly eat into your modeling profits.

Modeling income is fairly easy to keep track of. When you receive a paycheck, (from a job) make a copy of it. On the copy, list any and all names of people you worked with or met on the job, from makeup artists to photographers. Include their contact information (phone numbers, e-mail, addresses, etc.).

On rare occasions you will be compensated in cash. You will need to keep track of the cash amounts just as you do the checks.

A sample of a modeling income ledger is shown below. Refer to it each time you receive a paycheck. You don't need a fancy ledger or set of books to record your income; you just need to be consistent.

INCOME LEDGER

	JOB DATE		DESCRIPTION	CHECK #	AMOUNT PAID	YEAR TO DATE	
1	Feb	6th	Johnny's Clothing Photo Shoot	3226	400.00	400.00	1
2							2
3	Mar	13th	Ms. Jenny's Lunch Boutique	CASH	100.00	500.00	3
4							4
5	March	19th	Sal's Grand Opening	6310	150.00	650.00	5
6							6
7	April	10th	K-World Photo Shoot	9341	600.00	1250.00	7
8							8
9	April	28th	Photo Shop Gala	2875	400.00	1650.00	9
10							10
11	May	1st	Amy's Corporate Party	34216	800.00	2450.00	11
12							12
13	May	12th	Star Corporate Meeting	1063	875.00	3325.00	13
14							14
15	June	3rd	Redstone's Bridle Company	34951	1300.00	4625.00	15

When you volunteer as a model for any reason, from getting more experience to building your portfolio, you need to keep track of each job. As with paid jobs, it's important to write down any and all names of people whom you've worked with, or met on the job, from makeup artists to photographers. Be sure to also record their contact information.

In the first year or two, most models don't make a large profit. If your modeling expenses are greater than your modeling income in one calendar year January-December, your business will garner a net loss.

By keeping a travel log and accurate records of your expenses you will we able to calculate your profit, per each job. It's important to know what your overhead is, especially reguarding modeling jobs. out of town.

When working through an agency, you will have a "job voucher" for each assignment. When you join an agency ask your agent for a few, in advance. Job vouchers are, the time cards of the modeling industry. They show the type of work you've been hired to do (fashion, catalogue, etc.) along with your hourly rate of pay and the number of hours you're going to work. They should have your name and address along with your agency's name, address and phone number on them.

A few modeling jobs don't require vouchers, but most professionals and companies use them. Ask your agency what information should be enter on each job voucher, before the job starts. Also ask your agent the name of the person responsible for signing it.

Job vouchers have three copies. After they are filled out, both the client and the model signs them. The job voucher is your paycheck, if it's not signed and turned in, you don't get paid. The client gets the top copy, your agency gets the second copy and the model keeps the third copy.

Job vouchers also have a general "release" that the model signs. It protects the model from having the client publish pictures the model has not been paid for.

Do not show the job voucher to anyone, except the person authorized to sign it. Always present it after the photo-shoot. Never present it before or during any break time.

When your signature and the authorized signature are on the job voucher, tear off the top copy and with a closing, "thank you" hand it to the responsible party.

Your agency will bill the client, once you've returned the agency copy to them. This should be done within twenty-four hours.

If the job is out of town, call your agency and ask if they would like you to mail the voucher to them. The sooner your agency gets the voucher, the sooner you and your agency get paid.

Getting the job voucher signed, can be tricky. Some photo-shoots are very long and a tired crew can disappear in minutes. Keep your job voucher with you. Many photo-shoots are mobile and/or at more than one location. If you leave your job voucher behind, it's very hard to track down the signature later.

Always act professional and never interrupt your client for his or her signature. Even when you're in a hurry or late for another job or appointment. Being a professional means being courteous, calm and respectful to everyone around you.

You want to be hired again and words like "please and thank you" along with good listening skills, are a must and a very important part of your modeling career.

If you are asked to work more hours then your agency has agreed to/or if you're asked to work another job or another day on the job, you must refer these request back to your agency. Never negotiate your pay and never discuss your rate of pay with anyone on a job. Even with other models. Refer everyone and all request back to your agency.

Some clients try to bypass your agency by promising you more money and/or they ask for your home phone number for future work. Don't get caught up in this situation. Your agency gets the jobs and must negotiate any and all work with companies, today, tomorrow and next year.

In your local community there are small boutiques, young designers and photographers, all looking for models.

Occasionally you may get a job on your own, without your agency. These jobs offer you experience, exposure and sometimes a small paycheck.

Do not accept a job from anyone whom has hired or is affiliated with your agency, ever.

If you work on your own without an agency, you need to have a business plan. With each potential job, you need to know, and or ask the following information.

1) The name, address and phone numbers (office, cell) of whom you are working for or with.

2) The date, time and total hours of the job.

3) The address and location of the photo-shoot.

4) How much the job pays. (hourly, daily, etc.)

5) Who is in charge of the photo-shoot?

6) Who is responsible for paying you, and when will you get paid?

7) If the job is more then 100 miles away from your home, or overnight/how much will you get paid for accommodations and/or traveling expenses?

8) What kind of modeling will you be doing? (runway, print, demo's, etc.)

9) What clothes or shoes do you need to bring?

If your questions aren't answered to satisfaction, or if the answers you get, make you feel uncomfortable, or if you just don't feel the job is right for you, don't take it.

In the world of modeling, sometimes things aren't always what they seem. Knowing all of the facts about a job before you take it, is very important, for piece of mind and for personal safety, especially jobs, out of town.

Being a professional means, always being prepared. You should have the following items with you, at any and all modeling jobs. (even non-paid jobs.)

1) Zed cards, your portfolio, résumé and business cards, if you are working without an agent.

2) Makeup and makeup remover.

3) Strapless bra (women) boxer and brief shorts, razor (men.)

4) Emery board, nail polish and polish remover.

5) Lint brush, shoe brush.

6) A pair of pantyhose (women) Black and white dress ankle socks (men.)

7) Toothbrush and toothpaste.

8) Hair curling iron and hairdryer (women) Hair jell (men.)

9) Deodorant.

10) Safety pins, needle and thread.

11) Small hand towel and soap.

12) Hairpins, combs, brushes, hair supplies and hairspray.

13) Two to four pair, dressy shoes with 1–3" heels (women) One pair dressy black shoes (men.)

Most of these items are small and will fit in an oversized zipper purse or small carry bag. Put your name and address on the bag. Keep your essentials bag close by on photo-shoots. You never know when you will need it.

Many photo-shoots are done outside. The sun, wind and the rain have played havoc with the best of models.

If you work as your own agent, your job isn't finished at the end of a photo-shoot. Your next step is to bill and collect negotiated fees from your clients. Bills should be promptly sent out, within a day or two.

Fees should be paid within two to four weeks, although larger companies tend to stretch the time to eight weeks.

Always send your bills out with a postage paid return envelope. It looks professional and clients tend to pay faster, when return envelopes are attached.

If you were promised payment within a specific length of time (next week, Friday, the following Monday, etc.) and you haven't received the money, call your client and tactfully remind them the payment is past due, and you had sent them a postage paid return envelope for their convenience.

Keep notes on who you speak to, along with the date and time of day of each conversation

If you model for something other then money, such as designer clothes or professional photographs, follow up each job with a phone call, thanking the appropriate person for the job.

Log your travel mileage or any other expense you incur on all jobs, whether you're being paid and/or when you are working for free.

Keep notes of whom you worked for, the date of the photo-shoot, the length of time you worked, your total pay and the phone numbers of everyone involved in the job.

Review your list at least twice a year and ask yourself the following questions:

How many hours did I work?

How much did I get paid per hour?

How many expenses did I have to pay for?

If most of your jobs were for "free" you need to hire a modeling agency. Once the word gets out that a model will fork for free, you tend to constantly work for free. Having fun and enjoying your job doesn't mean you shouldn't be paid. "Thank you's" don't pay the rent or car payments.

Every six months send out updated zed cards, résumés and business cards to companies you enjoyed working for and who promptly paid you.

In the modeling profession, you are selling your "look." Modeling is a very competitive profession. Even if you have an agency, you should always be looking for work and referring potential clients to your agency.

7

MODELING & ETIQUETTE SCHOOLS

Modeling, etiquette & acting schools all have one thing in common: They all build self-esteem and confidence.

In the vast world of modeling, posing in front of a camera is just the beginning. Agencies are looking for talent, from acting to singing and dancing.

The more experience you have, the better chance you will have at getting work.

In this chapter modeling, etiquette and acting schools are listed alphabetically, first by state, then by school.

If you don't see a school listing for your city, get your local phone book out and look in the yellow pages as follows:

Modeling schools	look under …	"Modeling schools"
Etiquette schools	look under …	"Schools-general interest or etiquette instruction"
Dance schools	look under …	"Dancing-instruction"
Acting schools	look under …	"Schools-motion picture"
Voice schools	look under …	"Music-instruction-vocal"

For beginners most cities offer classes from ballroom dancing to ballet and country western, at their local community centers. The fees are generally low and experience is rarely needed to sign up.

If you have a community college in your area, they generally offer a wide range of classes, from acting to voice and dance instruction. Their fees are modest, and the teachers are quite versed in their professions.

The private sector offers more one-on-one training, which normally means higher fees.

Before you sign up or pay a school, you need to ask yourself a very important question: What do I expect to learn from this class?

For example: A modeling school. What are they going to teach you that you don't already know? Makeup, posing, clothes coordination?

If anyone promises you a job but first you must pay them and take their classes, then there probably is no job and it's a scam (See Chapter 9, Modeling Scams & Pitfalls).

Some of the larger franchised schools around the country are very aggressive with their promises. They have high-pressure sales pitches that feed off of your vanity (and pocketbook.) Avoid them or ask them for references—names and phone numbers of models who have graduated from their schools. Talk to family, friends and other models before you pay or sign up for any school.

Don't listen to sales pitches. If something sounds too good to be true, it probably is. Read all contracts very carefully before you sign them. If you don't understand a contract or need more time to read it, be honest. Ask for a copy to take home and study.

If a scouting agency or school tells you that unless you sign the contract immediately they won't have any room left for you, then smile at them and leave the room. You just saved yourself hundreds and possibly thousands of dollars on classes and lessons that are over priced and don't guarantee a modeling career.

Always remember your modeling career is a business and you need to run it like a business. Don't be afraid to ask questions. The more you understand, the more professional you will look.

A little common sense will carry you a long way in the modeling profession.

ALABAMA

CATHY LARSEN AGENCY 1675 Montclair Dr., #136 Birmingham, AL 35210 205-951-2445

C J'S DANCE FACTORY 816 Dozier Ave. Prattville, AL 36067 334-361-0554

FLORA MC GHEE CHARM SCHOOL 1614 11th Ave. N. Birmingham, AL 35204 205-324-6892

JOHN CASABLANCAS MODELING 1446 Montgomery Hwy Vestavia Hills, AL 35216 205-823-5114

PAMA AGENCY 721 Clinton Ave. W. Huntsville, AL 35801 256-536-5200

READY FOR THE WORLD MODELING 4429 Troy Highway Montgomery, AL 36116 334-2843006

SHIRLEY'S STUDIO OF DANCE 503 North Broadway Ave. Sylacauga, AL 35150 205-245-2453

STUDIO 4 MODELS & TALENT 2313 Thomas Ave Guntersville, AL 35976 256-582-6999

ARIZONA

ACT THEATRICAL & MODELING 3400 E. Speedway Blvd. Tucson, AZ 85716 520-795-4615

BARBIZON SCHOOL OF TUCSON 4811 E. Grant Rd. #255 Tucson, AZ 85712 520-323-5010

FLAIR MODELING & TALENT CTR. 6458 N. Oracle Rd. # 1 Tucson, AZ 85704 520-742-1090

FOSI'S ON CAMERA ACTING WKSHOP 2777 N. Campbell Ave. Tucson, AZ 85719 520-795-3534

JOHN CASABLANCA CTR. 7426 E. Stetson Dr. #220 Scottsdale, AZ 85251 480-941-4838

JOHN ROBERT POWERS CTR. 5225 N. Scottsdale Rd. Scottsdale, AZ 85250 480-424-7287

SINCERELY SANDRA IMAGE DEV. 2950 N. Dobson Rd. #4 Chandler, AZ 85224 480-899-2107

ARKANSAS

A CLOSER LOOK 2021 Rogers Ave. Fort Smith, AR 72901 501-783-4488

EXCEL MODELS & TALENT 8201 Cantrell Rd. #215 Little Rock, AR 72227 501-227-4232

STAGES 7509 Cantrell Rd. Little Rock, AR 72207 501-223-9224

CALIFORNIA

ACT MODELING SCHOOL 6464 West Sunset Blvd. #800 Los Angeles, CA 90028 213-466-2733

ADRIAN TEEN MODELS AGENCY 1021 E. Walnut St. #101 Pasadena, CA 91106 626-795-2560

AGENCY MODELS COMMERCIALS 4023 Jewell St. San Diego, CA 92109 858-274-4017

ALESE MARSHALL MODEL, TV 22730 Hawthorne Blvd. #201 Torrance, CA 90505 310-378-1223

ALLEGRIA DANCE THEATRE 14826 Whittier Blvd. Whittier, CA 90605 562-698-8861

AMBIANCE MODELS & TALENT 1733 E. G. St. #121 Ontario, CA 91764 909-931-3939

AMERICAN MODELS 542 College Ave. Modesto, CA 95350 209-526-6045

BARBIZON 591 Camino De La Reina #1150 San Diego, CA 92108 760-729-1322

BARBIZON AGENCY 445 Sutter St. San Francisco, CA 94108 415-956-3162

BARBIZON MODEL AGENCY 591 Kamino Dela Reina #1159 San Diego, CA 92108 760-352-1900

BARBIZON SCHOOL 4844 N. 1st St. #104 Fresno, CA 93726 559-225-4883

BARBIZON SCHOOL 701 Howe Ave. #H-50 Sacramento, CA 95825 916-920-4200

BROOKS COLLEGE 4825 E. Pacific Coast Hwy. Long Beach, CA 90804 562-597-6611

BUCKINGHAM IMAGES 16685 E. St. # 107 Fresno, CA 93706 559-233-5131

CATHY STEELE MODEL 1610 Oak Park Blvd. Pleasant Hill, CA 94523 925-932-4226

CHARM INC. 1456 W. Mendocino Ave. Stockton, CA 95204 209-464-3708

DAISY INNER BEAUTY 1100 Soquel Ave. Santa Cruz, CA 95062 831-459-9617

DE VORE ARTISTS 2224 N. Fine Ave. Fresno, CA 93727 559-255-2317

EMILY WALKER SCHOOL 2222 W. Manchester Blvd. Inglewood, CA 90305 323-759-5707

EXTRAORDINAIRE MODELS 200 New Stine Rd. Bakersfield, CA 93309 661-397-1157

FINESSE MODEL DEV. 20 Kientz Ln. San Anselmo, CA 94960 415-482-7980

FLAIR MODELING 12318 Saratoga Sunnyvale Rd. Saratoga, CA 95070 408-257-0448

FREDRICK'S MODELING SCHOOL 1031 McHenry Ave. #16 Modesto, CA 95350 209-527-0009

GIRALDO PATRICIA 8353 Cedros Ave. Panorama City, CA 91402 818-920-1304

GISELLE'S TALENT ACADEMY 1601 University Ave. Riverside, CA 92507 909-274-9247

HARVARD EXCEL CTR. 3807 Wilshire Blvd. #930 Los Angeles, CA 90010 213-386-1953

HOLLYWOOD FILMS SCHOOL 2500 Townsgate Rd. #K Westlake Village, CA 91361 805-496-5306

HOLLYWOOD INTL. STUDIO 6253 Hollywood Blvd. Los Angeles, CA 90028 323-856-4871

IN STYLE 2639 Terminal Blvd. Mountain View, CA 94043 650-318-0000

IZEL MODELING & ACTING 411 S. Associated Rd. Brea, CA 92821 714-672-6949

JEAN PIERRE INTL. 1349 Springfield CT. Fairfield, CA 94533 707-429-0802

JOHN CASABLANCAS 1011 Camino Del Rios #201 San Diego, CA 92108 619-299-7200

JOHN ROBERT POWERS ENT. 300 E. Esplanade Dr. #1640 Oxnard, CA 93030 805-983-1076

JOHN ROBERT POWERS 9220 w. sunset Blvd. Los Angeles, CA 90069 310-858-3300

JOHN ROBERT POWERS 30125 Agoura Rd. #G Agoura Hills, CA 91301 818-707-2602

JOHN ROBERT POWERS 27200 Tourney Rd. #120 Santa Clarita, CA 91355 661-286-1360

JOHN ROBERT POWERS 10570 Foothill Blvd. #230 Rancho Cucamonga, CA 91730 909-980-7673

JOHN ROBERT POWERS 16434 Beach Blvd. Westminister, CA 92683 714-375-4400

JOHN ROBERT POWERS 20 Independence Circle Chino, CA 95973 530-879-5900

JOHN ROBERT POWERS DEV CTR. 1600 Saratoga Ave. #109 San Jose, CA 95129 408-871-8709

JOHN ROBERT POWERS ENT. 8910 University Center Ln. #120 San Diego, CA 92122 858-824-0700

JOHN ROBERT POWERS 26 Ofarrell St. #6 San Francisco, CA 94108 415-362-8260

JOURNEY TO CTR. STAGE 5773 Pleasant Valley Rd. El Dorado, CA 95623 530-621-2809

JULIE NATION TALENT 2455 Bennett Valley RD. #110A Santa Rosa, CA 95404 707-575-8585

JUST 4 KIDS ENT.CO. 1111 Howe Ave. # 600 Sacramento, CA 95825 916-929-4386

KIDS ON CAMERA 1515 Vallejo St. San Francisco, CA 94109 415-440-4400

LARYSA PLAWAN SCHOOL 1900 Garden Dr. #321 Burlingame, CA 94010 650-342-9459

MACKER ENT CA. STUDIO 1111 N. Brand Blvd. #F Glendale, CA 91292 818-543-1211

MODEL U 2182 S. El Camino Real Oceanside, CA 92054 760-758-4884

MODELS CENTER 9281 Irvine Blvd Irvine, CA 92618 714-662-1000

MODELS WEST-ACTING 22808 Soledad Canyon Rd. Santa Clarita, CA 91350 661-290-2680

NORMA PAYTON SCHOOL 1361 Park St. Alameda, CA 94501 510-523-7000

ON CAMERA ASSOC. 14570 E. 14th St. San Leandro, CA 94578 925-600-7980

PROMOTIONS CO. 401 N. Brookhurst St. #200 Anaheim, CA 92801 714-491-7237

PROTOCOL SCHOOL 871 Ames Ave. Palo Alto, CA 94393 650-856-1970

ROLE MODEL PRODUCTIONS 33012 Pinnacle Dr. Trabuco Canyon, CA 92679 949-459-0268

SIMPLY CHARMING MODELING 1850 5th Ave. San Diego, CA. 92101 619-544-9880

SPOTLITE ARTS ACADEMY 7022 Village Pkwy Dublin, CA 94568 925-828-9722

STEPHANIE LLOYD TV 1170 N. Coast Hwy Laguna Beach, CA 92651 949-497-8274

STEPHEN MITCHELL STUDIO 11020 Ventura Blvd. #G Studio City, CA 91604 818-505-1676

SUZI'S FINISHING SCHOOL 20 El Viento Pismo Beach, CA 93449 805-773-0888

TROOP GROUP PRODUCTION 10519 S. Western Ave. Los Angeles, CA 90047 323-779-6519

TWISTERS GYMNASTICS 2639 Terminal Blvd. Mountain View, CA 94043 650-967-5581

VANCAT ENTERPRISES 1409 Harris Ct. Antioch, CA 94509 925-778-6983

VICKI CLEMENCE CENTER 14826 Whittier Blvd. Whittier, CA 90605 562-698-8861

WEST MODELING & ACTING 29134 Roadside Dr. #102 Agoura Hills CA 91301 818-889-3555

COLORADO

ASPIRE MODEL INC. 126 W. 5th Ave. Denver, CO 80204 303-733-3888

BARBIZON AGENCY 7535 East Hampden Ave. #108 Denver, CO 80231 303-337-7954

BELLA MODELS 2708 w. Colorado Ave. Colorado Springs, CO 80904 719-471-3030

JOHN CASABLANCAS CTR. 7600 E. Eastman Ave. #100 Denver, CO 80231 303-337-5100

JOHN ROBERT POWERS 14231 E. 4th Ave. #200 Aurora, CO 80011 303-340-2838

CONNECTICUT

ALLISON DANIELS AGENCY 1260 New Britain Ave. West Hartford, CT 06110 860-920-53125

BARBIZON SCHOOLS 135 Atlantic St. Stamford, CT 06901 203-359-0427

ETTIQUETTE USA 2505 Main St. Stratford, CT 06615 203-377-7109

JOHN CASABLANCAS CTR. 1263 Wilber Cross Hwy #2 Berlin, CT 06037 860-828-7577

DELAWARE

BARBIZON SCHOOL OF MODELING 17 Trolley Square # B Wilmington, DE 19806 302-658-6666

BARBIZON SCHOOL OF MODELING 909 N. Dupont Blvd. Milford, DE 19963 302-424-4500

CASE SCHOOL OF ETIQUETTE 310 Amorosa Way Newark, DE 19711 302-369-9471

CREATIVE IMAGES SCHOOL 222 Philadelphia Pike, Wilmington, DE 19809 302-764-9514

FLORIDA

ACADEMIA CRYSTAL 11455 S. Orange Blossom Trl. Orlando, FL 32837 407-858-9220

ACTORS &MODELS AGENCY 8181 NW. 36th St. Miami, FL 33166 305-591-8676

ACTORS SCHOOL FOR PERFORMING 9711 W. Sample Rd. Coral Springs, FL. 33065 954-753-2993

ALICIA FACCIO MODELING SCHOOL 8181 NW 36th St. #30 Miami, FL 33166 305-591-8166

ALICIA FACCIO MODELING 1822 N. University Dr. #B Plantation, FL 33322 954-423-2230

ARIANA'S ETIQUETTE SCHOOL 8441 SW 132nd St. Miami, FL 33156 305-234-9002

ASHLEY CAMILLE SCHOOL 909 Semoran Blvd. Casselberry, FL 32707 407-332-0195

ATTITUDE PERFORMANCE ARTS 5238 Norwood Ave. #15 Jacksonville, FL 32208 904-764-0606

BARBIE MODELING SCHOOL 1110 E. 8th Ave. Hialeah, FL 33010 305-888-6607

BARBIXON 1917 Boothe Circle Longwood, FL 32750 407-331-5558

BARBIZON INTL. 2240 WJ. Woolbright Rd. #300 Boynton Beach, FL 33426 561-369-8600

CHARMETTE CHARM & MODELING 53 Curtis Parkway Miami Springs, FL 33166 305-883-8252

CITRUS PERFORMING ARTS CTR. 2301 Carter St. Inverness, FL 34453 352-344-4422

DEBBIE'S DANCE CO. 11570 San Jose Blvd. Jacksonville, FL 32223 904-268-1410

DENISE CAROL MODELING STUDIO 2223 Atlantic Blvd. Jacksonville, FL 32207 904-398-6306

ELIZABETH HERNANDEZ IMAGE DEV. 5675 La Costa Dr. #D Orlando, FL 32807 407-273-3484

ELLEN MEADE SCHOOL 1323 63rd Ave. E. Bradenton, FL 3422203 941-755-1757

FAME INTL. 505 Deltona Blvd Deltona, FL 32725 407-860-0890

FINE ARTS STUDIO 436 SW 15th St. Ocala, FL 34474 352-622-7556

FIRESTONE MODELING SCHOOL 31 Barkley Cir. Fort Myers, FL 33907 941-939-3918

GEGEE'S STUDIO 706 E. Duval St. Lake City, FL 32055 904-752-4888

INTL ETIQUETTE SCHOOL 300 Palermo Ave. Coral Gables, FL 33134 305-446-7776

INTL MODELS INC. 8415 Coral Way # 205 Miami, FL 33155 305-266-6331

IT'S TOTALLY YOU 4427 SE 16th Pl. Cape Coral, FL 33904 941-541-9111

JOHN CASABLANCAS 1060 W. State Rd. 434 # 138 Longwood, FL 32750 407-265-1501

JOHN CASABLANCAS 10200 NW 25th St. #A105 Miami, FL 33172 305-716-0222

JOHN CASABLANCAS CTR 5215 W. Laurel St. #110 Tampa, FL 33607 813-289-8564

JOHN CASABLANCAS STUDIOS 8380 Baymeadows Rd. #14 Jacksonville, FL 32256 904-739-1118

JOHN ROBERT POWERS 1170 3rd St. S #C-203 Naples, FL 34102 941-430-0621

LISA MAILE IMAGES 999 s. Orlando Ave Winter Park, FL 32789 407-628-5989

LITTLE THEATRE SCHOOL 18822 NE. 29th Ave. Miami, FL 33180 305-936-9795
MAXINE'S MODELS CLIQUE 7795 W. Flagler St. #44 Miami, FL 33144 305-266-6263
MICHELE POMMIER ENT. 1916 Bay Rd. Miami Beach, FL 33139 305-674-1733
MODEL CENTRE 3201 SW 34th Ave. Ocala, FL 34474 352-237-1611
MODELS SCOUTS INC. 651 Rugby St. Orlando, FL 32804 407-420-5888
NATIONAL INST. OF ETHICS 1060 W. State Rd. 434 # 164 Longwood, FL 32750 407-339-0322
NEW IMAGES & CHARM 160 N. Florida Ave. Inverness, FL 34453 352-341-0050
PANACHE YOUTH OUTREACH 7896 Sonoma Springs Cir. Lakeworth, FL 33463 561-649-7779
S & S NETWORK 14765 NE 10th Ave. North Miami, FL 33161 305-354-7025
SESSIONS MODELING 10991 San Jose Blvd. #16B Jacksonville, FL 32223 904-292-4366
SET FIVE TALENT 714 Glenview Dr. Tallahassee, FL 32303 850-224-8500
STUDIO SASHAY 10387 Gandy Blvd N. St. Petersburg, FL 33702 727-570-2226
TURNABOUT MODELING 740 Beachland Blvd. Vero Beach, FL 32963 561-231-4579

GEORGIA

ABOUT FACES 3391 Peachtree Rd. NE. #410 Atlanta, GA 30326 404-237-9800
ATHENS MODELING 1052 Oliver Bridge Rd. Watkinsville, GA 30677 706-769-9341
BARBIZON SCHOOL OF MODELING 3340 Peachtree Rd. NE #120 Atlanta, GA 30326 404-261-7332
BAUDER COLLEGE 3500 Peachtree Rd. NE. #C. Atlanta, GA 30326 404-237-7573
HANDMAID PRODUCTIONS 2523 Roosevelt Hwy College Park, GA 30337 404-765-1788
JOHN CASABLANCAS 6255 Barfield Rd. NE. #165 Atlanta, GA 30328 404-705-9494
KIDDIN AROUND TALENT 1479 Spring St. NW. Atlanta, GA 30309 404-872-8582
LASHAY'S SCHOOL OF MODELING 6151 Old Natl. Hwy. College Park, GA 30349 770-996-0707
LIZ UNIQUE MODELS 1201 Williams St. #4 Valdosta, GA 31601 229-245-9934
LORREN & MACY'S SCHOOL 12 Riverbend Dr. SW. #235 Rome, GA 30161 706-235-1175
MADEMOISELLE MODEL 2901 University Ave. Columbus, GA 31907 706-561-9449

MILLIE LEWIS OF SAVANNAH 7011 Hodgson Memorial Dr. Savannah, GA 31406 912-354-9525

MODEL PRODUCTION 3604 Verandah Dr. Augusta, GA 30909 706-731-9889

MODELING & PAGEANTS 2200 Powder Springs Rd. SW Marietta, GA 30064 770-499-0934

MODELING IMAGES 2106 Chatou Pl. NW. Kennesaw, GA 30152 770-919-8285

MODELING SHOP 115 Marble Mill Rd. NW Marietta, GA 30060 770-424-6077

PREMIUM SCHOOL 3545 Peachtree Ind. Blvd. NW. #2B Duluth, GA 30096 770-232-1882

HAWAII

ISLAND FACES SCHOOL 1024 Kamalu Rd. Kapaa, HI 96746 808-822-7263

KATHY MULLER TALENT 619 Kapahula Ave. Honolulu, HI 96815

MODELS INC. 98-025 Hekaha St. #222A Aiea, HI 96701 808-484-1257

PREMIER AGENCY 1441 Kapiolani Blvd. #1206 Honolulu, HI 96814 808-955-6511

V TALENT AND MANAGEMENT 2153 N. King St. #323A Honolulu, HI 96819 808-843-0883

IDAHO

BLANCHE B EVANS SCHOOL 4311 Audubon P. Boise, ID 83705 208-344-5380

METCALF'S MODELING & TALENT 1851 Century Way # 3 Boise, ID 83709 208-378-8777

ILLINOIS

BARBIZON MODELING SCHOOL 541 North Fairbanks Court, Chicago IL 60611 312-321-6200

BARBIZON MODELING SCHOOL 1051 Perimeter Drive, Schaumburg, IL 60173 847-240-4200

BEST IMPRESSIONS 3939 Cumberland Dr. Quincy, IL 62301 217-222-6262

ELEMENTARY ETIQUETTE SOCIETY Glencoe, IL 60022 847-835-5247

ETIQUETTE PLUS 223 Brittany Dr. Fairview Heights, IL 62208 618-397-3805

GLAMOUR GIRL CHARM SCHOOL 2601 N. Mission Rd. Peoria, IL 61604 309-682-4266

JOHN ROBERT POWERS MODELING 27 East Monroe St. # 200 Chicago, IL 60603 312-726-1404

MANNERS MATTER 7306 Bunker Rd. Darien, IL 60561 630-322-9928

PATRICIA RAY MODEL ENT. 19 Willow Lane, Bristol, IL 60512 630-859-3444

PAULA PERSON INC. P.O. Box 148 Winnetka, IL 60093 847-251-3382

SOCIAL PRESENCE INC. 60 E. Chestnut St. #245 Chicago, IL 60611 312-951-6062

TALENT FORUM 450 Peterson Rd. Libertyville, IL 60048 847-816-1711

INDIANA

AAA MODELING & TALENT 736 10TH Pl. Mishawaka, IN 46544 219-247-9052

CHARMAINE SCHOOL 3538 Stellhorn Rd. Fort Wayne, IN 46815 219-485-8421

COVER SHOT MODELING 14370 State Road 23 Granger, IN 46530 219-271-1992

FINISHING TOUCH MODELING 2500 Harmony Way, Evansville, IN 47720 812-422-5064

FIRST CLASS PRODUCTIONS 230 E. Montgomery Ave. Clarksville, IN 47129 812-288-4631

MANNERS MATTERS 2033 Hamilton Ln. Carmel, IN 46032 317-843-2717

IOWA

ADA GAFFNEY SHAFF CHARM 2675 Tech Dr. #3A Betterdorf, IA 52722 319-332-6115

AVANT MODELING & TALENT 10546 Justin Dr. Urbandale, IA 50322 515-251-4199

KANSAS

ACTOR'S LAB 801 w. Douglas Ave. Wichita, KS 67213 316-265-2323

HOFFMAN INTL. 6705 w. 91ST. St. Shawnee Mission, KS 66212 913-642-1060

JACK & JILL PLAYERS 3928 w. 69th St. Shawnee Mission, KS 66208 913-831-2223

MODELS IMAGES 1619 n. rock Rd. Wichita, KS 67206 316-634-2777

SHERI'S CHARM SCHOOL 6124 sw 39th Circle Topeka, KS 66610 785-478-0845

THEATRE FOR YOUNG AMERICA 4881 Johnson Dr. Shawnee Mission, KS 66205 913-831-2131

WICHITA CHILDREN'S THEATRE 201 Lulu St. Wichita, KS 67211 316-262-2282

KENTUCKY

ALIX ADAMS MODEL SCHOOL 9813 Merioneth Dr. Jeffersontown, KY 40299 502-266-6990

BARBARANN'S SCHOOL OF MODELING 105 Princess Dr. Ashland, KY 41101 606-324-6683

CARLA RIGGS-HALL ENT. 202 Masters St. Elizabethtown, KY 42701 270-769-0255

COSMO MODEL & TALENT 7410 La Grande Rd. #204 Louisville, KY 40222 502-425-8000

DEBRA'S 117 S. 5th St. Paducah, KY 42001 270-442-2365

DIAMOND MODELS & TALENT 1195 SJ. Main St. #A. Madisonville, KY. 42431 270-821-0600

IMAGES MODEL AGENCY 163 E. Reynolds Rd. Lexington, KY 40517 859-273-2301

VOGUE OF LEXINGTON 1300 New Circle Rd. NE.# 112 Lexington, KY 40505 859-254-4582

LOUISIANA

ABOUT FACES MODELING 423 Jefferson St. Lafayette, LA 70501 337-235-3223

ENCHANTMENTS BY ELIZABETH 11010 E. Nickens Rd. Hammond, LA 70403 225-294-9100

FACE TO FACE 106 E. Kings Hwy Shreveport, LA 71104 318-868-2264

IDENTITY 4861 Magazine St. New Orleans, LA 70115 504-891-7443

JOHN CASABLANCAS 880 W. Commerce Rd. #103 New Orleans, LA 70123 504-818-1000

MODEL WORLD 602 Alex St. Houma, LA 70360 985-868-0613

OMA'S MODELING AGENCY 2318 ½ Walnut St. Rear Bossier City, LA 71112 318-861-2075

PHYLLIS NELSON PERFORMING ARTS 382 Robert Blvd. Slidell, LA 70458 985-641-0889

MARYLAND

BELLE CHARM 3911 Cotton Tree Ln. Burtonsville, MD 20866 301-989-9343

BELLE CHARM 23 Fieldstone Ct. Silver Spring, MD 20905 301-989-9343

CHARIOT OF ANGELS ACADEMY 7127 Allentown Rd. Fort Washington, MD 20744 310-449-1200

CHILDREN'S SPECIALTEAS 6205 Brookside Dr. Chevy Chase, MD 20815 301-654-5999

ELEGANT IMAGES 52 N. Main St. Bel Air, MD 21014 410-838-5206

ELEGANZA P.O. Box 416 Aberdeen, MD 21001 410-272-7409

FLAIR STUDIO OF DANCE 5602 Baltimore Nation Pike Catonsville, MD 21228 410-744-3901

GEDDINGS FASHION INSTITUTE 3613 St. Barnabas Rd. Suitland, MD 20746 310-899-2392

GFI STUDIOS 3613 Saint Barnabas Rd. Suitland, MD 20746 301-899-2392

JOHN CASABLANCAS CENTER 7801 York Rd. #303 Baltimore, MD 21204 410-821-6966

LA GAFFORD STUDIO 1303 Glenwielde Rd. Catonsville, MD 21228 410-744-8637

MODEL IMAGE STUDIOS 8001 Harford Rd. #B Baltimore, MD 21234 410-668-9200

MODEL'S WORKSHOP 9249 E. Parkhill Dr. Bethedsa, MD 20814 301-564-0883

VISIONS CHRISTIAN SCHOOL 8203 Harford Rd. Parkville, MD 21234 410-668-6868

YOLANDA VOSS STUDIO 8600 Foundry St. Savage, MD 20763 301-317-4007

MASSACHUSETTS

ANNMARIE'S STUDIO OF MODELING 347 n. Westfield St. Feeding Hills, MA 01031 413-789-3385

BARBIZON SCHOOL OF MODELING 607 Boylston St. Boston, MA 02116 617-266-6980

JOHN CASABLANCAS CENTER 1 Gateway Ctr. #180 Newton, MA 02158 617-969-2244

MICHIGAN

ADAMS MODELING & FINISHING 2722 e. Michigan Ave. #205 Lansing, MI 48912 517-482-4600

AMERICAN DANCE ACADEMY 32669 Warren Rd. #6 Garden City, MI 48135 734-261-6170

A PLUS DANCE 817 m 89 Plainwell, MI 49080 616-685-4444

ARRAND MODELING SCHOOL 13344 Wenwood Dr. Fenton, MI 48430 810-629-7161

BARBIZON SCHOOL 6230 Orchard Lake Rd. #110 West Bloomfield, MI 48322 248-855-5660

BRENDA'S DANCE ACADEMY 118 E. Lawrence Ave. Charlotte, MI 48813 517-543-8800

CARTALINA'S CHARM SCHOOL 19556 Grand River Ave. Detroit, MI 48223 313-534-3392

CENTER STAGE DANCE STUDIO 1930 W. Milham Ave. #C Portage, MI 49024 616-344-0114

CHARMELLE SCHOOL OF ETIQUETTE P.O Box 310378 Flint, MI 48531 810-732-5049

DANCE CONNECTION 1672 S. Lilley Rd. Canton, MI 48188 734-397-9755

DANCE ELECTRIC 24717 Crestview Ct. Farmington Hills, MI 48335 248-477-3830

FULL & FABULOUS 3544 Algonquin St. Detroit, MI 48215 313-862-0776

JOHN CASABLANCAS 40840 Van Dyke Ave. Sterling Heights, MI 48313 810-795-9800

JOHN CASABLANCAS CTR. 45185 Joy Rd. #101 Canton, MI 48187 734-455-0700

JOHN ROBERT POWERS SCHOOL 26500 Northwestn Hwy #33—Southfield, MI 48076 248-352-1234

MANNEQUIN MODELING CTR. 19148 E. 10 Mile Rd. Eastpointe, MI 48021 810-772-1940

MAXINE POWELL FINISHING SCHOOL 8106 e. Jefferson Ave. Detroit, MI 48214 313-331-4333

MPM PRODUCTIONS 19556 Grand River Ave. Detroit, MI 48223 313-534-7080

STELLAR MODELS 2739 Breton Rd. SE. Grand Rapids, MI 49546 616-977-1011

MINNESOTA

AGENCY WORKSHOPS 430 n. 1st Ave. #410 Minneapolis, MN 55401 612-338-1605
CARYN INTL MODEL 6651 Hwy 7 St. Louis Park, MN 55426 612-337-8400
DEBORA RACHELLE INC. 1017 W. Central Entrance Duluch, MN 55811 218-722-0340
IMAGE 1 PRO & ACTING 601 9th Ave. N. St. Cloud, MN 56303 320-251-0101
JOHN CASABLANCAS CTR. 1021 Bandana Blvd. E. #128 St. Paul, MN 55108 651-642-1222
JOHN CASABLANCAS CTR. 8200 Humboldt Ave. South Bloomington, MN 55431 612-948-9000
LA TERESE IMAGE 211 5th Ave. S. St. Cloud, MN 56401 320-654-6053
MAREY STUDIOS INC. 3450 Bonna Belle Ct. St. Cloud, MN 56301 320-259-1404

MISSISSIPPI

ALPHA SCHOOL OF DANCE 1016 24TH Ave. Meridian, MS 39301 601-693-2331
5TH Ave. MODELING SCHOOL 499 Gloster Creek Tupelo, MS 38801 662-840-5555
BARBIZON ACADEMY 931 Hwy 80 W. Jackson, MS 39204 601-355-0008
COLOR CAMPUS & ACTING 240 Eisenhower Dr. #12 Biloxi, MS 39531 228-388-2465
GRANT & CO. 499 Gloster Creek Tupelo, MS 38801 662-840-5555
KELLI'S SCHOOL OF DANCE 883 Howard Ave. Biloxi, MS 39530 228-432-0047

MISSOURI

ACADEMY OF PERFORMING ARTS 3600 Blue Ridge Ext. Grandview, MO 64030 816-761-7080
ACT UP DRAMA ACADEMY 1006 SW. Blue Pkwy Lees Summit, MO 64063 816-525-7744
ACTOR'S CRAFT STUDIO 4424 Campbell St. Kansas City, MO 64110 816-931-0099
AMERICAN HEARTLAND THEATRE 2450 Grand Blvd. #314 Kansas City, MO 64108 816-842-9999
BARBIZON SCHOOL OF MODELING 7525 Forsyth Blvd. St. Louis, MO 63105 314-863-1141

CHARACTERS & CO. 338 S. Kirkwood Rd. Kirkwood, MO 63122 314-822-6228

COMMERCIAL ACTORS STUDIO 1616 Westport Rd. Kansas City, MO 64111 816-5454

FLASH OF BEAUTY CHARM SCHOOL 3014 Montgall Ave. Kansas City, MO 64128 816-861-6849

GOLDEN STARS PERFORMING ARTS 4012 N. Newstead Ave. St. Louis, MO 63115 314-381-8082

ISBEN DANCE THEATRE 7221 N. Oak Trfy Kansas City, MO 64118 816-436-7277

JOHN CASABLANCAS MGMNT. 330 West 47th St. # 220 Kansas City, MO 64112 816-561-9400

JOHN ROBERT POWELL MODELING 711 Old Frontenac Sq. St. Louis, MO 63131 314-993-4097

KAY MODELING SCHOOL 1201 West 7th St. Joplin, MO 64801 417-781-4540

LEAPING LIZARDS PERFORMING ART 6907 Lansdowne Ave. St. Louis, MO 63109 314-645-6463

NORMA'S MODELING SCHOOL 3638 S. Campbell Ave. Springfield, MO 65807 417-882-2436

PATRICIA STEVENS AGENCY 2000 Baltimore Ave. Kansas City, MO 64108 816-221-1188

SAVOIR FAIRE PROGRAMME 7309 Natural Bridge Rd. St. Louis, MO 63121 314-381-9334

SCHOOL OF BALLET 508 ½ s. Joplin Ave. Joplin, MO 64801 417-782-4089

SCHOOL OF PERFORMING ARTS 22916 Perimeter Ln. Lebanon, MO 65536 417-532-3293

SPRINGFIELD LITTLE THEATRE 314 E. Pershing St. Springfield, MO 65806 417-831-9086

TALENT UNLIMITED 4049 Pennsylvania Ave. #300 Kansas City, MO 64111 816-561-9040

NEBRASKA

AMERICAN MODEL & TALENT 2806 S. 110th Ct. Omaha, NE 68114 402-399-8480

INTERNATIONAL MODELING SCHOOL 2806 S. 110th Ct. Omaha, NE 68144 402-399-8787

NANCY BOUNDS SCHOOL 11915 Pierce Plaza Omaha, NE 68144 402-697-9292

NEW JERSEY

ACTORS TRAINING INSTITUTE 91 Monmouth St. Red Bank, NJ. 07701 732-219-0055

ACTING WORKSHOP 2921 Atlantic Ave. Atlantic City, NJ 08401 609-347-0074

AMERICAN COED PAGEANTS 21 3rd St. Elmer, NJ 08318 856-358-6400

ATLANTIC CITY SCHOOL 8 S. Hanover Ave. Margate City, NJ 08402 609-822-2222

BARBIZON MODELING SCHOOL 440 State Rt. 17 Hasbrouck Hgts., NJ 07604 201-727-1034

BARBIZON SCHOOL 70 Park St. #A Montclair, NJ 07042 973-783-4030

BARBIZON SCHOOL of MODELING 300 Raritan Ave. Highland Park, NJ 08904 732-846-3800

BARBIZON SCHOOL OF MODELING 2103 Whitehorse Merc Rd. Trenton, NJ 08619 609-586-3310

BARBIZON SCHOOL OF MODELING 80 Broad Street Red Bank, NJ 07701 732-842-6161

CALIFORNIA MODELING SCHOOL 937 Brunswick Ave. Trenton, NJ 08638 609-393-3323

DIVAS PRODUCTION 553 61st St. West New York, NJ 07093 201-453-9090

GIRLS ON THE MOVE YOUTH 6805 Clark Ave. Camden, NJ 08105 856-486-4366

JO ANDERSON MODELING SCHOOL 1 Eves Drive Marlton, NJ 08053 609-596-7200

LA CRÈME CTR FOR MODELING 2331 Morris Ave. Union, NJ 07083 908-688-4411

LYONS ASSOCIATES 261 Bloomfield Ave. #C. Verona, NJ 07044 973-857-6200

MODEL TEAM 55 Central Ave. Ocean Grove, NJ 07756 732-988-3648

MODELS ON THE MOVE P.O.Box 4037 Cherry Hill, NJ 08034 856-667-1060

SANDERS CENTER FOR PERFORMING 586 Route 70 Brick, NJ 08723 732-477-9695

STARMAKER GYNMASTICS 718 W. Saint Georges Ave. Linden, NJ 07036 908-925-1155

TOP MODEL USA 4300 Bergenline Ave. Union City, NJ 07087 201-867-0190

NEVADA

AMERICA'S TOUCH OF CLASS 5437 Palmyra Ave. Las Vegas, NV 89146 702-313-9698

BARBIZON SCHOOL 1515 West Tropicana Ave. #785 Las Vegas, NV 89119 702-798-4120

CHARM UNLIMITED 880 East Sahara Ave. #106 Las Vegas, NV 89104 702-735-2335

J & J PAGEANTS & TALENT 3930 n. walnut Rd. Las Vegas, NV 89115 702-643-1006

JOHN CASABLANCAS CTR. 2080 E. Flamingo Rd. # 219 Las Vegas, NV 89119 702-733-8140

JOHN ROBERT POWERS 3010 W. Charleston Blvd. # 100 Las Vegas, NV 89102 702-461-9836

LAS VEGAS SCHOOL OF MODELING 3785 E. Desert Inn Rd. Las Vegas, NV 89121 702 433-7781

MIKEL'S DANCE ACADEMY 7514 Westcliff Dr. Las Vegas, NV 89128 702-256-4522

NEVADA STATE CINDERELLA 1780 n. Leslie St. Pahrump, NV 89060 775-727-0706

NEW MEXICO

JOHN ROBERT POWERS 2021 San Mateo Blvd. NE. Albuquerque, NM 87110 505-266-5677

NEW MEXICO FILM INSTE.6921 Montgomery Blvd. NE. Albuquerque, NM 87109 505-880-1095

NEW YORK

A L MODELS INC. 1011 Ave. Of The Americas New York, NY 10018 212-997-9371

AMBER DEENIE INTL INC. 3510 Union St. Flushing, NY 11354 718-321-2138

AMS MODELS & COORDINATORS P.O.Box 77 Clay, NY 13041 315-474-8466

BARBIZON SCHOOL OF MODELING 7163 Furnace Rd. Ontario, NY 14519 315-524-2800

BARBIZON SCHOOL OF MODELING 415 7th Ave. New York, NY 10001 718-230-0550

BARBIZON SCHOL OF MODELING 190 Post Rd. White Plains, NY 01601 914-428-2030

CAROLINA MODELING WORKSHOP 414 W. 53rd. St. New York, NY 10019 212-262-1292

CENTEREACH THEATRE ARTS 14 43rd. St. Centereach, NY 11720 631-467-0799

CHENEY TALENT ASSOC. 325 W. 38th St. #1407 New York, NY 10018 212-643-6924

CONWELL CAREER CENTRE 137 Summer St. Buffalo, NY 14222 716-884-0763

DIANNE LYNN DANCE THEATRE 3259 Winton Rd. S. Rochester, NY 14623 716-427-8800

GRAMERCY MODELS INC. 234 5th Ave. # 5 New York, NY 10001 212-598-1003

JOANNE'S FASHION & CHARM 2204 Pinnacle Dr. Utica, NY 13501 315-797-6424

JOHN CASABLANCAS CTR. 6902 Austin St. Flushing, NY 11375 718-997-0718

JUILLIARD SCHOOL 60 Lincoln Center Plaza New York, NY 10023 212-799-5000

JUNE 2 MODELING SCHOOL 2 Irving Pl. Buffalo, NY 14201 716-883-7672

L MODELS 1807 Elmwood Ave. Buffalo, NY 14207 716-874-3553

MARGO GEORGE MODELING SCHOOL 159 W. Main St. Goshen, NY 10924 845-294-8145

MARY THERESE FRIEL INC. 1251 Pittsford Mendon Rd. Mendon, NY 14506 716-624-5510

MODEL & TALENT MGMNT 415 7th Ave. # 170 New Yrok, NY 10001 212-239-6608

MODEL MERCHANDISING INTL. 111 E. 22nd St. # 4 New York, NY 10010 212-420-0655

NUAH PRODUCTIONS 25 Woodbury Rd. Hicksville, NY 11801 516-937-1735

OPHELIA DE VORE & ASSOC. 350 5th Ave. New York, NY 10118 212-629-6400

PERSONAL BEST 3653 Harlem Rd. Buffalo, NY 14215 716-831-3870

TYNANS SCHOOL OF PERFORMING 40 Russell Rd. Albany, NY 12206 518-459-9117

NORTH CAROLINA

AMRON SCHOOL OF THE FINE ARTS 1315 Medlin Rd. Monroe, NC 28112 704-283-4290

BARBIZON SCHOOL OF MODELING 4109 Wake Forest Rd. #400 Raleigh, NC 27609 919-876-8201

BARBIZON MODELING CTR. 8318 Pineville Matthews # 265 Charlotte, NC 28226 704-544-1550

CHANDLER MODELING & TALENT 5501 Executive Center #232 Charlote, NC 28212 704-531-1902

CHARLOTTE BLUME DANCE 1312 Morganton Rd. Fayetteville, NC 28305 910-484-3466

CITIES CLASSIC MODELS 1 Buffalo Ave. NW. #203 Concord, NC 28025 704-795-6049

D & S TALENT 101 S. Main St. Monroe, NC 28112 704-283-1659

FAMA MODELING & ACTING 1605 W. Vernon Ave. Kingston, NC 28504 252-526-0390

HIS IMAGE MODELING 4600 Park Rd. # 300 Charlotte, NC 28209 704-329-0780

JOAN BAKER MODELING SCHOOL 137 W. Mountain St. Kings Mountain, NC 28086 704-739-6868

JOHN CASABLANCAS MODELING CTR. 4326 Bland Rd. Raleigh, NC 27609 919-878-0911

JOHN CASABLANCAS MODELING CTR. 810 Tyvola Rd. # 100 Charlote, NC 28217 704-523-6966

JOHN ROBERT POWERS 4020 Westchase Blvd. #220 Raleigh, N 27607 919-828-9959

JOHN ROBERT POWERS 915 E. 4th St. #B Charlotte, NC 28204 704-358-9010

LIBBY STONE FINISHING SCHOOL 1819 Charlotte Dr. Charlote, NC 82803 704-377-9299

PROFESSIONAL MODELS GUILD 1819 Charlotte Dr. Charlotte, NC 82803 704-377-9299

SUZANNE'S STUDIO OF FINISHING 2502 E. Ash St. Goldsboro, NC 27534 919-734-7038

TOUCH OF CLASS MODELING SCHOOL 103 Whitney Pl. Goldsboro, NC 27530 919-736-7665

TOUCH OF CLASS MODELING SCHOOL 401 W. 1st St. Greenville, NC 27834 252-752-0509

VOGUE MODEL & DANCE STUDIO 7424 Chapel Hill Rd. # 204 Raleigh, NC 27607 919-816-9898

OHIO

AT EASE INC. 119 E. Court St. Cincinnati, OH 45205 513-241-5216

BARBIZON SCHOOL 6450 Rockside Woods Blvd Cleveland, OH 44131 216-351-8100

BARBIZON SCHOOL OF MODELING 1739 Arborhill Dr. Columbus, OH 43229 614-885-7200

ETIQUETTE CONSULTING 5091 Meadow Wood Blvd. Cleveland, OH 44124 440-442-3039

FASHION POINT MODELING 702 S. Main St. North Canton, OH 44720 330-494-1101

JOHN CASABLANCAS CTR. 5405 Southwyck Blvd. Toledo, OH 43614 419-866-6335

JOHN CASABLANCAS CTR. 6322 Busch Blvd. Columbus, OH 43229 614-847-0010

LILLIAN GALLOWAY AGENCY 6047 Montgomery Rd. Cincinnati, OH 45213 513-351-2700

MARGARET O' BRIAN'S MODELING 330 S. Reynolds Rd. # 12 Toledo, OH 43615 419-536-5522

MARIAN'S SCHOOL OF MODELING 831 Watervliet Ave. Dayton, OH 45420 937-252-0000

NATIONAL LEAGUE COTILLION 332 Sycamore Ridge Way Gahanna, OH 43230 614-428-8900

SIEBERT & ASSOC. 80 S. Liberty St. Powell, OH 43065 614-841-1188

SHERRY LEE AGENCY 7745 Cricket Cir NW. Massillon, OH 44646 330-833-2973

SONNIE'S SCHOOL OF DANCE 1211 Mitchell Blvd. Springfield, OH 45503 937-399-5855

TOMMYE'S NEW ATTITUDE 3710 E. 149th St. Cleveland, OH 44120 216-475-3388

URBANE ACADEMY 22 W. 7th St. Cincinnati, OH 45202 513-381-7371

OKLAHOMA

BASICALLY BOSTICK PROJECTS 600 NW. 23Rd. St. #122 Oklahoma City, OK 73103 405-521-8040

CHRISTIAN MODELS ALLIANCE 1916 S. Harvard Ave. Tulsa, OK 74112 918-712-9664

DAMAR SCHOOL OF DRAMA 3141 E. 15th St. Tulsa, OK 74104 918-749-6677

DANCE MASTERS BY CHRISTY 5616 SE 15ᵗʰ St. Midwest City, OK 73110 405-737-3171

JOHN CASABLANCAS 5009 N. Pennsylvania Ave. #200 Oklahoma City, OK 73112 405-842-0000

JOHN CASABLANCAS CTR. 6808 S. Memorial Dr. #334 Tulsa, OK 74133 918-622-2525

KENDI"S SCHOOL OF DANCE 500 N. Washington St. Weatherford, OK 73096 580-772-3938

KIRBY KASTING & MODELING 8136 South Harvard Ave. #A, Tulsa, OK 74137 918-491-3410

LI NDA LAYMAN AGENCY 3546 E. 51ˢᵗ St. Tulsa, OK 74135 918-744-0888

SHAWNEE ACADEMY OF BALLET 1318 E. Independence St. Shawnee, OK 74804

OREGON

ABC KIDS-TEENS ARTS CTR. 114 Willagillespie Rd. #1 Eugene, OR 97401 541-485-6960

ABC KIDS-TEENS PERFORMING 3829 NE. Tillamook St. Portland, OR 97212 503-249-2945

BARBIZON MODELING SCHOOL 4035 NE. Sandy Blvd. #225 Portland, OR 97212 503-282-1800

CINDERELLA'S MODELS AGENCY 317 Court St. NE. Dalem, OR 97301 503-581-1073

JOHN CASABLANCAS CTR. 9400 Beaverton Hillsdale, #130 Beaverton, OR 97005 503-297-7730

PENNSYLVANIA

ACTING & TV TRAINING 1244 W. Hamilton St. Allentown, PA 18102 610-820-5359

BARBIZON SCHOL OF MODELING 9 Parkway Ctr. #160 Pittsburgh, PA 15220 412-937-0700

BARBIZON SCHOOL OF MODELING 1033 Maclay St. Harrisburg, PA 17103 717-234-3277

BARBIZON SCHOOL OF MODELING 41 Oxford St. #1 Wilkes Barre, PA. 18702 570-823-3743

BARBIZON SCHOOL OF MODELING 22 Greenfield Ave. Ardmore, PA 19003 610-649-9700

CHARTREUSE TALENT WORKSHOPS 801 North 12th Street, Allentown, PA 18102 610-433-5448

ELITE UNLTD MODELING 933 N. Broad St. Philadelphia, PA 19123 215-769-5900

ENTOURAGE COMMUNITY DEVELOP. 1230 New Rodgers Rd. Bristol, PA 19007 215-781-8828

FRANJEAN MODELING & FINISH. 2100 E. Washington Ln. Philadelphia, PA 19138 215-769-5900

IMAGE INT. 4959 Hamilton Blvd. Allentown, PA 18106 610-391-9133

JOHN CASABLANCAS MODELING 920 Town Center Dr. Langhorne, PA 19047 215-752-8600

JOHN CASABLANCAS MODELING. 2101 Greentree Rd. #A109 Pittsburgh, PA 15220 412-276-7700

JOHN ROBERT POWERS MODELING 1528 Spruce St. Philadelphia, PA 19102 215-732-4060

KANE MODELING SCHOOL 1022 N. Main St. #2 Butler, PA 16001 724-287-0576

KARMA STUDIOS 325 Cherry St. Philadelphia, PA 19106 215-627-3245

KEYSTONES FOR SUCCESS Swarthmore, PA 19081 610-543-7020

MAIN LINE MODELS 1215 W. Baltimore Pike #9 Media, PA 19063 610-565-5445

MAIN LINE MODELS 160 N. Gulch Rd. King Of Prussia, PA 19406 610-337-2689

MARY LEISTER CHARM SCHOOL 539 Court St. Reading, PA 19601 610-373-6150

MISS CINDY'S SCHOOL OF DANCE 19 N. 7th St. Perkasia, PA 18944 215-257-4121

MITCHELL ORGANIZATION 234 Monroe St. Philadelphia, PA 19147 215-574-1666

QUEEN OF PRUSSIA SCHOOL 370 Crooked Ln. King of Prussia, PA 19406 610-278-0780

RUTH HARPER MODELING SCHOOL 1427 W. Erie Ave. Philadelphia, PA 19140 215-225-4268

RHODE ISLAND

JOHN CASABLANCAS CTR. 1 Lambert Lind Hwy Warwick, RI 02905 401-463-5866

SOUTH CAROLINA

BETTY LANE SCHOOL OF CHARM 250 Doyle St. Southeast, Orangeburg, SC 29115 803-534-9672

CAROLINA WINDS PRODUCTION 141 Gadsden St. Chester, SC 29706 803-581-2278

COLLINS MODELS & TALENT 1410 Colonial Life Blvd. W. #230 Columbia, SC 29210 803-216-0550

DREAMS UNLTD. 1249 S. Pleasantburg Dr. Greenville, SC 29605 864-676-1213

MILLIE LEWIS FINISHING SCHOOL 1228 S. Pleasantburg Dr. Greenville, SC 29605 864-299-1101

MILLIE LEWIS SCHOOL 1904 Savannah Hwy Charleston, SC 29407 843-571-7781

MILLIE LEWIS OF COLUMBIA 3612 Landmark Dr. #D Columbia, SC 29204 803-782-7338

SHAW'S MODEL & TALENT 200 Berkshire Dr. Columbia, SC 29223 803-699-0158

SOUTH DAKOTA

HAUNTE MODELING SCHOOL 1002 West 6th Street Sioux Falls, SD 57078 605-360-6772

TENNESSEE

ADVANTAGE MODELS & TALENT 4825 Trousdale Dr. #230 Nashville, TN 37220 615-833-3005

AMBIANCE MODELS 1096 Dayton Blvd. Chattanooga, TN 37405 423-265-2121

BARBIZON SCHOOL 10841 Kingston Pike Concord Farragut, TN 37922 865-777-4777

BARBIZON SCHOOL 5600 Brainerd Dr. Chattanooga, TN 37411 423-855-8883

BARBIZON SCHOOL 1890 n. Germantown Pkwy #104 Cordova, TN 38018 901-755-6800

BRENDA WILSON SCHOOL 2600 Fort Henry Dr. Kingsport, TN 37664 423-246-6838

CAROLYN'S FINISHING ACADEMY 522 S. Main St. Memphis, TN 38103 901-543-0803

DONNA'S STUDIO OF COMPETITIVE 1674 Dover Rd. Woodlawn, TN 37191 931-552-1258

JO-SUSAN MODELS 1817 W. End Ave. Nashville, TN 37203 615-327-8726

JOHN CASABLANCAS CTR. 4721 Trousdale Dr. #129 Nashville, TN 37220 615-781-2300

JOHN CASABLANCAS CTR 5028 Park Ave. Memphis, TN 38117 901-685-0066

RASMOC, PDE; OMG 5308 Middlebrook Rd. #B Knoxville, TN 37917 865-602-2002

VAL JA VAUGHN FINISHING STUDIO 354 S. Main St. Memphis, TN 38103 901-529-9933

TEXAS

ABILENE SCHOOL OF PERFORMING 3241 S. 1st St. #22 Abilene, TX 79605 915-673-7421

ACTORS WORKSHOP 1009 Charters St. Houston, TX 77003 713-236-1844

ACTORS WORKSHOP WEST 7600 Blanco Rd. San Antonio, TX 78216 210-344-9820

BARBIZON SCHOOL 4950 Overton Ridge Blvd. Fort Worth, TX 76132 817-294-0554

BARBIZON OF SAN ANTONIO 4600 NW. Loop 410 #190 San Antonio, TX 78229 210-731-8200

BARBIZON SCHOOL 12700 Hillcrest Rd. #142 Dallas, TX 75230 972-980-7477

BARBIZON SCHOOL OF MODELING 5433 Westheimer Dr. #300 Houston, TX 77056 713-850-9111

BOOGIE SHOES SCHOOL OF DANCE 125 W. Bear Creek Dr. Red Oak, TX 75154 972-274-2199

BRITE LITES ACTING STUDIO 7109 Woodrow Ave. Austin, TX 78757 512-459-1100

CAPERS FOR KIDS 12306 Park Central Dr. Dallas, TX 75251 972-661-2787

CHICK MODELING 4242 Medical Dr. #7250 San Antonio, TX 78229 210-614-2442

CINDERELLA MODELS & FINISHING 2910 Woodcrest Dr. San Antonio, TX 78209 210-832-8058

CREATIVE ARTS SCHOOL 1100 W. Randol Mill Rd. Arlington, TX 76012 817-861-2287

CYPRESS ACADEMY 11707 Huffmeister Rd. #B Houston, TX 77065 281-469-4599

D'LYN ACADAMY OF MODELING 14515 Briarhills Pkwy #118 Houston, TX 77077 281-589-2500

DIANE DICK INTL. 1410 S. Washington St. #B Amarillo, TX 79102 806-376-8738

DSM SCHOOL OF MUSICAL 1925 Elm St. #301 Dallas, TX 75201 214-969-7469

FRANCINE'S STUDIO OF MODELING 1103 Cardinal Ave. MC Allen, TX 78504 956-630-4420

HOUSTON TRAINING SCHOOLS 6969 Gulf Fwy #200 Houston, TX 77087 713-649-5050

JAM MODEL & TALENT CTR. 11551 Forest Central Dr. Dallas, TX. 75243 214-221-4683

JOHN ROBERT POWERS 9037 Research Blvd. #100 Austin, TX 78758 512-835-5089

JOHN ROBERT POWERS 6320 Camp Bowie Blvd. Fort Worth, TX 76116 817-738-2021

JONES 2000 656 The Meadows Pkwy De Soto, TX 75115 972-293-3931

JRC IMAGE & FASHION 2126 Simbrah Dr. Cedar Park, TX 78613 512-219-0521

K D STUDIO ACTORS CENTER 2600 N. Stemmons Fwy. # 117 Dallas, TX 75207 214-638-0484

KID'S ART CTR THEATRE 520 23Rd. St. Galveston, TX 77550 409-762-8644

LAKEWOOD PERFORMING ARTS 13050 Louetta Rd. #220B Cypress, TX 77429 281-655-5678

LONE STAR COMEDY 2600 N. Stemmons Fwy Dallas, TX 75207 214-630-7787

MARGO MANNING ENT. 14800 Quorum Dr. #200 Dallas, TX 75240 972-239-2882

MAXINE'S FINISHING TOUCHES 1220 Lano St. Pasadena, TX 77504 713-944-7672

MAYO HILL CTR FOR MODELING 7887 San Felipe St. #127 Houston, TX 77063 713-789-7340

MISS BARBARA' S DANCE SCHOOL 4566 FM 1960 Road East, Humble, TX 77346 281-852-4433

P S IMAGES 1105 Pueblo Midland, TX 79705 915-683-0844

PAGE PARKES MODEL CAMP 3303 Lee Pkwy #215 Dallas, TX 75219 214-528-0705

PAGE PARKES SCHOOL OF MODELING 2727 Kirby Dr. # 8th-Fl. Houston, TX 77098 713-807-8200

POISED FOR SUCCESS 13205 Cypress North Houston Rd. Cypress, TX 77429 281-469-6260

RHYTHM NATL. PERFORMING ART 700 S. Main St. Euless, TX 76040 817-283-1061

RISING STARS OF TEXAS 9200 Broadway St. San Antonio, TX 78217 210-828-7827

ROBERT SPENCE SCHOOL 4418 74Th St. #53 Lubbock, TX 79424 806-797-9134

SCHOOL OF FUN ARTS 3505 w. Lancaster Ave. Fortworth, TX 76107 817-737-5437

SCOTT ZACKERY THEATRE SCHOOL 1510 Toomey Dr. Austin, TX 78704 512-476-0594

STAGE 7906 Brookhollow Rd. Dallas, TX 75235 214-630-7722

STATE THEATER CO. 719 Congress Ave. Austin, TX 78701 512-472-5143

STUDIO 173 173 Pine St. Abilene, TX 79601 915-673-9484

TALENT INTL. 6060 Richmond Ave. Houston, TX. 77057 713-977-3648

THEATRE ARLINGTON 305 W. Main St. Arlington, TX 76010 817-275-7661

TOTAL PERSON 4982 Thunder Rd. Dallas, TX 75244 972-702-8166

UNICORN SCHOOL OF ACTING 11001 Delaney St. La Marque, TX 77568 409-935-3002

VIVIAN HARMON SCHOOL 1719 N. 23Rd. St. Mc Allen, TX 78501 210-687-3851

UTAH

COLLETTE'S DISTINCTIVE MODELING 1033 Revere Circle, Holladay, UT 84117 801-262-4262

EXECUTIVE MODEL SHOP 2900 S. State St. #300 Salt Lake City, UT 84115 801-487-2799

FINISHING TOUCH AGENCY 577 W. 3850 N. Ogden, UT 84414 801-782-5648

KUBY-MILLER'S MODELING & DANCE 273 E. 2100S. South Salt Lake, UT 84115 801-487-4238

MC CARTY AGENCY 1326 Foothill Dr. Salt Lake City, UT 84108 801-581-9292

SOLEIL MODEL & TALENT MGMNT. 4685 Highland Dr. #101 Holladay, UT 84117 801-274-3377

STYLE INC. 566 North 300 West, Salt Lake City, UT 84103 801-539-7703

VIRGINIA

ANN L SCHOOL OF MODELING 1925 E. Market St. #354 Harrisonburg, VA 22801 540-434-6664

CAROLE RIGGS STUDIOS 616 Leesville Rd. Lynchburg, VA 24502 804-237-7070

CHARM ASSOCIATES 144 Business Park Dr. #100 Virginia Beach, VA 23462 757-490-8340

COPELAND MILLS SCHOOL 1457 Mount Pleasant Rd. #102B Chesapeake, VA 23322 757-482-2528

JOHN CASABLANCAS CTR. 249 S. Van Dorn St. #210 Alexandria, VA 22304 703-823-5200

MODEL SOURCE INC. 601 Caroline St. #204 Fredericksburg, VA 22401 540-374-1935

NEW FACES MODELS 8230 Leesburg Pike #520 Vienna, VA 22182 703-821-0786

RAVEN PRODUCTIONS 5599 Seminary Rd. Falls Church, VA 22041 703-671-2590

RHAPSODY MODELING AGENCY 3801 Pheasant Hollow Dr. Richmond, VA 23231 804-795-2885

WHITE HOUSE OF CHARM 7954 Fort Hunt Dr. Alexandria, V. 22308 703-765-8292

YOUNG PEOPLES GUILD SCHOOL 2117 High St. Portsmouth, VA 23704 757-397-5763

WASHINGTON

BARBIZON SCHOOL OF MODELING 1501 4th Ave. #305 Seattle, WA 98101 206-223-1500

DREZDEN INTL. MODELING 3121 N. Division St. Spokane, WA 99207 509-326-6800

FINAL TOUCH FINISHING SCHOOL Des Maines, WA 253-946-3313

FLORANCE IBEA MODELING & DEVELOPMENT Marysville, WA 360-659-4624

FUTURE STARS MODEL & TALENT 610 Industry Dr. Tukwila, WA 98188 206-575-7922

JOHN CASABLANCAS CTR. 50 116th Ave. SE #100 Bellevue, WA 98004 425-646-3585

NORTHWEST FASHION INSTITUTE 19009 33Rd. Ave. W. #100 Lynnwood, WA 98036 425-775-8385

PJ & CO MODELS AGENCY 24622 E. Moffat Rd. Newman Lake, WA 99025 509-226-2135

WASHINGTON D C

ENCHANTE MODEL INC. 39 New York Ave. NE. Washington, DC 20002 202-547-0265
D C YOUTH ENSEMBLE 1006 Pennsylvania Ave. SE. #2 Washington, DC 20003 202-393-3293
ROYAL ETIQUETTE 6008 Utah Ave. NW. Washington, DC 20015 202-237-7004

WISCONSIN

CAROL WAITE P.O. Box 4 North Lake, WI 53064 262-966-2450
CSL IMAGE INC. 2821 N. 4th St. Milwaukee, WI 53212 414-263-1780
ETIQUETTE ESSENTIALS 2962 Green Crest Ct. Madison, WI 53711 608-274-6542
JOHN CASABLANCAS CTR 200 N. Patrick Blvd. #700 Brookfield, WI 53045 262-879-1200
JULIE'S TOUCH OF SILVER 2070 W. 20th Ave. Oshkosh, WI 54904 920-231-8414
MARILYN SCHOOL OF DANCE 329 Division St. La Crosse, WI 54601 608-785-1447
PREMIER FASHION NETWORK 8933 N. Spruce Rd. Milwaukee, WI 53217 414-247-1170

8

AGENCY AND UNION REPRESENTATION FEES, COMMISSIONS, AND TRAVELING EXPENSES

In the modeling industry a good agent and agency are worth their weight in gold. As a whole, this industry is generally unregulated and has no union representation.

Your modeling agency negotiates each and every working contract for you. Your agent's job is to be available on a moment's notice and must have qualified models in all shapes and sizes available. Your agent receives casting calls daily by phone, fax, and e-mail.

Modeling agents live on the telephone. Casting and open calls occur like lightening: they strike fast and furiously.

Modeling agencies know what each of their models "special look" is. When a casting call comes in that fits the description of one of their models, the agency immediately mails, faxes, or e-mails specifics about the model to the interested parties.

When models are picked for a job, an agent within the agency locate the model and confirms with him or her that they are available to work on a specific date and time.

Next, your agent calls back the interested parties and confirms the model is available. Then the contract negotiation begins. Do you make $25 an hour with an eight hour guarantee, or are you being paid $250 to $2,500 per day?

Other factors are always in question. Models get sick or hurt, or have personal problems and cancel at the last minute. Or a director changes the shooting time or date.

Last, but most importantly, is the billing process. Each model, each job, large or small, must be separately billed, collected, and distributed to staff and models.

To update or promote the talent they represent agents also attend specialized modeling industry functions and parties. Modeling agencies do not get paid unless they find you work. They are on the phone night and day, promoting you, the model.

Your agency receives a percentage of your compensation, which is called a commission. Agencies charge between 10 percent to 25 percent commission, with an industry average of 20 percent.

If a job contract is for $1,000 the model will receive a check for $800. Your agency will keep their percentage, or in this example; $200 (20 percent commission rate).

Well-known modeling agencies have an established clientele. Their contracts tend to pay higher compensation than a lesser-known smaller agencies. Large agencies are very picky about whom they represent. They tend to work with experienced models who have already proven their sellable "look."

Don't judge your agency by the size of their office, large or small. Judge your agency by how much work they get for you.

Modeling and television commercials go hand in hand. Agencies who represent models also represent talent, voice overlays, and actors. If you sing or dance or if you have any other talents, be sure to let your agent know about it. The more your agent knows about you, the more they can "sell" you.

Modeling jobs are not unionized, so compensation varies greatly, from state to state and from job to job. All pay is negotiable.

If you're making less than $25 per hour as a model, you need to find out why. Do you need a different look? Perhaps a new hair style or makeover? Or is the problem your agency? Are they working hard enough for you? Be realistic. Ask yourself, what can I do to enhance or further my modeling career?

It usually takes a year or two to become established in the world of modeling, which means you're going to be doing a lot of driving to open calls and interviews. When traveling to or from an audition or open call, you pay for all of your own expenses, from car gasoline to meals and parking fees. Your agency does not reimburse you for any of these expenses. For this reason it's wise to work with an agency (no matter how large or small) located close to your home or immediate area.

Once your name gets out in the industry and you become more established, your agency will be able to book you jobs just by showing your zed cards to his clients, thus you won't have to travel as much to open calls and callbacks.

Driving is a big part of this industry. You should be prepared for anything when you travel. Keep your car's gas tank filled with gas, and routinely check your tires and car battery.

Often when your agency calls you, you'll seldom have more than a day's notice to drive to a job. There is an old saying in this profession: "Being at the right place at the right time" is the key to success in this industry. Most of the time, you're called the same day of the interview.

Keep a pillow, blanket, jacket, change of clothes, bottled water, and energy bars in your car, at all times.

Having your car break down on a busy freeway or running out of gas on an isolated road early in the morning is an experience you do not need.

Casting studios are located everywhere, from small offices inside huge buildings to dimly lit warehouses and private homes. If you're not familiar with an area, get directions. Two good sources to find any location are:

www.mapquest.com and www.mapblast.com

Ask your agency for the phone number of the casting studio. If you get lost call your agency first. As a last resort call the studio.

Being late for a casting call can mean loosing the job. Always know where you are going and how to get there.

Some modeling jobs last more than a day. Newcomers in this industry rarely get paid for a hotel room or travel expenses. You get paid a set amount, which generally is for a preparation day, and a set amount of compensation for the actual photo shoot day.

The first day is for clothes fittings, styling or coloring of hair, and/or rehearsals. Typically, the next day, the photo shoot, begins early in the morning and is often at a different location from where the first day's activities took place.

For beginners, compensation will be anything from $200 per day to $1,500 per day. If you work conventions or product demonstrations the pay is generally lower, but the advantage here is that there is more steady work in this area. The pay ranges from $25 an hour to $75 an hour, with bookings lasting from one to ten days.

When your agency books you a job out of his or her city or state, they negotiate travel expenses for you. Typically, the hotel and airfare are included. Your agency negotiates a travel allowance for meals and incidentals. Travel allowances are negotiable, but aren't handed out very often.

When you travel out of town for a modeling job, you are responsible for paying your own bills, from meals to taxi cabs and tips. When you travel by plane, you generally fly with a group of models and photographers, all hired for the same job.

At the hotels you are paired up with a roommate (or two) and you are responsible for all of your own meals or anything else you might need. Hotel accommodations are clean, upscale, and close to, if not at, where the photo shoot will take place.

If you are a teenager and you want a parent to travel with you, have your agency negotiate whatever allowance they can for the parent, which might include airfare and hotel accommodations. Parents are welcome and expected to travel with their teenagers, but normally they are required to pay for their own expenses.

For toddlers or young children, the rules are different. Hotel and airfare are part of the negotiated fees for the parent or guardian.

Traveling with small children is at best, hectic. A bubbly toddler today could become a monster tomorrow. (After traveling long distances) For this reason, the modeling industry tends to hire toddlers or young children from local modeling agencies located in the immediate area of the photo shoot.

Modeling and acting go hand and hand. Many models get their first job on a television commercial or music video.

Four major unions govern the television and radio industry:

1) The Screen Actors Guild, commonly referred to as "SAG," represents film and television performers.

2) The America Guild of Musical Artists commonly referred to as "AGMA," represents live music and variety performers.

3) The American Guild of Variety Artist, commonly referred to as "AGVA," represents live music and variety performers.

4) The American Federation of Television and Radio Artists commonly referred to as "AFTRA," represents film, television, and radio artists

All four of these unions are affiliated with the AFL-CIO, national union. None of the above unions have contracts with and/or represent the modeling industry.

Your agency will tell you whenever you're hired for a union job.

Union jobs allow non-union members to work under a union contract, without joining the union, for a maximum of thirty days. After working thirty days on a union job, you must join the appropriate union to remain on the union job or to get any other union work at any time in the future.

Often young models and actors join unions early on in their careers in the hopes of earning higher wages and guaranteed work. This is a mistake. Unions do not guarantee work. Their main goal is to provide competitive wages and a safe working environment for their members.

Once you've joined the Screen Actors Guild, or any other affiliated union, you may no longer work non-union work of any kind.

It doesn't matter if the job is for a non-profit community learning experience, educational or any other production. Unless the production has signed a contract or letter of agreement with the appropriate union, you may not work on it.

When you're new to the modeling profession, any and all working experiences are crucial. The more experience you have, the more jobs you will attain, and the more professional your portfolio will become.

Is working a union job worth giving up all of the learning experiences you will have to pass up in the future? Will the union job pay enough to cover the cost of having to join the union and pay a steep yearly dues?

The initiation fee to join the Screen Actors Guild is $1,474. It is payable in advance by cash, cashier check, MasterCard or Visa credit cards.

Union dues are paid semi-annually or twice a year. They are based on the total of your Screen Actors Guild Union earnings in the prior year (12 months). Members pay 1.85 percent of the first $200,000 they earn per year and 0.05 percent on other earnings from $201,000 to $500,000.

If you haven't earned any wages during a twelve-month period, there is a minimum annual dues of $100 per year. Dues are paid on the first day of May and November of each year.

To join the Screen Actors Guild union, you must be in a principal speaking roll in a SAG film, videotape, television program, or commercial. Or you must have worked for a minimum of three workdays as an extra background person, by a company signed to a SAG background player's agreement and in a SAG film, videotape, television program, or commercial (after 3/25/90).

You must have proof of employment from the Screen Actors Guild job before you can join the union.

Below is a list of both SAG and AFTRA union pay national contact information:

Screen Actors Guild: East Coast: 360 Madison Ave., 12th Floor, New York NY 10017 (212) 944-1030

Screen Actors Guild: West Coast: 5757 Wilshire Blvd., Los Angeles, CA 90036 (323) 954-1600

AFTRA: East Coast: 260 Madison Avenue, New York, NY 10016 (212) 532-0800

AFTRA: West Coast: 5757 Wilshire Blvd., 9th Floor, Los Angeles CA 90036 (323) 634-8100

9

MODELING SCAMS & PITFALLS

The modeling industry is a multi-million-dollar business that is not regulated by the federal government. and most states don't even require agencies to have a license. That means that just about anyone can open a modeling agency or school just about anywhere in our country.

Scams, phony agencies and schools along with bogus talent scouts, are out there in force and have given the industry a bad name.

However there are thousands of legitimate agencies, schools and talent scouts all over the country, also.

This chapter will help you understand the difference between the legitimate and phony ones, along with the scams they use.

The modeling industry generally is made up of a younger, naive group of people who are following a dream and have stars in their eyes. All of this adds up to easy prey for con artists. They know you aren't stupid, but they also know exactly what to say and how to say it to you.

Always remember that if something sounds too good to be true, then it probably is.

First of all, legitimate modeling agencies DO NOT charge you for anything, from registration fees to zed cards or portfolios. They get paid when they find you work. It's that simple. They pay you. You do not pay them.

Many an agency out there have twisted things around. They find it's a lot easier to make money off of you versus having to find you work. Avoid them.

A large and growing area of scams in this industry are the fake scouts that are out there.

Typically, they place ads on your local radio stations, usually with the stations that cater to the younger crowds. They also put ads in your local newspaper that say something like this "Model search for national company. We are looking for new faces, no experience necessary." They usually mention that representation from top modeling agencies will be there to "discover you."

The scouting companies visit towns, usually only for a day or two and rent a room or banquet area from a larger hotel chain.

They have "open calls or auditions" at a set hour. This is where the scam begins.

These companies know that the ads will bring in a lot of hopeful, dreamy-eyed teenagers. They herd you into the small rooms until the rooms are full. Then they start their scam.

They line you up or they herd you into groups. This is done to keep you distracted and excited at the same time. What they are actually doing is checking you out to see if you look gullible enough to take money from.

To keep the energy high in the room, they usually pick a tall male or female right away and they tell that person to go to a different part of the room. They know the rest of you hopefuls will be closely watching, and they know you will watch this tall person as he or she walks over to a table and chairs in another area of the room. This is part of the scam.

Then, one, by one they pick individuals and tell them, "You have the look that we are looking for." They ask you to go over to the same set of tables and chairs that the tall man or woman that was picked a few minutes ago did.

Of course, they can't pick everyone, so they tactfully tell others that are lined up, "Thank you for coming, you're beautiful (handsome) but you don't have the look that we need right now."

They tell the teenager hopefuls that have been rejected to come back to the next model search because the "Look" constantly changes.

What they are really doing is hoping that you will come back to their next search, which will help them get a larger crowd.

The energy of a large group of good looking, vain teenagers is enough to feed on itself. The bigger the group, the more they sign up.

Every con is different, but what always happens is: When you get picked, you pay the company money.

Sometimes you pay them for seminars where an agent could discover you. Other times the company insists that you need to have zed cards made up by their photographer.

Many of these companies make a very good living insisting that you need training, from dance instructions to makeup application.

Words like, "guaranteed" or "Your deposit is fully refundable" are thrown around.

No matter what line they give you, the bottom line is that all of these companies are making money off of you.

They travel town to town and do the same thing over and over again. This is how these companies make their living. Their so-called scouts are just sales people that make a commission on each and every one of you starry-eyed people.

Legitimate modeling agencies DO NOT place ads in the newspaper.

Legitimate modeling agencies DO NOT place ads on the radio stations.

Legitimate modeling agencies DO NOT charge you for registration fees and DO NOT insist that you buy pictures or zed cards from them.

Legitimate modeling agencies get paid when they find you work. It's that simple. They represent you and find you modeling jobs. When you finish a modeling job, they get paid a commission or a portion of your pay, usually fifteen percent.

Modeling agencies should not be making money from selling you anything.

Some of these agencies insist that you buy their makeup. Others insist that you use their photographers and buy expensive portfolios from them. Some even insist that you buy special clothes from a specific store. All of these agencies are bogus.

They are making money off of you. They usually have no intention of finding you work. Why should they? All they have to do is sit in a room and answer a phone. That's a lot easier that being a real agent.

Just remember, a legitimate agency does not get paid until they find you work, which means they are out there working very hard because they want to make money.

Another area of the modeling industry you should be cautious with is: Modeling Schools.

First of all, to become a model you DO NOT need to go to a modeling school.

If you want to build your confidence and you decide to sign up for a modeling school, then you need to ask yourself, "What am I going to learn here that I already don't know? What do I want to learn from this class? How will this class help my career?"

There are thousands of schools around the country for everyone from children to adults. Some of them promise they will have work waiting for you once you have taken their classes. These schools are overpriced and usually shut down or are run out of town after a year or so. Needless to say, they don't find you work, either.

Always ask a school how long they've been in business. A school that has been in business for a long time, in the same location, with the same owners, will probably teach you more and charge you less than a new company that has fancy fliers and pushy salesmen.

High-pressure sales people are, salesmen. They get paid a commission when they sign you up for whatever it is that the company is selling, sometimes modeling classes, sometimes overpriced zed cards. Avoid these people and their schools.

Legitimate schools want you to succeed. They answer all of your questions and don't have pushy sales people.

You are paying these schools to educate you in a new profession. Don't be afraid to ask questions, and don't sign a contract unless you completely understand it.

If you are young and pretty or good looking and hang around the mall, there is a fairly new scam out there that you probably will be approached with.

If you are "discovered" by a modeling scout at a mall or highly traveled area, walk away.

These men and women prey on pretty young faces. They approach you and hand you a business card. Their lines include: "I'm a modeling scout and you have the look that my agency is looking for."

They are always well dressed, charming, and they can't throw enough compliments toward you. What they are really doing is sweeping you off of your feet and putting stars in your eyes. Their business card refers you to a modeling agency.

These (so-called) scouts get paid a commission for each and every person that goes to the agency and signs up.

The agencies spend the first ten minutes or so interviewing you to see if you are good enough to be let into their (so-called) agency. Most of their talk is flattery and you almost can't resist them when they tell you that you are very good and with just a little training you will be on your way. That's their scam.

Overpriced modeling classes, exorbitant registration fees, expensive photographer and zed card fees. These so-called agencies make their money off of you, not the work that they are supposed to be finding you.

Some unscrupulous photographers are part of the scams within an agency. The agencies tell you that they cannot get work for you unless you have better pictures. They recommend a professional photographer that works with them.

The photographer is usually inexperienced and charges you two to three times (or more) more than what an honest photographer would have charged. The pictures are always mediocre, and you probably would have gotten better pictures from your own camera.

Legitimate modeling agencies DO NOT insist that you use their photographer.

Sometimes they will supply you with a list of photographers they have worked with in the past who take good pictures and are reliable. This is done as a convenience for you, not for a commission or referral fee.

Some dishonest photographers tell model hopefuls that you must have lots of professional photographs taken before you can become a model, and that no modeling agency will even talk to you unless you have professional pictures taken first. This is not true.

Other photographers scam adults by snapping picture after picture of babies for proud parents who dream of seeing their little ones on the cover of magazines. The photographers insist that without a professional portfolio of pictures your baby has no chance of becoming a model. This is not true.

Modeling agencies for infants to adults DO NOT insist upon, and in many cases don't even want to see professional photographs, especially pictures of infants and toddlers.

Casual snapshots that are current are all that is required, especially for infants.

Chapter Two explains all the ins and outs of what pictures you need to have in order to succeed.

Chapter Five explains how and where to take your baby or toddler to get them started into the world of modeling.

Modeling conventions can be a very positive experience, although a growing number of models say that they are overrated and way too expensive.

The idea behind them is to get representatives from many well-known modeling agencies from around the country to meet all in one place, usually in New York or Los Angeles.

Thousands of models fly in and attend these conventions hoping to be discovered. Most of them spend thousands of dollars on everything from photographs to clothing and makeup.

There is no list of "discovered super models" to prove or disprove that anyone was discovered at these conventions.

Many aspiring models say that they enjoyed the experience, even though it was expensive and even though they weren't " discovered" at the convention.

Ask your family, friends and other models about any conventions they have attended.

This is your career. It's your money. Do you want to spend thousands of dollars for a good experience? The more you know, the further you will go.

The newest scams out there are radio ads promising you work, dancing with famous movie stars or famous bands. The ads are placed on local radio stations that cater to teenagers. They mention a few dance styles that most every teenager is familiar with. The ad tells you to come in and try out for the job. It entices you by telling you that anyone can apply and they will give you a free evaluation just for showing up.

When you arrive you are herded into small rooms and you are required to fill out a card with your name address and phone number information. This is the start of the scam.

You will be asked to dance a few steps while all the other hopefuls watch you. Sometimes the room is plastered in pictures of famous bands and people. After a few steps you are thanked for coming and told that they will call you back in a day or so to let you know if you got the job.

They call you back within a day or so. They also call every other person that showed up for the interview. They tell you all the same thing.

This is the scam. They call you and congratulate you for being picked for the job. They make you feel very special then they casually mention that you need to take a few dance lessons to learn the steps that the band or famous people will be using. Then they mention that if you can't afford the lessons, it's ok, they have a runner up picked.

Next they sign you up for dancing lessons that are very expensive and that are offered at your local community center, or even through private instructors for a lot less money.

Some of the studios work with sleazy photographers and insist that you need professional pictures taken. Exorbitant fees are charged for simple snapshots, and the photographer splits the profits with the dance school.

When it comes time to make your television debut or appear with the famous rock star you are always told the same thing. "Someone else got the job because they danced better than you, it's ok though, because another dance job is coming up, and you only need a few more lessons for that job."

Similar scams are used for acting lessons, along with modeling and singing lessons.

They all promise the same thing: that once in a lifetime shot at stardom. Don't be tempted by these radio ads. Legitimate companies are always looking for talent and a good way to find them is word of mouth or through local instructors that have been in business for a long time.

Beauty pageants and contests from babies to teenagers have become a popular avenue in introducing your child into the world of modeling.

Usually an ad is placed in your local newspaper. Sometimes you are invited to attend the pageants by getting a letter in the mail.

These contest are almost all self-perpetuating, which means they are making a profit off of you or that they are supporting the people that run them.

Money is generated from the paying of entry fees. For toddlers you pay an entry fee for each classification you enter your toddler into.

Each contest has different categories ranging from "most photogenic" to "best dressed" and "most talented." Sometimes there are as many as fifteen categories you can enter your child into.

For younger children you pay between $15.00 and $150.00 for a general entry fee to the pageant. Then you pay an additional fee for each and every category that you enter your child into. These fees differ from contest to contest, but are progressively higher if you are invited to a state or national beauty pageant.

On the national level a few of these companies award large savings bonds, but with most of the smaller companies your child wins large trophies and lots of applause.

If you have the time and the money, these contests are a great way to test the waters of the glitz and glamour that your child will be exposed to in the modeling world.

Your child will learn many important skills here, from speaking directly to an adult to correct posture. If they have shy tendencies a contest or two could really help boost their self-confidence. Seeing other kids their age on stage at the same time really changes some children.

Just remember, winning these contest doesn't guarantee your toddler fame, money or a career. There are no super agencies waiting behind the stages to sign your talented toddler up, no matter how many of these contests your little one has won.

Some of the contests boast television exposure. This sounds great, but most of the time the television exposure is limited to your local broadcast.

Having copies of these tapings, are priceless especially for grandparents.

In chapter five we have listed a few of the well-known companies that put on these pageants.

These contests should be approached as a fun learning experience for both you and your toddler.

Nude modeling is rarely talked about, but it's very much alive in the modeling pitfall area.

Be leery if you are promised unusually high pay or if you are offered a dream job outside of the country by someone other then your agency. These are warning signs that something isn't quite right.

Some unscrupulous companies that call themselves international agencies use high-pressure tactics once they get you out of the country. They insist that you pose nude for them, and in many cases, they won't let you go home unless you have sex with them or with some of their special clients.

Don't let a lot of instant cash blind your common sense. Turn around and walk away from these people. They use every person, place and thing in their path. Doing them one tiny favor will lead you down the wrong path and will not help your career.

Nude pictures travel very fast in the wrong circles. They can and have ruined many a promising model's career.

If you have a perfect body and want to get into nude modeling, make sure you have an established reputable agent.

Lights, camera, action. At a photo shoot don't get too caught up in the excitement. You need to always remember what you were sent there to do.

Loud music, flashing camera strobes and a captive audience awed by your every move in front of the camera sometimes gets the best of you.

"That's great! Much better. Show a little more breast. Perfect! Now show a little more hip … beautiful!"

Don't take your clothes off in front of a camera unless that is what you are being paid to do. Some photographers get carried away, and if you get lost in the excitement, you could easily strip naked without even realizing it. This sounds unbelievable, but it happens all the time.

One nude picture in the wrong hands can ruin a career or send it down a spiraling path.

If you were hired to wear a bikini, wear it. If you were hired to wear sexy lace stockings, wear them.

If anyone insists that you take your clothes off or partially off for any reason, question them.

Remember, your agency pays you, not the people behind the camera.

In the glitz and glamour of the modeling world there are parties, lots and lots of parties.

Don't be tempted by the party hounds out there. Only attend functions that your agencies send you to. Go to parties that will give you exposure, not to meet (so called) movie stars or film producers.

Late nights and alcohol can quickly take their toll on an aspiring model.

Makeup can hide dark circles, but bad habits are hard to break at any age.

The biggest temptation in this area is after a successful photo shoot. Everyone is full of energy, and usually someone in the crew offers to have everybody over. Avoid these parties; they won't get you any more exposure.

The more professional you are, the more you will get noticed.

Everybody loves the party animals in this industry, but they don't last long in the world of modeling.

The scams that have been mentioned in this chapter constantly change.

Con artists keep up with the times and modify their scams as you become leery of them.

Always, always ask questions, get all promises in writing, and never forget that if it sounds too good to be true, it probably is.

Don't open your wallet or purse just because "you have been picked" or because, "it's the last opening and you're the lucky one it's been saved for."

It's your money, never forget that! Who and what are you paying for?

If you feel you are being pressured into signing something, then take a deep breath, count to ten, slowly let it out, and look around the room. Regain a real perspective of what is happening around you.

Take contracts home and study them before you sign them. If you're told "someone else will get the spot if you don't immediately sign a contract," let them give the spot away.

You probably just saved yourself hundreds and possibly thousands of dollars. If the company is legitimate, waiting a day or so to sign a contract shouldn't matter. Keep copies of everything you sign.

If a salesperson is evasive about what kind of training you are going to get, ask him or her for names and phone numbers of people who have graduated from the class. If they won't give you this information, walk away. It doesn't matter how many people in line behind you sign up. You just exposed their scam, they will ask you to leave because they don't want the next person in line to hear what you asked.

Call your local Better Business Bureau and ask them if the company has had any complaints filed against it.

Some of these companies change their names as they move from city to city, so always talk to your family, friends and others in the modeling profession.

Listen; really listen to what other models have to say. Don't ignore them or discount their experiences because you are taller or prettier than they are. A scam is a scam is a scam.

978-0-595-47660-2
0-595-47660-0

www.ingramcontent.com/pod-product-compliance
Lightning Source LLC
Chambersburg PA
CBHW080408290526
45791CB00008BA/2196